THE
EVERYTHING®

ANGELS BOOK

Discover the guardians, messengers, and
heavenly companions in your life

M.J. Abadie

Adams Media Corporation
Avon, Massachusetts

An Everything® Series Book.
Everything® is a registered trademark of Adams Media Corporation.

Published by Adams Media Corporation
57 Littlefield Street, Avon, MA 02322. U.S.A.
adamsmedia.com

ISBN: 1-58062-398-0

Printed in the United States of America.

J I H G F E D C B

Library of Congress Cataloging-in-Publication Data
available upon request from the publisher.

291,215

This publication is designed to provide accurate and authoritative information with regard to the subject matter covered. It is sold with the understanding that the publisher is not engaged in rendering legal, accounting, or other professional advice. If legal advice or other expert assistance is required, the services of a competent professional person should be sought.
— From a *Declaration of Principles* jointly adopted by a Committee of the American Bar Association and a Committee of Publishers and Associations

Illustrations by Barry Littmann.

This book is available at quantity discounts for bulk purchases.
For information, call 1-800-872-5627.

Visit the entire Everything® series at everything.com

Dedication

This book is lovingly dedicated
to my own personal angel

Mary Orser

in appreciation of her many contributions to my life.

Contents

PART ONE
ANGELS IN HISTORY ✧ 1
chapter one ✧ Ancient Angels ✧ 3

chapter two ✧ The Old Testament View of Angels ✧ 15

chapter three ✧ The New Testament View of Angels ✧ 27

CONTENTS

Permissions

Grateful acknowledgment is made to the following for permission to reprint the following exerpts:

"Close to the Edge," by LouAnn Thomas. Reprinted with permission from *Angels on Earth* (Sept./Oct. 1999). Copyright © 1999 by Guideposts, Carmel, New York 10512.

"Do Angels Exist?" by Mary Orser, from her forthcoming book *What Is Reality?* Reprinted with permission from Mary Orser.

"The Motel Angel" and "Angels on the Road," by M. J. Abadie, from her forthcoming book *Everyday Angels*. Reprinted with permission from M. J. Abadie.

"The Day We Saw the Angels," from A LIFE AFTER DEATH by S. Ralph Harlow. Copyright © 1961 by Doubleday, a division of Bantam Doubleday Dell Publishing Group, Inc. Used by permission of Doubleday, a division of Random House, Inc.

We Are Not Alone

Angelic Presences

We not only live among men, but there are airy hosts, blessed spectators, sympathetic lookers-on, that see and know and appreciate our thoughts and feelings and acts.
—Henry Ward Beecher, *Royal Truths*

Angels, it seems to me, are a very private matter. Seldom do we encounter them collectively, though there are stories on record of such encounters. Mostly, the experience of these heavenly beings is an individual matter.

Therefore, this discussion of angels must begin with the claim that I personally have had direct experience of angels, as have many, many others, as attested to by the countless "angel stories" that have been published. There are also, no doubt, an equal number that have not been made public but have been held in memory's privacy.

The issue of whether angels exist or not has been debated extensively, not only by those opposing factions of religious or scientific bent, but also by different sects of various religions, most specifically Christians, who, as a whole, do not agree on much of anything about angels. It is not the purpose of this book to convince anyone of any particular belief system concerning angels. My intention is to provide information to serve as a guide to those interested in pursuing the subject of angels, for whatever reason.

When I was a child, I held conversations with angels on a regular basis and found the experience neither odd nor disturbing.

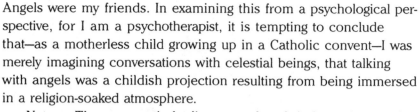

Angels were my friends. In examining this from a psychological perspective, for I am a psychotherapist, it is tempting to conclude that—as a motherless child growing up in a Catholic convent—I was merely imagining conversations with celestial beings, that talking with angels was a childish projection resulting from being immersed in a religion-soaked atmosphere.

Not so. The nuns actively discouraged such independent spiritual activity, as a result of which I became extremely secretive about my angels. According to my much older brother, to whom I occasionally mentioned talking to angels, I was "extremely reluctant" to disclose what the angels said to me.

In working with people who have had angelic encounters, I have discovered that my reaction of secrecy is commonplace. Those who have "seen" or "talked to" angels are almost always hesitant about disclosing the details of their experiences. Many feel they will be disbelieved or, worse, ridiculed. Others simply find the experience to be of such awe-inspiring dimensions that they choose to keep it private. Everyone, it seems, who has an encounter with an angelic presence wants to save and savor that precious experience and not have it tarnished by the disbelief of others. They *know* that they have—perhaps just for a brief moment—seen a veil slip open to reveal another, exceedingly potent, reality.

Today, unfortunately, I have no exact memories of my early conversations with angels. Yet, angels have kept me company in one form or another for most of my life. When I was a child, other than being told that I, like every other person, had been assigned a guardian angel at birth to look over me, the subject of angels was rarely mentioned in my religious education.

Billy Graham says that when he wrote *Angels, God's Secret Agents* (1975), he found almost nothing contemporary had been published on the subject. Today, the subject of angels is an increasingly popular topic. Not only are dozens of books about them rolling off the presses regularly, but stories about them, both fictional and true, appear on popular nighttime television programs that draw huge audiences, such as the immensely popular TV series *Touched by an Angel*. Hollywood, too, has acknowledged angels on occasion, one of the most famous angel films being *It's*

a Wonderful Life, in which a rather befuddled angel named Clarence lovingly convinces a suicidal man, played by Jimmy Stewart, that his life is worth living and that he must remain true to his principles. Throughout his life, Stewart maintained that this role was his particular favorite. Another film, *Field of Dreams,* while only subtly invoking angel spirits, made such an impact on the public that the baseball field in Iowa, where it was filmed, attracts thousands of tourists yearly.

In pondering this development, I can only surmise that the angels have, for whatever reason, decided that it is time for them to come forward and reveal themselves. My feeling is that they are doing so in response to many heartfelt prayers from people from all faiths and all walks of life.

Another reason for this extraordinary resurgence of interest in angels—and apparently for their increased appearances and interactions with human life—may well be as a counterweight to the heavily mechanistic life resulting from our burgeoning—and all too often soulless—electronic technology.

Could it be that the angels are now taking a more active role in our lives for the simple reason that we *need* them? Have we gone so far in our detachment from our own inner selves and our deep spiritual needs that we need their intervention and guidance more than ever before?

I can't claim to know the answers to these questions, but I think they are valid ones to ask as we venture to investigate the subject of angels in our lives. From my own experience, I can attest that angels, as guides and teachers as well as rescuers and performers of many other beneficial functions on behalf of humans, come in many forms and that individual contact with them is equally varied, as the true stories that appear throughout this book will demonstrate.

Angels can appear either as personages or as events; they can contact us while we are sleeping and dreaming, or they can put in an appearance while we are wide awake and functioning in our normal everyday world. There is a mystery here, and it is very deep, as well as intensely intriguing. To encounter an angelic presence in any manner is to touch the hem of the divine plan.

Many traditions claim that we have certain angelic guides with us from birth until death, as well as a personal guardian angel. It is my own personal experience that these angelic guides and teachers can come and go, changing according to our needs and level of spiritual progress.

Any discussion of spirit, or that which is spiritual, is fraught with complexity. Just what is spirit? And, where is it? Is it "out there," a great God in the sky? Or is it "in here," located somewhere within us? Are we spiritual only when we are present in our formal place of worship, or are we so also when we are actively praying to God? Does spirituality require a formal discipline, a prescribed practice? Can anyone be spiritual, or is this quality difficult to attain?

The simple truth is that we are *all* spiritual beings. The problem is that all too often we are not fully awake to our own sacred dimension and that of the world around us.

Unfortunately, many of us are cut off from this vivifying flow of spirit. We are hampered and hamstrung by the notion that what we seek exists somewhere in time and space, or is to be found in a specific place of worship. Today, many are seeking the wellspring of their own inner spirituality in their own individualized way. It is my opinion that the rise in our seeking a more personalized spirituality is more than a little responsible for the sudden rise of, and interest in, angelic encounters. More and more people are discovering that it is the *quality* of the encounter that is significant.

This question inevitably arises: What are angels? No one knows for sure, but I believe that they are celestial intelligence given form; some say they are beings of pure light who vibrate at a very high rate that ordinarily makes them invisible to us. Unlike ourselves, however, they have the ability to change their vibrations at will and assume different forms. When they lower their vibrations to the approximate rate of human vibration, they become visible to us or make us aware of their presence in some other way. We become aware of them through thoughts, ideas, and experiences, especially in dreams and altered states of consciousness such as meditation.

Accordingly, we must now explore more fully the nature of our relationship with angels, for even the most casual encounters are

fraught with enormous significance, not only for the individual, but also for the entire planet. Our most prominent physicists have declared that we live in a cosmos that is itself alive, and in a living cosmos, all communication is a sacred act. Every meeting, however chanceful it might seem, even with what appears to be nonliving (or inorganic) matter, bears within it the possibility of communion with the divine presence, which is everywhere and in all things. It is through our observations and how we relate to them that we learn to see the soul inherent in whatever we behold. Thus, in some sense, we commune with angels all the time, whether or not we are aware of it.

For example, the evening of the first day I spent writing this book, after I had finished a long and tiring day's work and left my studio—my head fairly spinning with angel matters and the long daunting task ahead—I sat at the small table where I sort through my mail, on which there is a lamp with a pink shade. Suddenly, the most beautiful moth I have ever seen (and there are many of these creatures who upon examination look like works of art) flew straight at me and landed on the lampshade. It was a chilly night, and all the windows and doors were closed, as they had been all day. How had this flying fellow gained entry? As I gazed at the beautiful, winged visitor who had calmly settled in utter stillness with the rosy glow of the lamp as its background, mere inches from my face, I realized that it was an angel come to call, as if to approve of my day's work and encourage me in my endeavors. It was no mere insect, not at all—but a divine visitation. And just as an eraser cleans chalk off a blackboard, my fatigue vanished, and I felt elated and energized for the continuance of the work begun.

Angels, then, though they can appear in extraordinary circumstances—such as when they save lives—are actually the inner life and light of familiar things. It doesn't make a bit of difference whether angels are "real" in the sense of being discrete entities separate from ourselves, or whether they are abstract powers or energies operating in ways we can never comprehend. What is important is that they speak to us in many ways, on many levels. They exist simultaneously in various forms, expressing their own, and our human, extraordinary range of diversity. Just as no two

humans are exactly alike, no two angels are alike either. As physicist David Bohm tells us, it is how we relate to our experiences that enables us to see what we see, or even to participate in the creation of that which we see.

Therefore, it is necessary for humans to begin to cooperate with the angels' intentions. We must, as Jesus is reported to have said in one of the Gnostic gospels (discovered in 1945 at a village in upper Egypt called Nag Hammadi), realize that "the kingdom of the Father is spread over the earth and men do not see it."

And, in truth, the divine is everywhere, and angels are its closest representatives to us. We have only to look and listen, to pay attention to the small details, to become *aware*, for the possibility is that an angel is *always* nearby, just waiting to be recognized.

Through our communion with angels, we have the rare opportunity to envision heaven in the here and now, to intuit the eternal as part of ourselves as individuals. We have only to learn to be watchful in new ways, to open our eyes and our hearts to the elegant potential of spirit that dwells in the most interior, sacred, part of our beings. Through our encounters with angels, we part the veil that separates us from the realization of our own divinity and get a privileged glimpse—if only for a brief moment—of the illusionary division between heaven and earth.

The Sufi tradition tells us that there is a hidden meaning in all things, that every thing has an outer as well as an inner meaning, and that every external form is complemented by an inner reality that is its hidden eternal essence.

Treat your life in all its parts, the good and the bad, with compassion, gentleness, patience, and respect, and you will find the sacred all about you in your daily life, with all of its mundane activities. You may be surprised at all the positive change that can come about as you open to the sacredness of every day and discover that the living spirit is everywhere, unbounded. And in so doing, you will surely find yourself in the companionship of angels.

Part One

Angels
in History

CHAPTER ONE
Ancient Angels

*T*he many books being written about angels today attest to a renewed and burgeoning interest in them. Angels have a long tradition. We don't know if they appeared to prehistoric man—although they may have been more apparent to people who lived in close communion with nature and relied more on their intuition than on rational thought—but when history begins to be recorded, we find images of them in many cultures around the world. These images suggest that the notion of angels is embedded in our psyches.

From the city of Ur, in the Euphrates valley, c. 4000–2500 B.C.E., comes a stele depicting a winged figure who has descended from one of the seven heavens, pouring the water of life from an overflowing jar. Some scholars maintain that this is the earliest known representation of an angel, but there are other precursors. In Mesopotamia, there were giant winged creatures, part human, part animal, known as griffins. And in Egypt, Nepthys, the twin sister of the goddess Isis, is shown in paintings and reliefs enfolding the dead in her beautiful wings.

Images of angels appear all over Asia Minor, in different cultures in the ancient civilized world, and westward into Greece and Italy. Iris, "the rainbow of Zeus," and Hermes, messenger of the gods and guide of souls, both wear wings and serve angelic functions, carrying messages and giving humans aid. The famous Greek sculpture Winged Victory was a precursor to the Italian Renaissance representations of winged angels in the form with which we are today familiar.

Angels are arranged in a hierarchy radiating downward from God or heaven. One of these orders of angels is the cherubim (a plural noun), from the Assyrian *karibu*, which means "one who prays" or "one who communicates." The Islamic form is *el-karrubiyan*, meaning "brought near to Allah." Cherubim praise God unceasingly night and day.

In Assyrian art, cherubim are the figures we call griffins, with wings and human or lion faces and with bodies of eagles, bulls, or sphinxes. Highly symbolic, these griffins combine in one body the four signs of the zodiac that mark the solstices and equinoxes of

the earliest period of Mesopotamian astronomy: the Bull (Taurus, or the spring equinox and eastern quarter); the Lion (Leo, or the summer solstice and southern quarter); the Eagle (Scorpio, or the autumn equinox and western quarter); and the Water Carrier (Aquarius, or the winter solstice and northern quarter).

These figures often carry little pouches, symbolic of the elixir of immortal life. They were guardians, as were the angels who stood at the gates of the Garden of Eden with flaming swords, after the expulsion of Adam and Eve, to prevent them from returning to eat the fruit of the Tree of Immortal Life. However, the more ancient angels did not prevent humans from enjoying the Tree, but rather, they fostered its care. A cylinder seal (700–600 B.C.E.) in the Morgan Library in New York City depicts two winged figures, or genii, fertilizing the Tree of Immortal Life from the elixir in their pouches.

The word *angelos* in the original Greek means "messenger," and in this respect, angels may be related to the function of Mercury, or Hermes, one of whose daughters is called "angel" by Pindar. A daughter of Zeus, Iris, the goddess of the rainbow, is also described as an angel by the writer Hesiod. Such terms suggest that an angel is a special carrier of messages from the gods, an idea that permeates the writings about angels of many cultures, including those that precede the biblical stories.

Without doubt, based upon archeological evidence and other prehistoric information, there were angels long before Christianity appeared on the religious stage. Angels are most ancient, predating even early Judaism. In addition to Hermes, who wore wings on his heels, and Iris, from the Greek tradition, we have angel-type figures, often called griffins, in many ancient cultures. An Etruscan tombstone dating from about 100 B.C.E. has kneeling beside it two enormous stone figures with great wings springing from their shoulders. However, even such remarkable examples are recent when compared to the figures of ancient Egypt, Mesopotamia, the Hittites, and the Persians.

In Egypt, for example, the goddess Nepthys, considered along with Isis and Osiris to be one of the progenitors of the world, often

Messenger of the Gods

"The mysterious figure of Hermes, the Greek god who was the guide of souls and messenger of the gods, is the perfect paradigm for the guides and teachers [angels] we encounter on 'the other side' during our journeys into the mysterious realm of our selves.

"Hermes, whom the Romans renamed Mercury, is first known to us through the Greek epics of Homer, the *Iliad* and the *Odyssey*. He is most powerful, the mediator between the worlds of being and nonbeing, of reality and unreality, of conscious and unconscious."

—M. J. Abadie, *Your Psychic Potential*

appears as a winged figure. She is seen thus on the inner right-hand door of Shrine III in the tomb of Tutankhamen, c. fourteenth century B.C.E. (in the Cairo Museum). Tall and erect in the Egyptian fashion, she spreads her slender arms, to which her intricately carved wings are attached (as opposed to the usual shoulder blade rendition), in a sweeping motion forward, as if to encompass the dead pharaoh and protect him from all harm. It is interesting that this angelic representation is on the inside of the shrine and would thus not be visible when the shrine doors were shut, as they surely would have been when the young Tut was buried.

Other early cultures featured winged lions and bulls with human heads who warded off evil and stood between the realm of the myriad gods of the era and their human worshippers. Sometimes, griffins were entirely human in appearance, as is the case of the two winged genii fertilizing the Tree of Life, depicted on a cylinder seal from Assyria c. 700–600 B.C.E., mentioned above.

The ancient Egyptians believed that each person born into the world had a supernatural double, called his or her ka, who was born alongside the person and stayed as a part of his or her life ever after. The ka was in one sense what we today call a guardian angel, but it also represents the soul, or that part of the human being that is able to separate from the body and travel around on its own. To what we refer to as "out of body" experiences these days, the old Egyptians would simply say that their ka was off somewhere else than attached to the body and would find nothing unusual about it.

A Complete World

The classical scholar Walter F. Otto tells us that "the world of Hermes/ Mercury is a complete one . . . a world in the full sense which Hermes animates and rules, a complete world, and not some fragment of the sum total of existence."

Akhenaton

One theory about the evolution of ancient angels is a result of the reign of the Pharaoh Amenhotep IV, commonly known as Akhenaton, whose wife was the beautiful Nefertiti. Akhenaton, though he had been raised with the entire multifold pantheon of the Egyptian gods and goddesses, decided that there should be a single deity over all to whom the others should become subordinate. He chose Ra, or the Sun, for this role. Since Akhenaton was the supreme ruler, the people had no choice but to go along with this extremely unorthodox change in their centuries-old religious practices and beliefs, and while Akhenaton lived and reigned, Egyptians worshiped Ra as their only god.

No fool, Akhenaton knew that he could not simply erase centuries of multiple gods and goddesses in one stroke, although he made an effort to do so by having their various names erased from the monuments. To appease his uneasy subjects, he allowed the former gods and goddesses to remain in the pantheon, but in a diminished stature; according to one chronicler, they were left "hanging about like reduced officers and doing odd jobs for the chief god . . . angels in the making."

Since ancient tradition is extremely hard to root out, Akhenaton's premature effort at establishing monotheism failed in the end, dying with him and his elegant queen.

Zoroaster

A similar fate befell the gods of ancient Persia in the sixth century B.C.E. (there is scholarly disagreement on this date; Professor Eduard Meyer dates the prophet c. 1000 B.C.E.), when the prophet Zoroaster announced that from thenceforth there would be one and only one god—named Ahura Mazda.

As with Akhenaton, Zoroaster, for all his power over the populace, couldn't manage to eradicate the whole pantheon of deities his people had been honoring for centuries, a pantheon that included winged bull-men, a god named Nebo, a moon god, and others called sukalli, or angel messengers, who were the sons of the deities. Therefore, he came up with the ingenuous idea of assigning them other roles in his new religion. He declared them to be either "bounteous immortals," or good spirits, or else to be demons. By either designation, they all stayed on, another troop of angels in the making.

As indeed Buddha would do half a millennium later, Zoroaster sought to establish a form of monotheism based on ethical principles that emphasized goodness over evil—good thoughts, words,

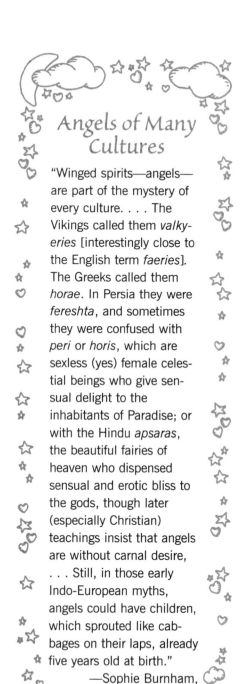

Angels of Many Cultures

"Winged spirits—angels—are part of the mystery of every culture. . . . The Vikings called them *valkyries* [interestingly close to the English term *faeries*]. The Greeks called them *horae*. In Persia they were *fereshta*, and sometimes they were confused with *peri* or *horis*, which are sexless (yes) female celestial beings who give sensual delight to the inhabitants of Paradise; or with the Hindu *apsaras*, the beautiful fairies of heaven who dispensed sensual and erotic bliss to the gods, though later (especially Christian) teachings insist that angels are without carnal desire, . . . Still, in those early Indo-European myths, angels could have children, which sprouted like cabbages on their laps, already five years old at birth."
—Sophie Burnham, *A Book of Angels*

Zoroaster the Prophet

Zoroaster, or Zarathustra (the name meaning "rich in camels"), dates sometime between 1000 and 600 B.C.E. Born in Media and active in Bactria, Zoroaster was a prophet who sought to revise the religion of the era, which was quite likely related to the Hindu Vedas, which included the worship of fire and the sacrifice of cattle. It probably also included the worship of the Great Goddess (which had not yet died out completely) in Her various forms, which in Hinduism are many, and may have included the reverence of Ba'al or Ba'lim.

deeds. He formulated the then-new idea that the world is polarized in a perpetual battle between the forces of good and evil and that it is the charge of humans to choose between them.

Thus, in the religion of Zoroastrianism, good is ruled by the supreme god Ahura Mazda (or wise lord), who represents the supreme pure light. Ahura Mazda is assisted by archangels or holy spirits that represent the seven fundamental moral ideas proposed by Zoroaster. His opposite is Angra Mainyu, or Ahaitin (an early form of Satan); he is the progenitor of evil, the dark principle, or evil spirit. This evil god is surrounded by demons.

One authority translates the seven moral ideas proposed by Zoroaster as Good Knowledge (Wisdom), Truth (or The Way), Piety, Salvation, Immortality (or Delight in Beauty), Obedience, and Deserved Good Luck. Each of these amesha spenta is assigned to protect something. Wisdom protects the Earth, Truth protects Fire, Delight in Beauty protects Plants, and so forth.

Another angel in Zoroaster's system is Ashi, the Good Angel of Blessings. Ashi is the feminine form of Asha, who rules over Truth, Justice, Virtue, Holiness, Cosmic Law, and Order. Ahura Mazda, as head god, bestows blessings on those who follow Asha, or Truth and Divine Law (as defined by Zoroaster).

In turn, Armaiti, the Angel of Devotion, or Love of God, protects Ashi and her three brothers: Sraosha, the Angel of Divine Intuition; Rashnu, the Angel of Justice, who—like the Goddess Maat in the Egyptian pantheon, who places the "feather of truth" on the opposite side of the scale upon which holds the dead soul in order to judge its right to enter the Underworld of Osiris—weighs the good and evil deeds of the soul when it reaches the underworld of death; and Meher, the Angel of Light and Mercy, who comforts the soul during its journey into the Underworld (not unlike the Greek Hermes, who serves as the soul's guide). Clearly, there are all sorts of interminglings among the formulations of these early religions.

Zoroaster's teaching of certain powers proceeding from the Creator also included other angels, or yazatas, one of which was Psychopomp (here again an echo to Hermes, who is also known

as Psychopomp), who was the "Celestial Escort, or Lord of the Material Plane." Another was known as Vata, who ruled the Air and the Winds. A third, Mithra—he of the ten thousand eyes—was considered to be the angelic mediator between heaven and earth, judge and preserver of the world.

Interestingly, as the pre-Zoroastrians sacrificed cattle, Mithra is seen represented on ancient monuments as a handsome youth plunging a dagger into the neck of a bull! In a fascinating precursor to later Christian practice, Mithra was worshiped in underground catacombs in a ceremony that involved baptism, the eating of consecrated bread and water, and anointing with honey.

Prior to the time of Zoroaster, there had been no division of the Supreme Being into good and evil: the Ultimate Source, by whatever name (and certainly the Great Goddess), were presumed to contain *both* good and evil, without any concept of right or wrong attached to either. In essence, it was assumed that although people perceived their experiences on earth to be either beneficent or malignant, the Supreme Deity saw to it that they contained the seeds of both. It was not an either/or situation but one that was all inclusive. It was not until the advent of Zoroastrianism that the world became split in two—one part good, the other part evil, and the two always at war with one another. This duality has plagued humanity ever since—good angels arranged on one side, with evil spirits on the other, in eternal battle for the souls of humans.

As it happened, the Greeks were hot on the heels of Zoroaster's followers, and in 330 B.C.E., Alexander the Great all but wiped out Zoroastrianism when he marched triumphantly across the Levant. The seventh century C.E. Muslim conquest of Asia Minor exterminated what few followers remained, and the once great Ahura Mazda was declared dead—though oddly enough, those names live on today as a lightbulb and an automobile. The small pockets of remaining worshippers eventually migrated to India in the tenth century C.E., and became known as the Parsees; they still exist as a dwindling sect today, mostly assimilated into the Hindu culture.

Zoroaster's Legacy

Zoroaster, according to Professor Meyer, was "the first personality to have worked creatively and formatively upon the course of religious history." Although Akhenaton had gone there first, "his solar monotheism did not endure." As a result—and in contrast to the enduring metaphysical religiosity of the Orient, which saw the cosmic order as an ever-cycling, unchanging majestic process that could never be changed or altered by the hand of man—the religion propounded by Zoroaster can, according to Joseph Campbell, "be heard echoed and re-echoed, in Greek, Latin, Hebrew and Aramaean, Arabic, and every tongue of the West."

Mithraism

Mithra was restored to full godhead in his own right by the later Persians, who installed the religion called Mithraism, a syncretic cult that became the chief religion of the empire, a sort of Zoroastrian heresy that was, in the Roman period, a formidable rival of Christianity both in Asia and in Europe. Mithraism reached as far north as to the south of Scotland. Interestingly, the neophyte was known as Raven, another of our winged friends.

Angels in Different Faiths

Angels are found also in the oriental cultures represented by Buddhism and Taoism. The angels of ancient Assyria and Mesopotamia were a tradition that was carried down through Manichaean, Judaic, Christian, and Islamic lore, all of which influenced each other's faith in angels. Without question, the idea of angels appears everywhere in Asia Minor, our ancient civilized world, from where it extended into the Mediterranean basin of Greece and Italy, where it would be transformed.

In Greece, the idea of angels transformed into the famous Winged Victory "Nike"; this sculpture served as a model for the Renaissance angels that proliferated into the Middle Ages, firmly establishing the concept of angels in that period. The once fierce cherubim changed from the vastly awesome beings of Ezekiel's vision—those terrifying creatures with swords of fire who guarded the Garden of Eden against the return of the expelled Adam and Eve—into putti, or cute little pink baby cherubs. Childlike in form and appearance, cherubs usually floated like little Cupids around beautiful, serene women, who are often pregnant or with small children.

Shamanism

Even the world's oldest religious practice, shamanism, such as was practiced by Native Americans, incorporates intercourse with winged beings. These often come in the form of eagles or ravens or spirits and are not usually associated with the later angelic iconography.

Among Native Americans, great birds—Raven and Eagle—were believed to help humans, to heal or bring fire, or to carry messages from God. In this tradition, too, friendly spirits, or familiars, walk among the people and guard them from harm. These winged creatures are considered to be of great help to the tribal shaman in his work.

We cannot ever know if the idea of angels arose in different cultures independently, if the idea traveled from culture to culture, or which cultural ideas seeded those of others. All over

Asia, from Byzantium to Cathay, for thousands of years, merchants and mercenaries, wise men and priests, prophets and pagans, and those uprooted by famine or war wandered and intermingled. Ideas are rootless, often seeming to come from out of nowhere. Thus it is that we find the concept of angels in the mythologies of nearly every ancient culture of which we have knowledge. The angel concept courses through the centuries like a single thread on which each culture hung its own variations of the same theme.

Doubtless, however, in the long and meandering river of thought about angels that finally reached the West, the most important and enduring figure—the real prototype of what became Judeo-Christian-Islamic versions of angels—is the towering figure of Hermes Trismegistus of the Greeks, whom we know as Mercury.

The great classical scholar Karl Kerényi says that Hermes "is called *angelos* . . . the messenger of the Gods." The deeper expression of Mercury's role as messenger of the gods is that he mediates or delivers messages between the conscious mind and the unconscious realm (or altered states of consciousness such as dreams). This is a more subtle meaning than is usually encountered in discussions of angels, but it is one of the most important factors in understanding how angels operate, especially as guides and teachers.

To embark upon the spiritual journey is to invite unseen forces to interact with us. These creative energies manifest in many ways, a principal one of which is as angels. Angels bring us into grace and show the way. To encounter an angel—and they come in many guises—is to enter another realm, a place of great powers and, sometimes, of great secrets. This realm belongs to the invisible world, although its denizens come in human or animal form. To interface with this world is to be impacted in a way that is life changing. With angels, we enter a world of supreme power—not the power of the material world but of the invisible order that supports and nourishes our world and our lives here. It is the realm of the sacred.

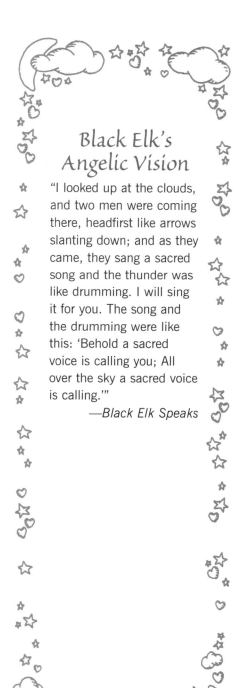

Black Elk's Angelic Vision

"I looked up at the clouds, and two men were coming there, headfirst like arrows slanting down; and as they came, they sang a sacred song and the thunder was like drumming. I will sing it for you. The song and the drumming were like this: 'Behold a sacred voice is calling you; All over the sky a sacred voice is calling.'"

—*Black Elk Speaks*

Classical Greek Hermes, the "guide of souls," is emblematic of such angels. In answer to the question, "What appeared to the Greeks as Hermes?" Kerényi states:

. . . he is the supra-individual source of a particular world-experience and world configuration [that] is open to the possibility of a transcendent guide and leader who is also able to provide impressions of consciousness, but of a different kind: impressions that are palpable and manifest, that in no way contradict the observations and conclusions of natural science, and yet extend beyond the attitude which is the common one today . . . . The sum total of pathways as Hermes' playground; the accidental "falling into your lap" as the Hermetic material; its transformation through finding . . . . They are the world and they are *one* world, namely, *that* world which Hermes opens to us.

Kerényi speaks also of the "activity of Hermes" as referring to "alternatives of life, to the dissolution of fatal opposites, to clandestine violations of boundaries and laws." In other words, the overturning of the rational-mind-dictated world and the discovery of the magical powers of both the inner and outer worlds in which we live and have our being.

The Bible on Angels

"For He will command His angels concerning you to guard you in all your ways; they will lift you up in their hands, so that you will not strike your foot against a stone."
—Psalms 91:11,12

Seven Ancient Angels

Unity minister Catharine Ponder identifies the following seven types of ancient angels to whom one can appeal for specific purposes related to *other people*:

1. The angel of *Ephesus*, for those who are appealing but hard to reach
2. The angel of *Smyrna*, for those who are lovers of beauty and adornment who tend to get into financial trouble
3. The angel of *Pergamum*, for those who are closely knit in family or business relationships, wary of strangers, new friends, and new ideas
4. The angel of *Thyatira*, for those who are idealistic but have trouble producing actual results
5. The angel of *Sardis*, for those who are timid, apprehensive, fearful, indecisive, hypochondriac
6. The angel of *Philadelphia*, for organizations that espouse brotherly love but don't practice love
7. The angel of *Laodicea*, for unstable, unsettled, changeable wanderers seeking new doctrines, new places

For a full exposition of angel-writing techniques, case histories, and examples of letters to the seven types of angels, see Ponder's *The Prospering Power of Love*.

CHAPTER TWO

The Old Testament View of Angels

How Many Angels Are There?

Angels crisscross both the Old and New Testaments. They are mentioned directly or indirectly about three hundred times, according to Billy Graham. It is told that David recorded twenty thousand angels coursing through the stars in the sky. Even without modern telescopes—or even binoculars—he managed to note, in Psalms 68:17, that "the chariots of God are twenty thousand, even thousands of angels."

Some biblical scholars believe that angels can be numbered in the millions, based on the comment in Hebrews 12:22, which refers to "an innumerable company of angels."

Abraham and Sarah

In Genesis 21:14–20, angels are introduced by an amazingly dramatic scenario that could have come from a Hollywood production. Imagine the following: A young woman finds herself pregnant by an important man who has a powerful wife. The wife, to her dismay, is infertile. This unfortunate girl is in a most inferior position, lower even than a servant; she is a slave. And it is the wife herself who has presented the girl as a gift—a concubine—to her husband, who is not a young man himself. As we know, men can father children at a far later age than women can bear them, and so in due course, the young slave girl cum concubine, named Hagar, found herself "in the family way."

True to dramatic form, the wife, Sarah, was less than pleased to find her gift concubine impregnated with her husband's seed. In fact, Sarah made poor Hagar's life a living hell.

When the poor girl could take no more of Sarah's abuse, she ran away. At this time, there were, of course, no women's shelters, only the wilderness, full of wild beasts and all manner of other dangers. And Hagar had no money, though money wouldn't have helped much in any case.

During her flight, she found a spring on the road to Shur and stopped there to rest and refresh herself. Here she had her first of two encounters with angelic presences, called holy ones by the Jews. The Bible reports that "the angel of the Lord found her . . . and said to her, 'Return to your mistress, and submit yourself to her authority [for] you are with child, and you shall bear a son; and you shall call his name Ishmael.'"

Not knowing what else to do, Hagar obeyed the angel and returned to Abraham's house and gave birth to a boy, naming him Ishmael as she had been directed. In time, Hagar once again found herself alone in the desert, not a runaway, but an outcast. At some distance, lying under the sparse shade of a shrub, lay her son Ishmael, dying of thirst. Fearful for her son's life, Hagar prayed as she had been taught to do; as she did, she heard the voice she had heard earlier:

"What is the matter with you, Hagar? Do not fear, for God has heard the voice of the lad where he is," said the voice

Isaiah on Angels

"Anyone who doubts [the grandeur of angels] should read a first-hand description of angels as they were in Old Testament times, such as what Isaiah said of these heavenly creatures:

"'In the year that king Uzziah died I saw also the Lord sitting upon a throne, high and lifted up, and his train filled the temple. Above it stood the seraphims: each one had six wings; with twain he covered his face, and with twain he covered his feet, and with twain he did fly.'

"Another passage comments that every seraph has *four faces* . . . There is a Syrian depiction in sculpture of a demon that exactly meets Isaiah's standards; it dates from the eighth century B.C. It has six wings, holds a serpent in each hand, and is terrifying . . . . Some scholars have pointed out that the Hebrew *saraph*, possibly the origin of the word "seraph," means "serpent." *Seraphim* is translated as "burning ones." . . . but let us return to Isaiah:

"'And one cried unto another, and said, Holy, holy, holy, is the Lord of hosts: the whole earth is full of His glory. And the posts of the door moved at the voice of him that cried, and the house was filled with smoke. Then said I, Woe is me! . . . Then flew one of the seraphims unto me, having a live coal in his hand, which he had taken with the tongs from off the altar: And he laid it upon my mouth, and said, Lo, this hath touched thy lips; and thine iniquity is taken away, and thy sin is purged.'"

—Emily Hahn, *Breath of God*

*of the angel of God, and Hagar took heart hearing this call
from heaven.*

*"Then God opened her eyes and she saw a well of water; and
she went and filled the skin with water, and gave the lad a drink.
And God was with the lad."*

Abraham, too, entertained angels, as we are told in Genesis,
but these appeared as ordinary men. They came and sat down to
dinner with Abraham and his wife Sarah, who was promised a
baby of her own, despite her advanced age.

These angels, three of them, one of which was said to be
Yahweh himself, partook of the meal, even eating some of the meat
course, although this detail has been hotly debated for centuries by
biblical scholars who specialize in angelology. Angels, you see, are
supposed to eat nothing but manna, that same substance that was
fed to the starving followers of Moses during their flight from Egypt.

Be that as it may—and no one will ever know for certain—
Genesis tells us that as the angels were departing, they informed
Sarah that she would bear a child, a son named Isaac, whose
descendants would found a great Hebrew nation. It was this star-
tling announcement, considering the circumstances of the aged
couple, that made Abraham realize he had been visited by holy
ones, or angels.

A Wife for Isaac

When Abraham and Sarah's son Isaac grew to marriageable age,
Abraham assigned the job of finding a proper bride for his son to
his trusted servant. In so doing, he said, "The Lord, the God of
heaven, who took me from my father's house and from the land of
my birth and who spoke to me, and who swore to me, saying 'To
your descendants I will give this land,' He will send his angel
before you and you will take a wife for my son from there"
(Genesis 24:7).

Apparently, the angel performed as promised, going before
Abraham's servant and acting as matchmaker to arrange the perfect
wife for Isaac, the comely Rebekah. Who's to say just what the

An Army of Angels

In the Jewish Kabbalah, the
number of angels is listed at
49 million, while by another
count there are 496,000
angels, ranked into seven
divisions like an army. In a
vision, Daniel saw that
"thousands of thousands
ministered to him and ten
thousand time a hundred
thousand stood before him."

angel whispered in her ear when the servant popped the question as to whether she would go with him to be the wife of Isaac. When asked, "Will you go with this man?" she replied without hesitation, "I will go." And thus was a large chunk of Jewish history made. One might say this was a marriage made in heaven.

Meetings with angels seemed to run in this family, for Abraham's nephew, Lot, who was a resident of the city of Sodom, was visited by two strangers, who turned out to be angels. The men of the city came to Lot's house and threatened to attack and rape his guests. In retaliation for such inhospitable behavior, the angels "smote the men with blindness." The next morning, as they took their leave, thanking him for his hospitality, they told him to get out of town, and to be quick about it. The startled Lot asked why and was told that God had marked Sodom for destruction because of all the sinful tomfoolery going on in the city. Realizing this was sound advice from a supernatural source, Lot packed up and left town and saved his life. Unfortunately, his wife, who had been explicitly warned not to look back as they fled, did so and was instantly turned into a pillar of salt! But the obedient Lot and his two single daughters were saved when Sodom and Gomorrah went up in flames, the same angels being the arsonists who caused the destructive blaze. This story illustrates the idea that the "holy ones" can serve the dual purposes of salvation and destruction.

Jacob

Abraham's grandson, Jacob, had a difficult experience with an angel, wrestling with him all night in the dark. He hadn't a clue who his adversary was, for the angel apparently appeared as an ordinary man with nary a wing in sight.

Now it had happened that, as a young man, Jacob had cheated his brother Esau out of his inheritance by deceiving their blind father. He had also tricked his uncle Laban out of all his wealth and possessions, after which he decamped and went on to marry twice, as a result of which he had twelve sons (we are not informed of the number of his daughters, if any). In addition,

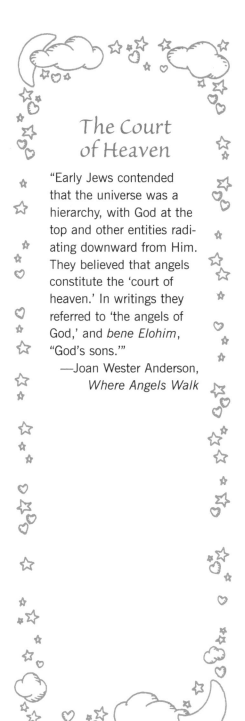

The Court of Heaven

"Early Jews contended that the universe was a hierarchy, with God at the top and other entities radiating downward from Him. They believed that angels constitute the 'court of heaven.' In writings they referred to 'the angels of God,' and *bene Elohim*, "God's sons.'"

—Joan Wester Anderson, *Where Angels Walk*

he had liaisons with numerous maidservants who produced his illegitimate children. After all this procreating, Jacob decided to return home. After what he'd been up to, he wasn't quite sure of his welcome, so he set up camp half-a-day's camel ride from Esau's encampment and began sending gifts—entire herds of sheep and goats, thirty she-camels for milking, along with their young, twenty female asses and their ten offspring, and forty cows just for good measure. Milk was much appreciated in the desert climate.

Even after sending all these elaborate peace offerings, Jacob's mind was not at rest; he knew he'd done wrong. He feared Esau might kill him when he discovered he was nearby. One night, an angel came. Jacob wrestled with the angel all night long, not knowing who his adversary was. In the end, Jacob prevailed. He then demanded a boon (blessing) from the angel, who gave it without ever identifying itself. But Jacob figured out that his struggle had been with a supernatural being, and since he had won, he concluded that all would be well with his brother.

The next day he arranged to meet Esau. He took all of his various wives, servants, livestock, and other riches, much of which he had in the form of precious metals, tapestries, woolen goods, jewelry, and the like, and traveled down into the valley and across the plain to where his brother awaited him. Esau arrived with an armed guard of 450 men, but he offered Jacob peace and forgiveness and professed to be glad to be reunited with this brother.

Jacob's angel never returned. From a psychological point of view, we might view this encounter as a struggle with inner conflict between right and wrong, especially since Jacob had clearly wronged his innocent brother, who had trusted him. No matter. Nowhere is it explicitly stated that angels are exterior or interior. Personally, I am sure they can be either or both.

Apparently Jacob learned from these experiences to recognize angels when they presented themselves. We have this passage from Genesis 32:1,2: "And Jacob went on his way, and the angels of God met him. And when Jacob saw them, he said, 'This is God's host' and he called the name of that place Mahanaim.''

Jacob was clearly deeply involved with angelic presences all through his life, and when he reached the end of it, reviewing his experiences with the holy ones, he in wonder exclaimed, "God . . . has been my shepherd all my life to this day, the angel who has redeemed me from all evil."

This same Jacob is the one famous for "Jacob's ladder." He saw in a vision the multitude of angels ascending and descending a ladder that reached up to heaven. By this time, he had become used to recognizing angelic presences. The Bible does not report whether or not the angels on the ladder in Jacob's vision had wings, but one would presume not, since they were climbing up and down the ladder.

None of these angels had any unusual garments or characteristics that would distinguish them from ordinary men. They had no halos (these would be introduced later in medieval art) and wore no "shining garments of the Lord." They were just working angels in plain clothes and nothing more.

Such angel visitations are similar to those reportedly made by the Greek gods to favored mortals. Hermes (or Mercury, as he was known to the Romans) appeared often as a youthful stranger, showing the way or being helpful in some manner.

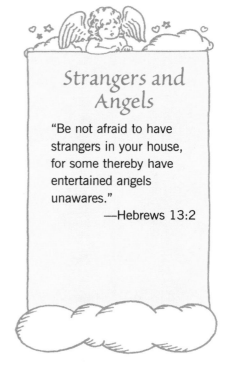

Strangers and Angels

"Be not afraid to have strangers in your house, for some thereby have entertained angels unawares."

—Hebrews 13:2

Abraham and Isaac

One of the most famous biblical stories of angels has to do with Abraham and his son Isaac. One day, Abraham heard the voice of God—spoken through an angel (for being messengers is one of their prime duties)—calling to him. In Genesis 22:11, we are told, "And the angel of the Lord called unto him out of heaven, and said, 'Abraham, Abraham' and he said, 'Here am I.'"

The voice instructed him to sacrifice his son Isaac. It ordered him to take the boy to the top of a remote mountain and slit his throat in the manner of the usual sacrificial lamb

and to let his blood run out as an offering to prove to God that Abraham was a true and complete devotee. Giving up that which was most dear to him, his only child, would show God that Abraham's devotion included complete surrender to God's will.

Without questioning this heavenly dictum, Abraham made preparations for a sacrifice, sharpening his knife and gathering wood for a fire. Revealing his aims to no one, not even his wife (one can imagine what might have happened if he had revealed to her God's peculiar message), he took his son and, accompanied by one servant, went off into the wilderness.

Leaving the servant at the bottom of the mountain, Abraham went ahead with the boy, who trustingly tagged along, expecting to help his father sacrifice a lamb.

At one point Isaac realized there wasn't any animal with them and asked, "Father?" to which Abraham answered, as he had to the angel, "Here I am, my son."

The boy said, "We have the knife and wood for the fire, but there is no lamb."

"God will provide," answered Abraham, knowing that God had already provided the sacrificial lamb in the person of his beloved son. One can only wonder what this man must have been thinking and feeling as he prepared to do the unthinkable. At a certain point, Abraham and Isaac built an altar of stone and laid the fire and lit it. When it was going well, Abraham suddenly took hold of the boy and bound him hand and foot. Laying him across the altar, he raised the keen-edged knife in his hand and put it against his son's throat. As he was about to slice into flesh of his flesh, the angel's voice stopped him. "Lay not thy hand upon the lad," commanded the voice. Abraham obeyed, no doubt thankfully, and at that moment, he spotted a sheep with its woolly fleece entangled in the thorns of a bush. He caught it and sacrificed it, offering it up to God in place of his son.

Was the voice of the angel purely interior, or did Abraham actually hear someone? We'll never know.

Moses

In later years, as the children of Israel began the seemingly impossible task of overcoming the mighty nations of Canaan in order to take possession of their lands, Yahweh spoke to Moses to assure him there was nothing to fear. "Behold," he said, "I am going to send an angel before you to guard you along the way, and to bring you into the place which I have prepared . . . for My angel will go before you and bring you into the land" (Exodus 23:20,23).

As it happened, the process of being brought "into the land" had actually begun more than 40 years before, when the Israelites were in bondage in Egypt and the all-powerful Pharaoh refused to free them from their slavery.

Moses, desperate for his people to achieve their freedom, declared, "But when we cried out to the Lord, He heard our voice and sent an angel and brought us out of Egypt" (Numbers 20:16).

After having delivered the people of Israel from Egypt and overseen their emancipation from the Pharaoh, the angel did not forsake them but went along to sort of manage the trip. It even divided the waters of the Red Sea so they could pass through without getting wet.

Then, with the powerful army of Egypt in hot pursuit, the "angel of God, who had been going before the camp of Israel, moved and went behind them; and the pillar of cloud moved from before them and stood behind them. So it came between the camp of Egypt and the camp of Israel and there was the cloud along with the darkness, yet it gave light at night. Thus the one did not come near the other all night." (Exodus 14:19,20).

Angel of Death

Oddly enough, the only angel mentioned by name in the history books of the Old Testament is the Angel of Death. This angel, true to its name, was an agent of destruction, presumably acting under direct orders from God.

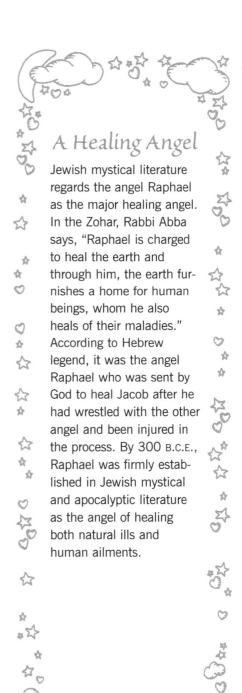

A Healing Angel

Jewish mystical literature regards the angel Raphael as the major healing angel. In the Zohar, Rabbi Abba says, "Raphael is charged to heal the earth and through him, the earth furnishes a home for human beings, whom he also heals of their maladies." According to Hebrew legend, it was the angel Raphael who was sent by God to heal Jacob after he had wrestled with the other angel and been injured in the process. By 300 B.C.E., Raphael was firmly established in Jewish mystical and apocalyptic literature as the angel of healing both natural ills and human ailments.

Interior Guides

"In those days angels acted more as the kind of interior guides that people work with today in their dream journals rather than as external beings. They could be counted on to appear when you called on them, and if Jacob wrestled all night with an angel who would not reveal its name, what do we learn from this strange tale except that even in that nomadic time men (and women, too, I hope) wrestled with their guilty inner selves?"

—Sophie Burnham, *A Book of Angels*

At the time of David, it destroyed 90,000 people, and on another occasion, in the Assyrian army camp that was arrayed against the Jews, it came along and killed 185,000 of King Sennacherib's soldiers as he was about to invade Judah, with his armies camped outside Jerusalem. This last was considered to be such a miraculous intervention that it is mentioned at length, described in a most fulsome way. Here is one description:

And it came to pass that night, that the angel of the Lord went out, and smote in the camp of the Assyrians a hundred fourscore and five thousand; and when they arose early in the morning, behold, they were all dead corpses.

Not surprisingly, Sennacherib returned to Nineveh and thenceforth left the Jews of Judah in peace.

Elijah

In an earlier tale from I Kings 18:22–40, Elijah, one of Israel's greatest prophets, flung down a gauntlet of challenge to the prophets of the heathen god Baal. It was a contest in which the losers would perish, for in those days they played for keeps.

It was at a time of severe drought, and Elijah proposed that the two contending sides build altars for sacrifice and call upon their separate Gods to inflame them. The priests of Baal erected an altar upon which they placed the customary bull for sacrifice and then, calling upon Baal to send fire, retired from the scene while Elijah's followers built their altar. This was duly accomplished, and the sacrifice was placed thereon. However, as a finishing touch, Elijah had his men dig a trench around the altar and fill it with water. Then, they drenched the altar itself—the wood, the stones, the bullock.

Elijah called upon Yahweh (Jehovah) to send fire, and in an instant, a huge sheet of flame arose into the air from Elijah's wet altar with such force and heat that it consumed the entire edifice, leaving only a pile of dust.

After this rather dramatic demonstration, the priests of Baal were captured and killed alongside the brook Kishon. And in the wake of these murders, came the rain—a regular deluge, after the long and disastrous drought.

Although Elijah had the courage of his conviction that Yahweh would send fire when asked, when he received word that an angered Queen Jezebel was planning to kill him in retaliation for the slaying of her prophets, Elijah turned tail and fled for his life.

Accordingly, the Queen's army took the lives of 450 of the Hebrew priests. Feeling responsible for their deaths, Elijah took to wandering in the wilderness in a sort of self-imposed penance. A victim of self-pity and self-recrimination and ready to give up, he prayed, "It is enough; now, O Lord, take my life, for I am not better than my fathers."

Then he lay down to what he supposed would be his last sleep but was awakened by someone touching his shoulder—an angel, of course. The angel had brought food for Elijah and commanded, "Arise and eat." Amazed at his deliverance, "he looked and behold, there was at his head a bread cake baked on hot stones, and a jar of water. So he ate and drank and lay down again. And the angel of the Lord came again a second time and touched him and said, 'Arise, eat, because the journey is too great for you.' So he arose and ate and drank, and went in the strength of that food forty days and forty nights to Horeb, the mountain of God" (I Kings 19:1–8).

Daniel

Last but not the least of the Old Testament angelic interventions is the story of Daniel in the lion's den. King Darius, a man who could recognize piety and courage when he saw it, predicted that Daniel's faith would save him from being eaten. He came to Daniel just before he was to be tossed into the den of the starved lions and said, "Your God whom you constantly serve will Himself deliver you."

Archangels of the Ten Sefiroth

1. Methattron, for Kether (crown)
2. Ratziel, for Chokmah (wisdom)
3. Tzaphqiel, for Binah (understanding)
4. Tzadqiel, for Chesed (mercy)
5. Khamael, for Geburah (strength or fortitude)
6. Mikhael, for Tipereth (beauty)
7. Haniel, for Netzach (victory)
8. Raphale, for Hod (splendor)
9. Gabriel, for Yesod (foundation)
10. Methattron, or the Shekinah, for Malkuth (kingdom)

—S. L. MacGregor Mathers, *The Kabbalah Unveiled*

In the morning, apparently somewhat worried about what might have transpired during Daniel's night with the hungry beast, the king approached the den and called out, "Daniel, servant of the living God, has your God, whom you constantly serve, been able to deliver you from the lions?"

Alive and well, Daniel was able to answer the worried king, saying, "O king, live forever! My God sent His angel [into the den before Daniel got there] and shut the lions' mouths, and they have not harmed me" (Daniel 6:16–23).

C. Leslie Miller, in *All about Angels*, says of this angelic visitation, "The Holy One knew just what Daniel needed, so he gave all the lions a temporary infection of lockjaw and to the prophet a good night's rest."

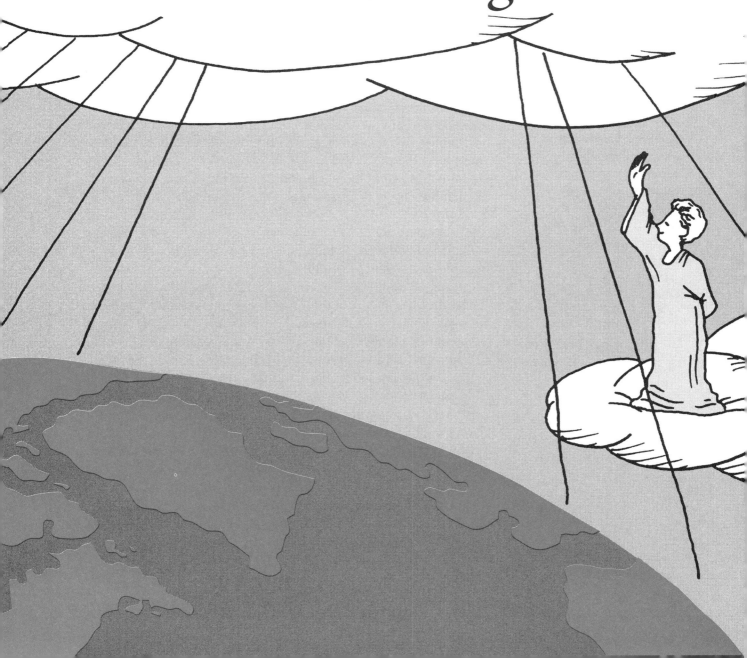

CHAPTER THREE

The New Testament View of Angels

Angel Battle

"Christians believe that God made angels at or about the time He made the world (Saint Augustine thought the two acts of creation were simultaneous), but before He created human beings. They were given minds and wills, like us, but had no bodies. At some point, according to the Book of Revelation, some of the angels wished to be gods and there was a terrible battle in heaven. The defeated angels then became evil spirits, headed by Satan, who roam the world to this day."
—Joan Wester Anderson, *Where Angels Walk*

With the advent of the New Testament, angels change dramatically. Gone are the Angels of Death and Vengeance, and also gone are the heroic deeds of angels. No longer do angels bring death and destruction upon such sinful places as Sodom and Gomorrah, nor do they go about killing the firstborn of unbelievers, as they did on that night when, to save their own, the Jews marked their lintel posts with the blood of a sacrificed lamb and, thus notified, the dread angel passed by their houses. Angels no longer bring plagues and disease, as they did in Egypt when the recalcitrant Pharaoh refused the Jews their freedom from bondage.

It was the encounters between the patriarchs, apostles, and angels that formed the basis for the early church fathers to develop the foundation and framework for angelology. These biblical references were the precedent for much of the most important angelological issues. All of the angelology of the early Christians passed through the angels of Scripture and the church fathers' interpretations of them.

Thus, the early church's readings of the angels of the Bible are of utmost importance, as they form the basis for the later Middle Ages view of angels, which inherited the previous interpretations and enlarged on them.

Most of the angels of the Old Testament were fairly bland creatures without personalities—messenger boys or God's agents. But Luke's narrative about Gabriel and the Annunciation offers images of angels that are more personalized. It is quite possibly this train of thought that caused the view of angels that has evolved from the Old Testament through the Middle Ages and into modern times to take on the qualities of personality, even quasi-humanness. From being purely abstract extensions of God, angels became *friends* to human beings, powers that could be called upon in times of stress or need.

Michael, for example, in Jude 9, fought with a demon over the soul of the deceased Moses. This passage seems to be the basis of the early Christian idea that angels would fight with evil spirits on behalf of humans. Also, Michael was seen as escorting souls to heaven, an idea that quite probably derived from the Greek Hermes, who served to guide souls after death.

Another important idea was that an angel not only would carry the dead soul to heaven but also would there crown it—an appealing notion to say the least. Imagine being crowned in heaven by an angel!

Angels constantly enjoy the company of God. As Matthew 18:10 tells us, they "always behold the face of [the] Father." This is especially true of guardian angels. It was the reading of Matthew 18:10, Acts 12:15, and Tobit 3:25 that convinced clerics to assert that God assigns an angel to stand by and watch over the welfare of each individual soul. This is the concept of the "guardian angel" that we know so well. This guardian angel is supposed to be with every person from birth throughout life.

There are two texts in Matthew that indicate angels will be a part of the Last Judgment. In 24:31, it states, "And he [the son] will send out his angels with a loud trumpet call, and they will gather all his elect from the four winds, from one end of heaven to the other."

And says Matthew in 13:41–42, "The Son of man will send his angels, and they will gather out of his kingdom all causes of sin and all evildoers, and throw them into the furnace of fire; there men will weep and gnash their teeth." Not a pretty picture. Not only will the good Christians be saved by the angels, but the angels will round up the bad guys and see that they get their just desserts.

But it is important to remember that early Christianity was preoccupied with the end of the world, or the Apocalypse. Jesus himself was an apocalyptic preacher, and his followers thought the end of the world was quite near. Naturally, angels would be important participants in this event.

Angels are found throughout Revelation, the last book of Scripture, which gives us this grand vision of final victory:

And war broke out in heaven; Michael and his angels fought against the dragon. The dragon and his angels fought back, but they were defeated, and there was no longer any place for them in heaven. The great dragon was thrown down, that ancient serpent, who is called the Devil and Satan, the deceiver of the whole world—he was thrown

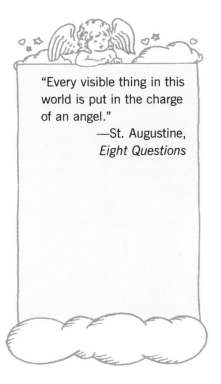

"Every visible thing in this world is put in the charge of an angel."
—St. Augustine,
Eight Questions

Heavenly Messenger

"In the original languages of the Old and New Testaments, the words translated *angel* literally and simply mean *messenger*. And this is how we most often find angels at work in the Bible: carrying a message. When they poke their celestial heads into stories of the Bible, more often than not it is to say something, guide a wandering nation, trumpet astonishing news, or set somebody straight."

—Timothy Jones, *Celebration of Angels*

down to the earth, and his angels were thrown down with him. Then I heard a loud voice in heaven, proclaiming,

> *Now have come the salvation and the power*
> *and the kingdom of our God*
> *and the authority of his Messiah,*
> *for the accuser of our comrades*
> *has been thrown down,*
> *who accuses them day and night before our God.*
> *But they have conquered him by the blood of the Lamb*
> *and by the word of their testimony,*
> *for they did not cling to life even in the face of death.*
> *Rejoice then, you heavens,*
> *and those who dwell in them!*
> *But woe to the earth and the sea,*
> *for the devil has come down to you*
> *with great wrath*
> *because he knows that his time is short.*

—Revelation 12:7–12

Angel Terminology

There is some confusion that was handed down to the New Testament writers from the Old Testament's view of angels, and that is in the matter of terminology (i.e., exactly what an angel was and how they were called) and of wings. Even though Tertullian stated flatly that "every angel and demon is winged," he was a latecomer in the field, having been born in the second century C.E., and he may not have been aware of all the angelic history that preceded his life. Wings actually come in after the conversion of Constantine.

Annunciation

Of course, the most important angelic visitation in the view of the early Christians, is the Annunciation, the speaking of those famous

words: *Ave Maria, gratia plena, Dominus tecum: Hail Mary, full of grace, the Lord is with thee.*

Although Mary didn't quite understand what the angel meant, she realized the message was of great importance and kept puzzling about what it might mean. Then the angel came to her and said, "Do not be afraid, Mary; for you have found favor with God. And behold, you will conceive in your womb, and bear a son, and you shall name him Jesus. He will be great, and will be called the Son of the Most High; and the Lord God will give Him the throne of His Father David; and He will reign over the house of Jacob forever; and His kingdom will have no end."

When Mary's pregnancy became obvious, Joseph, her husband, who was a much older man, was much embarrassed by this situation and wanted to quietly put her away somewhere so that her condition would not cause him and his family shame. But an angel of the Lord appeared to him in a dream, saying, "Joseph, son of David, do not be afraid . . . for that which has been conceived in her is of the Holy Spirit. And she will bear a Son; and you shall call His name Jesus, for it is He who will save His people from their sins."

After the birth of the Savior, the angel of the Lord continued to look after the family's safety. Herod, the Roman-appointed ruler of Jerusalem, heard rumors that the newborn might be a threat and became jealous of the babe and what his birth might mean, and made plans to have the child killed.

Once again, the angel appeared to Joseph in a dream and warned him, saying, "Arise, and take the Child and His mother, and flee to Egypt, and remain there until I tell you; for Herod is going to search for the Child to destroy Him." Later, after Herod died, the angel appeared again to Joseph in another dream and told him, "Arise and take the Child and His mother, and go into the land of Israel; for those who sought the Child's life are dead."

Angels comfort Jesus Christ when he is exhausted from his 40 days and 40 nights in the desert, where he was tempted by Satan, but the New Testament has little or nothing to say about angel activities until after the crucifixion of Christ.

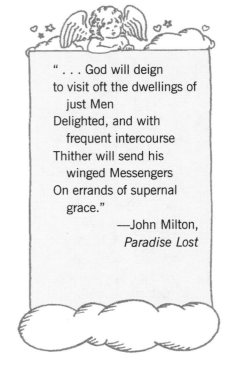

" . . . God will deign to visit oft the dwellings of just Men Delighted, and with frequent intercourse Thither will send his winged Messengers On errands of supernal grace."

—John Milton, *Paradise Lost*

Angels after the Crucifixion of Christ

The Gospel of Matthew does mention that two angels—without wings but with "a countenance like lightning" and "garments white as snow"—were found sitting inside the cave in which Christ had been laid in burial, possibly as mourners, as they appeared sad to the women who saw them.

On this occasion, Mary Magdalene and Mary (the mother of James, not the Virgin Mary) went to the tomb to care for the dead body and—lo and behold!—there was no body to be seen anywhere. It had disappeared. One of the angels informed the amazed and startled women that the reason there wasn't a corpse was that Christ had "risen up from the dead."

Not knowing what to think about this extraordinary occurrence, the women rushed back to where the men were waiting (it is not explained why the women went to the tomb, unless washing and dressing a dead body for burial was considered to be "women's work") and related their tale of wonder. Naturally, the men were skeptical, but they rushed up the hill to take a look for themselves and indeed found the tomb empty. This story is told in many different versions by different Gospel writers, but the basic elements are the same.

Angels and the Law of Moses

The earliest Christians were at pains to distinguish between the revelation of Christ's new covenant and the old covenant of Moses. For this reason, the early Christians believed that it was angels, not God himself, who had given the law to Moses. The flame of the burning bush, which guided Moses in the desert, is identified as an angel in Acts 7:30–38 of the New Testament. Further, Galatians 3:19 flatly states that the law was "ordained by angels," leaving God out of the matter entirely.

It would seem that just as the law handed down from Moses prepared the people to receive the Gospel—and it must be remembered

God's Wrath

The Christian derives a firm conviction about God's power from more than angel stories. Of Christ's death on the cross and resurrection, Paul says that God "disarmed the rulers and authorities and made a public example of them, triumphing over them in it" (Colossians 2:15).

that all of the early Christians were Jews, prior to their conversion to Christianity—so did angels serve to prepare the congregation for the advent of Christ.

Although at the time of Christ, Jews agreed that angels had presented Moses with the law, it was absolutely crucial for the new early church to draw a firm line of distinction between Christ and angels, who were considered to be the lesser intermediaries between God and his people. No doubt, angels had their work to do delivering messages from God, or the Lord, but it had to be Christ who was the prime mediator—a sort of CEO of the corporation of angels.

Paul's Angel

In Vision of Paul, in *New Testament Apocrypha*, Paul is guided by an angel on a complicated and confusing journey through the territory of heaven and hell. The narrative shifts back and forth between beauty and horror: he sees hell and several blessed abodes. He has visions of utter bliss, and visions of terrible punishments. The vision provides a wealth of imagery and an interesting role for his angelic guide. Finally, the angel leads Paul to the door of the third heaven. Paul says, "And I looked at it and saw that it was a golden gate and that there were two golden tables above the pillars full of letters. [These letters are the names of the righteous, already inscribed in heaven while they still live on earth.] And again the angel turned to me and said: 'Blessed are you if you enter in by these gates.'"

After entering the gates of paradise, Paul encounters the ancient prophet Enoch, who issues a warning to Paul not to reveal what he has seen in the third heaven. Then, the angel descends, with Paul in tow, to the second heaven and thence to the earthly paradise, where the souls of those deemed righteous await the resurrection.

In this place, Paul sees the four rivers of paradise, which flow with milk, wine, honey, and olive oil, and on the banks of each river, he meets those souls who have exhibited some specific virtue in their lives: The river of milk is for those who are innocent and chaste; the river of wine, a reward for those who have shown

Angels of the New Testament

"Then the angel showed me the river of the water of life, bright as crystal, flowing from the throne of God and of the Lamb through the middle of the street of the city. On either side of the river is the tree of life with its twelve kinds of fruit, producing its fruit each month; and the leaves of the tree are for the healing of the nations."
—Revelation 21:1–2

hospitality to strangers; the river of honey, for those who have submitted their own will to the will of God; and the river of oil for those who have renounced earthly pleasure and gain for love of God.

The angel puts Paul in a golden boat, and the narrative continues: "And about three thousand angels were singing a hymn before me until I reached the City of Christ."

Sinners who have repented of their crimes are gathered in a forest, where they abide during the time between death and resurrection. The City of Christ is made with twelve walls, each exceeding the one before in greatness, and he goes into the center of this apparent maze and says:

I saw in the midst of this city a great altar, very high, and there was [David] standing near the altar, whose countenance shone as the sun, and he held in his hands a psaltery and harp, and he sang psalms, saying Alleluia. And all in the city replied Alleluia till the very foundations of the city were shaken. . . . Turning round I saw golden thrones placed in each gate, and on them men having golden diadems and gems: and I looked carefully and saw inside between the twelve men thrones in glorious rank . . . so that no one is able to recount their praise. . . . Those thrones belong to those who had goodness and understanding of heart and made themselves fools for the sake of the Lord God.

Paul is occupied looking at the trees of heaven when he sees two hundred angels preceding Mary and singing hymns. Mary informs him that he has been granted the unusual favor of coming to this place before he is dead.

(It is to be noted that "thrones" are also a type of angel [to be discussed in Chapter 10]).

Isaiah's Angel

The story of the Ascension of Isaiah (in *New Testament Apocrypha*) is far less complex. The prophet is taken out of his body and led by an angel to the first heaven above the sky: "And I saw a throne in the midst, and on the right and on the left of it were angels [singing praises]." He asks whom they praise, and is told by the angels, "It is for the praise of him who is in the seventh heaven, for him who rests in eternity among his saints, and for his Beloved, whence I have been sent unto [you]."

The "heaven above the sky" is the first heaven, (of seven), and the angel then takes Isaiah to the second heaven, where once more he sees, as before, a throne and angels to the right and to the left. Awed by the situation, the holy prophet prostrates himself to worship the angel on the throne (there is some confusion here about a throne being an angel and an angel being on a throne) but is told not to do that. Angels are not to be worshiped.

Ascending further, each of the succeeding heavens is more filled with glory than the one before, and the sixth heaven is of such glorious brightness that it makes the previous five dark by comparison. Naturally—in common with those who have reported near-death experiences—Isaiah wants to remain in this place of wonders and not be sent back to a dull life encased in earthly flesh. But the angel explains that Isaiah's time on earth isn't finished: "If [you] already rejoice in this light, how much [will you] rejoice when, in the seventh heaven, [you see] that light where God and his beloved are, whence I have been sent. . . . As for [your] wish not to return to the flesh . . . [your] days are not yet fulfilled that [you may] come here."

Poor Isaiah! But Jesus himself allows Isaiah to enter the seventh heaven, of which he reports: "And I saw there a wonderful light and angels without number. And there I saw all the righteous from Adam . . . I saw Enoch and all who were with him stripped of the garment of the flesh, and I saw them in their higher garments, and they were like the angels who stand there in great glory."

However, he continues, "But they did not sit on their thrones, nor were there crowns of glory on their heads." This was because the blessed of the Old Testament would not be fully glorified until the Word is made flesh in Christ.

The vision ends with Christ escorting Isaiah down through all the heavens to earth to witness the Annunciation and the Incarnation.

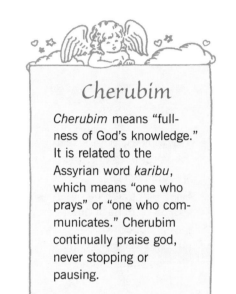

Cherubim

Cherubim means "fullness of God's knowledge." It is related to the Assyrian word *karibu*, which means "one who prays" or "one who communicates." Cherubim continually praise god, never stopping or pausing.

The End of Wingless Angels

The wingless angels seen in the tomb of Christ soon sprouted wings, superceding the literal gospel account of how angels appeared to humans. Wings became a distinguishing characteristic of angels, making easy to recognize as such.

After the conversion of Constantine the Great (306–337), who was the emperor of Byzantium, angels become winged, the idea most probably taken from the Greek tradition as represented by the Winged Victory. Constantine had a vision of a cross in the sky, and it was powerful enough to cause him to convert to Christianity, which was still a minority religion at the time. The martyrdom of those Christians killed in the Roman games by lions or in other horrible ways only served to encourage more people to become members of the despised sect. Soon, the church was growing like an untended field full of wildflowers. Constantine's conversion convinced a lot of those not otherwise inclined toward Christianity that it would be a smart move to join up. Constantine's own mother made a pilgrimage to the Holy Land and returned with a splinter from the true cross and, most amazing, one from the same little peasant manger in which the Christ child had been cradled. There's nothing quite like a mother's influence.

However, perhaps due to the influx of non-Jews and others into the early church, theological arguments were breaking out all over the place. It was at the first Ecumenical Council at Nicea, held in 325, that the doctrine of "coinherence" was adopted. This dogma was formulated to separate body and soul in no uncertain terms. Soul was all; whatever was corporeal (i.e., the body and the physical and material world) was of no value at all.

Angels were a difficult matter for the early church, especially concerning whether they had bodies or were incorporeal, or pure spirit. While Scripture clearly states that angels appear as men, it also states plainly that angels are *spiritus* (Hebrews 1:14). There also was serious debate about the angels who visited Abraham and Sarah to inform them of her impending pregnancy and who were supposed to have shared a meal with them. Did they really eat meat? Angels, of course, are only supposed to eat angel food, or manna, so this question had to be dealt with so as not to set a bad precedent.

No doubt Constantine had a lot to do with the renewed interest in angels, due to the addition of wings, for the folk were used to fairies, and it was a short step from a winged fairy to an angel with wings. What concerned the church fathers was that the common people were worshipping angels, which was a definite no-no, since only God and His Son could be worshiped.

This dilemma was settled by St. Paul, with his usual "I know what's best here" attitude—call it zeal if you will. Paul attacked "the worship of angels which some enter into blindly, puffed up by their mere human minds," in no uncertain terms.

Nevertheless, the First Council of Nicea in 325 decided that belief in angels was to be church dogma. Apparently, this decision unleashed a rampant renewal of the angel worship that St. Paul had so detested. It was proclaimed idolatry in 343, less than 20 years after Nicea, by another council.

Finally, in 787, to end the controversy, the second Council of Nicea, called the Seventh Ecumenical Synod, was held. It declared a *limited dogma* of the archangels, which included their names, their specific functions, and also formally legitimated the depiction of angels in art (with or without wings).

These events suggest that while the authors of Genesis certainly did not provide all the answers that troubled the early church fathers, most early Christian theologians who speculated on these matters, differing significantly in their conclusions, did feel that the angels had some form of natural body, whether it was solid, etheric, or fiery.

It would be the job of the coming Middle Age theologians to settle the questions about angels once and for all time.

"Do not forget to entertain strangers, for by so doing some people have entertained angels without knowing it."
—Hebrews 13:2

"The Son of man will send his angels, and they will gather out of his kingdom all causes of sin and all evildoers, and throw them into the furnace of fire; there men will weep and gnash their teeth."
—Matthew 13:41–42

CHAPTER FOUR

The Christian Medieval View of Angels

*A*s Christianity progressed from its early and contentious days, it became evident that the type of angel that satisfied the Jewish patriarchs and their followers wasn't at all appropriate to the burgeoning new religion of Christ. Thus, the various church authorities—theologians, historians, and those who made sacred art and illuminations—evolved the concept of angels into something entirely different from what the books of the old prophets had offered.

As the Catholic Church increased both in membership and in temporal power, an entire angelology grew along with it. Throughout the Middle Ages, angels not only were extremely popular (as they are today in their new resurgence), but also were a topic of hot and intense debate among those responsible for making decisions about what the church approved and what its members were allowed to believe.

Today, it may seem ridiculous that grown men—and serious scholars at that—spent their time debating such issues as whether angels were made of pure light. But people took such matters quite seriously, just as today scholars (and politicians) hotly debate certain questions and throw around all sorts of mud at those who disagree with them. In those days, however, since so much was at stake, and as the church was the supreme arbiter of almost every facet of life for ordinary people (by now, there was little or no religious competition in Europe, except for the few remaining Jews who were sequestered and subject to special laws, such as the one that prevented them from owning property), those arguing could toss around such phrases as "heretic" against their opponents.

No doubt there was popular opinion on the subject as well, for the ordinary folk had long been accustomed to encountering the angels of Scripture in a wide variety of media—liturgical, devotional, and pictorial. Prayers, sermons, records of visions, theological textbooks, and iconographic traditions indicate that both clerics and laypersons addressed and discussed the topic of angels in Scripture, making such discourse and speculation a vital and regular element of medieval Christendom.

For all these reasons, the medieval Christians wanted to know about angels in specific terms; they wanted to know their own relationship to nature and to their "Lord of hosts." The Middle Ages had inherited the early church's readings of the angels of the Bible and built on it in a manner that was amazing for its continuity. For example, Isidore of Seville, who wrote *Etymologiae*, defers to Gregory the Great and Saint Jerome in their discussion of angels, raising no new questions. Often there were traditional responses to the most frequently discussed questions about angels, such as why they have wings (the answer is that it makes them swift as messengers).

Another writer, Honorius of Autun, dating from the early twelfth century, raises no significantly new questions concerning the traditional view of angels in his treatise on the creation and fall of the angels. The patristic readings—though enlarged upon and debated—remained essentially in place until the thirteenth century. Prior to that, most theologians, even when in disagreement, were asking similar questions within the same framework regarding the traditional readings of angels from Scripture.

During the twelfth and thirteenth centuries, scholastics revolutionized the Christian view of angels and their nature. According to Marcia L. Colish, who has studied Peter Lombard and other theologians of the period, this era was divided into three stages.

Angels and Creation

In the first of these periods, the scholastic theologians—realizing a need for a systematized method of teaching theology—determined that angelology would be considered in the context of the creation. Speculation about angels from then on centered around the different accounts of creation—causing debates over the harmonies and conflicts among the various versions—Genesis and the Platonic and Neoplatonic writings such as the *Timeaus*. Although these scholastics were, in most instances, merely reiterating the traditional answers to these problematic ideas about angels, at least they were coming at the subject from new perspectives by using a distinct methodology, which, in the end, caused a complete transformation of angelology. This stage culminated in the work of the Italian the-

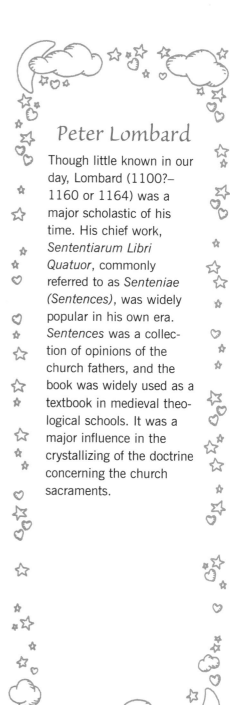

Peter Lombard

Though little known in our day, Lombard (1100?–1160 or 1164) was a major scholastic of his time. His chief work, *Sententiarum Libri Quatuor*, commonly referred to as *Senteniae (Sentences)*, was widely popular in his own era. *Sentences* was a collection of opinions of the church fathers, and the book was widely used as a textbook in medieval theological schools. It was a major influence in the crystallizing of the doctrine concerning the church sacraments.

ologian Peter Lombard, who was bishop of Paris in 1159. Lombard wrote *Sentences*, which Aquinas would discourse upon.

During the second period, approximately the second half of the twelfth century, notes Colish, "the interest in angels [was] quite muted." Apparently, the theologians had moved on to other, more pressing matters.

Alexander and Bonaventure

The third and last stage of this progression dates to the first quarter of the thirteenth century, when scholastics such as William of Auxerre and Alexander of Hales took up the study of angels and applied to it new philosophical categories, which led them to new metaphysical and epistemological problems. Bonaventure, who had been mentored by Alexander, carried through on Alexander's exploratory work, which ultimately led to the great medieval angel-ogical syntheses.

However, when it came to questions of angelic nature and metaphysics, the fur began to fly in earnest. In the thirteenth century, two rival schools had sprung up. One of these was represented by the Scottish theologian John Duns Scotus. The second was represented by Thomas Aquinas (who was canonized, or granted sainthood, in 1323 by Pope John XXII, less than 50 years after his death), who at that time was an Italian scholastic philosopher, known as the "Angelic Doctor," as a result of his brilliant discourses on angels. He was also called "Prince of Scholastics," in acknowledgment of his superior intellect and mental abilities.

The basic and burning question addressed by these two schools of thought was, What are angels made of?

John Duns Scotus

Scotus's point of view held that angels were composed of "spiritual matter," and quite difficult to identify or pin down, nebulous as that might seem. Further, Scotus said they were "incorporeal and immaterial," while at the same time they were made of denser material than God, who was, it seemed to Scotus, a being of sheer nothingness. Scotus also held that angels were able to think and reason just as humans do and that, like horses or dogs, they were a distinct species within which existed countless numbers of individuals with individual personality traits—not unlike ourselves. This point of view must have been comforting to those who liked the idea of angels as warm and fuzzy beings, not totally different from people but just better and more perfect while still being approachable and not distantly divine, existing in the upper sphere above humanity. In other words, they were closer to us and therefore more accessible to supplications for assistance, providing a kind of celestial unconditional love, like that of a mother.

By this time, also, angels had acquired a new look; no longer the scary apparitions of Old Testament visions, they had acquired the human number of eyes, the same as the pair we gaze into when we look in a mirror or into the eyes of another person. And though they were supernaturally beautiful and radiant, they had faces that were recognizable as faces. The addition of wings wasn't so far-fetched either, as we see flying creatures we call birds all the time. People like wings and have always been fascinated by them and by the prospect of flight. The great Leonardo da Vinci made copious notes regarding wings and flight in his notebooks, accompanied by many drawings speculating on how flight was accomplished by the nonsupernatural winged beings. And he declared, "Man shall have wings. He shall fly. He shall be as the gods." He wasn't wrong either, as anyone who has ever watched a 747 in the air can attest. Of course, men don't fly *individually*—but, oh, how we wish we could! Still, it *is* flight, and it does involve wings. Leonardo's fascination with wings took him far into the future, though I doubt that even the great da Vinci could have anticipated flight that would land men on the moon.

Thomas Aquinas

Thomas Aquinas held a totally different point of view. This he professed to the public in a series of lectures, in 1259, at the

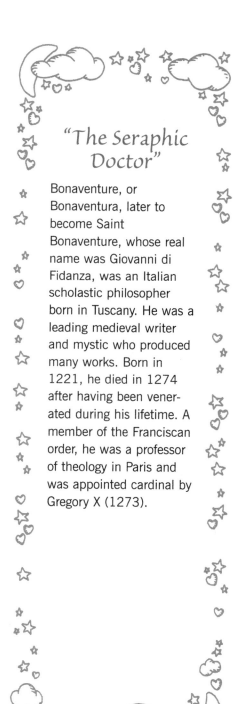

"The Seraphic Doctor"

Bonaventure, or Bonaventura, later to become Saint Bonaventure, whose real name was Giovanni di Fidanza, was an Italian scholastic philosopher born in Tuscany. He was a leading medieval writer and mystic who produced many works. Born in 1221, he died in 1274 after having been venerated during his lifetime. A member of the Franciscan order, he was a professor of theology in Paris and was appointed cardinal by Gregory X (1273).

University of Paris. It is to be remembered that at this time there were few books, and most of these were handwritten by monks and kept in monasteries. The general public was illiterate; they could not read for the simple reason that there were no books to read. (Gutenberg's printing press was still more than 175 years in the future.)

Thus, those who liked thinking and wanted education and the ability to use their minds attended lectures almost as a spectator sport, for afterward they could argue among themselves the topic and opinions of the lecturer.

The great teachers of the day were all great orators, like Abelard and Thomas Aquinas, and their events attracted great crowds eager to hear them discourse on all matter of topics. The multitudes favored lectures on subjects that were contentious, with arguments and counterarguments, especially those that concentrated on long quotations from Scripture or classic writings from the past. They especially enjoyed hearing the speakers display complex use of logic (being French, this was built in!). The attendees much appreciated the style of a speaker and his clarity of thought, just as aficionados of the opera dote upon a singer's interpretation of an operatic role, debating the merits of one over the other as Aida or Madame Butterfly. In a sense, these lectures not only were for edification but also were a major entertainment of the day, a kind of verbal football game.

Giving fifteen lectures over a period of a week, the fleet-minded Aquinas set forth everything known or ever asked about angels, taking questions from the audience and giving answers. Here is one of Aquinas's convoluted arguments:

He asks whether angels grieve for the ills of those whom they guard (*Summa Theologiae* 1.113–7) and then answers that "it would seem that angels grieve for the ills of those they guard." Quoting from Isaiah 33:7, "The angels of peace shall weep bitterly," he reaches the conclusion that since grief is the result of things that happen against the person's will and because angels' wills are aligned perfectly with God, nothing can happen to angels against God's will (or their own, if they have wills). Thus, Aquinas states flatly and emphatically, "Angels do not grieve." He then proceeds to resolve the discrepancy between the quoted Scripture and his own rational deduction thusly:

These words of Isaiah may be understood of the angels, that is, the messengers of Ezechias, who wept on account of the words of Rabsaces, as related . . . This would be the literal sense. According to the allegorical sense the angels of peace are the apostles and preachers who weep for men's sins. If this passage be expounded of the blessed angels according to the anagogical sense, then the expression is metaphorical, and signifies that, universally speaking, the angels will the salvation of mankind. For it is in this manner that we attribute passions to God and the angels.

As was common in those days, his lectures, as he spoke, were taken down in writing, which was fortunate, for his ideas have formed the base of our "knowledge" about angels to this day.

In Aquinas's considered opinion—hardly to be doubted—angels were "all intellect," not a surprising conclusion for a man who was himself perhaps the greatest intellect of his time, and certainly one of the greatest of all times. The psychologist of today might say that Thomas was "projecting" himself onto the angels, seeing in them, as in a mirror, what he was himself.

Whether or not this was the case, he firmly declared angels to be pure intellect and nothing else—no matter or material body. However, he also believed that angels could assume bodies at will and even eat real human food (the question of whether they actually partook of the meal with Abraham and Sarah now being answered).

Aquinas's statements and arguments are all drawn directly from Scripture—from his application of logic and reason to the passages referring to angels—and not from an experiential knowledge of them. (Mystics who have actual experiences of angels couldn't care less about these logical arguments; they are primarily interested in the contact, whether through apparition or dream or inner voice, and the message that the angel brings.)

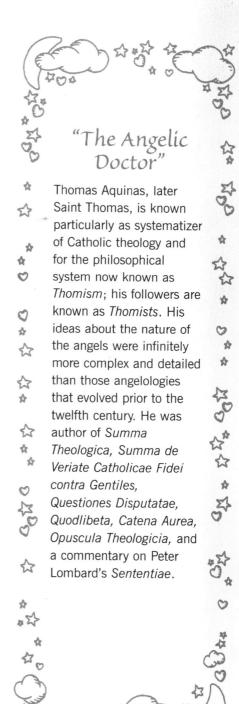

"The Angelic Doctor"

Thomas Aquinas, later Saint Thomas, is known particularly as systematizer of Catholic theology and for the philosophical system now known as *Thomism*; his followers are known as *Thomists*. His ideas about the nature of the angels were infinitely more complex and detailed than those angelologies that evolved prior to the twelfth century. He was author of *Summa Theologica, Summa de Veriate Catholicae Fidei contra Gentiles, Questiones Disputatae, Quodlibeta, Catena Aurea, Opuscula Theologicia,* and a commentary on Peter Lombard's *Sententiae*.

Another question essential to the Middle Ages was, Are angels eternal? Are they, like stars and humans, born only to die, or do they belong to the immortals? The church fathers took up this question and gave many hours of discussion to it. They also gave much time to the ancillary questions to which it gave rise, If angels are born and die, do they also evolve into progressive stages of angel being? If they are "all intellect," does that mean they have the capacity to think, as do humans, to use logic and reason? This was seen as a vital point, for it brings in the question of free will. Do angels have free will? Can they of their own volition choose between God and Satan? Do "good angels" sometimes decide to become bad, or fallen, angels?

Aquinas believed that although angels are "pure intellect," they do not have the power of reason or of choice, that the decision is made in one brief moment of free will as they are created, their perfection causing them instantly to opt for God as their life choice. For Aquinas, angels were part of a higher sphere than humans, not belonging to an angel species but each being a distinct individual substance, what might be called a one-of-a-kind species. Aquinas's belief was the accepted concept of angels at that time.

However, in 1277, just three years after Aquinas's death, the Condemnations denounced certain teachings, including some which Aquinas had advanced. This was the result of a shift of the teaching centers from the monasteries to the universities, and of the dominance of Aristotle, who had by then been rediscovered, having been translated into Latin from the Arabic, in which language the original Greek writings had been preserved over the centuries.

The universities of the thirteenth century played a major role in making fundamental changes in theological thinking that served to greatly transform the medieval Christian view of angels.

First, under the influence of Aristotle, new techniques and methodologies based on sheer logic were introduced and formalized. The dialectical method took over as the primary form of exploration, leading to new questions about angels and to speculation on old questions in greater depth.

Under the influence of the great Greek philosopher, the twelfth and thirteenth centuries experienced a tremendous increase in interest regarding the exact nature of creatures, and scholastics began to use philosophical and metaphysical categories to explore these natures.

Thus, during this crucial period, angels were studied not only as themselves (as messengers) or from the perspective of their job descriptions but also from the perspective of their actual natures, or their existence as "intelligences" or substances with separate natures, or "spirits." So great was this influence that the study of angels acquired a definite role in formal university training. No longer just a topic for general discussion, from now onward the study of angels would be requisite for every student of theology, forming an important part of the training for this profession.

Interestingly, Aquinas and Bonaventure died in the same year, 1274, having both been major players in the era's questioning about angels and its confrontations with specific problems concerning angels and their natures. Despite the Condemnations of 1277, these two men were in large part responsible for the fact that the angelologies of the thirteenth-century scholastics remained in place throughout the remaining years of the Middle Ages.

Primarily, however, it was the sheer thoroughness of the nit-pickingly detailed work of Aquinas and Bonaventure, and their development of systematic and comprehensive angelologies addressing all of the major natural and metaphysical issues regarding angels, that discouraged any further development. They had simply left no territory uncovered, with the result that their successors had little or nothing left to explore in the field of angelology. As David Keck puts it, "The major questions had been asked, and the revolutionary philosophical concepts and questions had been incorporated. The science of angels became complete in the thirteenth century."

Angels, angelology, the discussion of angels, the belief in angels, the arguments about angels, all permeated the European Middle Ages, a world so different to what modern people know that if anyone today could travel back there in time, they would feel as if they were on a different planet—perhaps carried there by an angel!

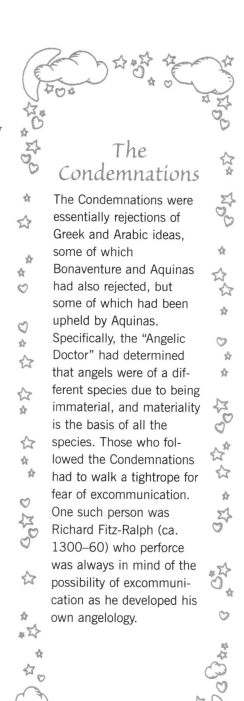

The Condemnations

The Condemnations were essentially rejections of Greek and Arabic ideas, some of which Bonaventure and Aquinas had also rejected, but some of which had been upheld by Aquinas. Specifically, the "Angelic Doctor" had determined that angels were of a different species due to being immaterial, and materiality is the basis of all the species. Those who followed the Condemnations had to walk a tightrope for fear of excommunication. One such person was Richard Fitz-Ralph (ca. 1300–60) who perforce was always in mind of the possibility of excommunication as he developed his own angelology.

CHAPTER FIVE

Angels in Non-
Christian Cultures

Enoch's Vision of Angels

"I saw . . . a structure built of crystals; and between those crystals tongues of living fire. And my spirit saw a ring which encircled this structure of fire. On its four sides were rivers [the four rivers of paradise] full of living fire which encircled it. . . . Moreover, seraphim, cherubim, and ophanim . . . also encircled it . . . and I saw countless angels . . . encircling that house."

—*The Book of Enoch*

The Jewish Tradition of Angels

While all the furious debate about angels was going on in the predominantly Christian world in Europe, a Jewish population lived side by side with their Christian neighbors, yet remained totally isolated from them. It's hard to see just how any metaphysical or theological ideas might have been exchanged between the two communities, one clearly superior in number and political clout. Thus separated, and trying to maintain their own identity as a people through their language and traditional culture, medieval Jews lived in a religious vacuum.

The Kabbalah

Their great book, the *Kabbalah* (also *Kabala, Kabbala, Cabala, Cabalah*), apparently never made any contact with the great Christian masters of theology we have been discussing. The term *Kabbalah* derives from the Hebrew root *kbl*, which means "to receive." And it refers to matters that are occult (meaning "hidden") or mystical knowledge so secret that it is rarely written down but rather transmitted from master to neophyte, or student, orally, in order to protect the secrets from being revealed to those not prepared to receive them, or unworthy to do so.

The sacred book of Jewish mystical writings is exceedingly complex and extremely difficult to comprehend. It is based on infinitely complicated numerical formulations, for the belief was that numbers themselves had created the world.

Although the Kabbalah dates back to the first century C.E., when it flourished in Palestine, the major texts did not appear until the twelfth and thirteenth centuries, alongside the Christian expositions of angels. These were primarily seen in Spain, which at that time had a large Jewish population. One in particular, *Zohar*, or the Book of Brightness, dates from that period in Jewish history.

Various other books, apparently written between the third and the sixth centuries, beginning with the *Sefer Yetzira*, or Book of Creation, also appeared around that time. The thirteenth century

also saw the appearance of the Book of Splendor and the Book of the Image.

All of these books of the Kabbalah constitute a system of guidance to the path to God, on which the believer is taken through a series of heavenly halls guided by angels. It is replete with long descriptions of how to make the journey safely up through a tree of angels, and it gives the secret passwords to bypass demons encountered along the path.

Angels played central roles in the Merkabah, or Throne Chariot of God, as well as in other Kabbalistic traditions. One doctrine from the twelfth century taught that there are four worlds, each deriving from God.

In the Kabbalah are ten sefirot, or angels, considered to be the fundamental channels of divine energy. Their names are Foundation, Splendor, Eternity, Beauty, Power, Grace, Knowledge, Wisdom, Understanding, and Crown. They are arranged in the shape of a tree and called the Tree of Life.

The top of this tree is occupied by the singular angel Metatron, and beyond all of this is the mystical contemplation of God. It is so distant and removed from the human sphere as to be incomprehensible, for humans can never know God directly but only experience Him through His angels.

The Hebrew Bible

According to Jeffery Burton Russell, in *A History of Heaven*, the dating and authorship of the Hebrew Bible is vigorously debated. Says Russell:

The oldest materials date as far back as the eleventh century B.C.E. The reforms of Josiah in 622 B.C.E. established some of the texts, but most recensions occurred in and after the Babylonian Captivity of 586–538 B.C.E. The distinction between revelation and inspiration is essential in Jewish and Christian thought. Many writers may be divinely inspired, but revelation is restricted to the Bible alone. The Biblical writers received not only inspiration but also direct revelation of truth from God.

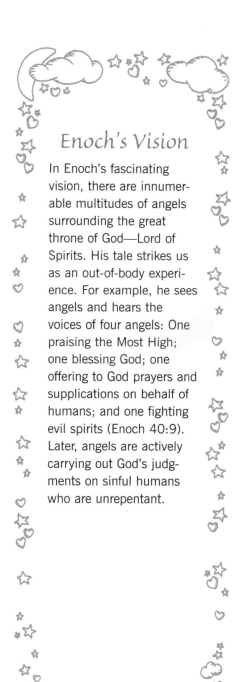

Enoch's Vision

In Enoch's fascinating vision, there are innumerable multitudes of angels surrounding the great throne of God—Lord of Spirits. His tale strikes us as an out-of-body experience. For example, he sees angels and hears the voices of four angels: One praising the Most High; one blessing God; one offering to God prayers and supplications on behalf of humans; and one fighting evil spirits (Enoch 40:9). Later, angels are actively carrying out God's judgments on sinful humans who are unrepentant.

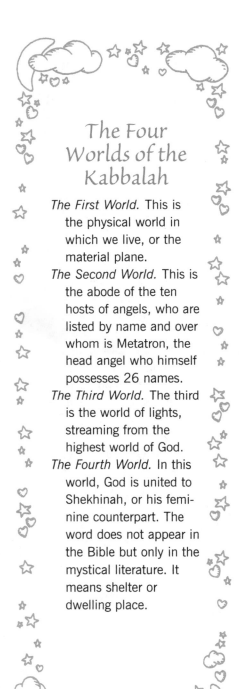

The Four Worlds of the Kabbalah

The First World. This is the physical world in which we live, or the material plane.

The Second World. This is the abode of the ten hosts of angels, who are listed by name and over whom is Metatron, the head angel who himself possesses 26 names.

The Third World. The third is the world of lights, streaming from the highest world of God.

The Fourth World. In this world, God is united to Shekhinah, or his feminine counterpart. The word does not appear in the Bible but only in the mystical literature. It means shelter or dwelling place.

The glorified earthly Jerusalem was the model for, and gradually merged with, the heavenly city of Jerusalem. The idea that the just have the heavens as their eternal abode appears in the Hebrew Bible only indirectly by association with God and the *angels* [emphasis added]. The Ark and Temple do not appear in heaven until after the Biblical period. The Hebrew word for heavens is the word for sky: *shamayim*, from *shama*, "the high place." Metaphorically it is the place of God and of the angels and was sometimes used as a synonym for God.

There is little doubt that the exile of the Jews in Babylon, during which time Zoroastrianism was the primary religion of the region, highly influenced their concepts of angels. In fact, much of our present Western lore regarding angels dates from this period.

Prior to Zoroaster, the Supreme Deity—no matter what name was used—contained within itself both good and evil, but with Zoroastrianism came the concept of good angels on one side and bad angels, or demons, opposite, in an eternal tug of war. This notion, new to the world at the time, quite probably influenced the Jewish tradition of bad, or fallen, angels, and that worked its way into Christianity.

The Story of Zoroaster's Vision

Zoroaster had an experience similar to that of Jacob. However, instead of wrestling with an angel, he battled a devil. The story is told that the soon-to-be prophet wrestled mightily with his own inner feelings, angered by what he considered to be superstition and primitive fear, which blighted the lives of his people. In addition, his people were being attacked by the Turanians, creating a state of utter misery for them. So deep was his despair and his state of emotional conflict that he retired to a cave in the mountains to think things through.

In a flash of (divine?) inspiration, he saw the answer to his question, Why is this happening? It was the work of a malignant spirit, the devil himself. This inner revelation began the split between good and evil in the divinity; it has trickled down through the centuries and is still with us today.

Unlike Jacob, who never did get the name of the angel with which he had wrestled, Zoroaster took it upon himself to name his demon Angra Mainyu, or the Prince of Lies, or Demon of Doubt and Despair. A psychiatrist today would realize he was deeply depressed and would prescribe Prozac, but there weren't any such remedies for his state of mind at the time, not even the popular St. John's wort herbal preparation. Lacking such, he solved his problem by inventing a new religion that was slated to have far-reaching effects.

In his inner agony, having identified the source of his own troubles and those of his people, he determined that he would fight the demon, or evil spirit. Said he, "This great demon of darkness will be conquered by the god of light," who he forthwith named Ahura Mazda and set out to preach this new version of what life is all about to the folk, now that he knew who to blame for their troubles, including the raids on their cattle. Declared the newborn prophet, "I will go forth and . . . tell them that their old gods . . . are but agents of the great Lie Demon, Angra Mainyu. I will tell them that the Turanians are raiding our cattle because they are sent by this evil one."

However, he must have been an optimist at heart, for he also determined that he would proclaim the demon's demise: "I will also proclaim that the time is coming when Angra Mainyu will be completely vanquished by Ahura Mazda, the supreme god of light and truth." Like later prophets and seers, he saw God in a vision and afterward felt purged of his despair and agony, for now he understood the source of it and resolved to deal with it.

As the story goes, at daybreak after his long dark night of the soul, Zoroaster stood upon the bank of the third channel of the sacred river Daitya and filled his hands with its holy water. As he lifted his cupped hands to drink, he was nearly blinded by a shining figure approaching from the south, carrying a staff of light. This turned out to be the archangel Vohu Manah, who was nine times the size of a human. This angel—or apparition perhaps—told

Thus Spake Zarathustra

Zoroaster was also called Zarathustra, meaning "rich in camels," and Friedrich Nietzche, the great German philosopher and poet (1844–1900) titled one of his most well-known books *Thus Spake Zarathustra*, a work that introduced the concept of the uber mensch, or superman.

Zoroastrian Chronology

Later writers described Zoroaster's vision of God in great detail, dating their chronology from this unique moment in time, which occurred at dawn on the fifteenth day of the month Artavahisto (to us, May 5, 630 B.C.E.). Thus, by their reckoning, the 31st year of King Vishtaspa, who occupied the temporal throne, was called the First Year of the Religion (1 A.R.).

the amazed Zoroaster to leave his body behind and follow him to the presence of the great Ahura Mazda and all of his holy angels (such out-of-body experiences are common in vision stories).

Doing as he was bade (it isn't explained exactly how Zoroaster accomplished this feat), the prophet followed the shining angel and was led to the audience chamber of God and all of his holy angels, who all shone as brightly as did his escort. In their presence, he noticed that he cast no shadow but attributed this anomaly to the brightness and radiance of the Holy Host, apparently not realizing that he had left his material self, his body, down by the riverside.

He never figured out that he was now incorporeal, but this didn't seem to matter; he simply approached the "seat of the enquirers" and was taught the cardinal principles of his new religion. He received mysterious signs and was made privy to secrets that foretold the future of his new religion, soon to be known as Zoroastrianism. After receiving all this instruction, he floated back down to earth, hopped back into his body, and set forth to preach this revolutionary new gospel for the next two years.

Ugarit

The remains of Ugarit, an ancient kingdom and capital city, were discovered on an archaeological site in the small Arab village of Ras Shamra, near modern Latakia, in 1931. Tablets were found dating from the fourteenth century B.C.E. These tablets were written in Ugaritic, which has been identified as a Semitic language that is related to classical Hebrew.

This once-powerful kingdom located on the Mediterranean seacoast of northern Syria worshiped a pantheon of gods, including the highest god El and his consort Atirat, the storm god Baal and his sister Anat, plus other divinities.

Of interest here is that the religion of Ugarit included angels! This was discovered when the long and discursive texts discovered at Ras Shamra were deciphered. The texts mention the "messengers of god" as part of the "divine council," or *puhru ilani*. This divine

When Did Zoroaster Live?

In November 1754, a young Frenchman, Abraham Hyacinthe Anquetil-Duperoon (1731–1805), who was a private in the French army, set sail for India in hopes of finding what remained of the works of the fabled Persian prophet Zoroaster. His quest was a success, and in 1771, he published the *Zend Avesta,* which detailed what was known about Zoroaster and his important religious innovation.

Since that time, says Joseph Campbell in *Occidental Mythology*, "the progress that Oriental scholarship has since made toward an understanding of the relationship of those texts to the doctrines [including angels] of both Christianity and Islam has been—though extremely slow—secure and convincing."

The Persian prophet's words have come down preserved like gems in the setting of a later liturgical work known as the Yasna, "Book of offering," which is a priestly compilation of prayers, confessions, invocations [to angels], and the like, arranged according to the rituals in which they were employed."

Professor L. H. Mills, in the introduction of his translation of the Yasna, dates the Gathas between c. 1500–900 B.C.E. Another professor, Hans Heinrich Schaeder, dates them to the seventh century B.C.E. However, there is some dispute about the dating. A King Vishtaspa [the presumptive ruler in Zoroaster's day] is named in the Gathas with King Darius's father, Hystaspes. If so, this would place the prophet as late as c. 550 B.C.E. According to Campbell, the problem is extremely complicated, with arguments and arguers on every side.

From The Koran

"In the name of god, most gracious, most merciful,

"Praise be to God, the cherisher and sustainer of the worlds: most gracious and most merciful, Master of the Day of Judgment.

"Thee do we worship and Thine aid do we seek. Show us the way that is straight, the way of those on whom Thou hast bestowed Thy grace, whose portion is not wrath, and who go not astray."

—*Koran* 1:1–7

council of angels were advisers to the chief divinity El. Curiously, these messengers are called by the identical term often used in Hebrew scriptures for angels, that is, *mal'akim.*

However, since Ugarit, a seaport nation, traded with the known world, there is every possibility that there was considerable intermingling that would have included ideas about angels. Nonetheless, the similarities are astonishing. The functions of the angels of Ugarit correspond to what the Hebrews defined as angelic job descriptions: they served as messengers of the gods in two capacities; between the various gods and between the gods and the human population.

In addition, the angels are subordinate to the highest god of Ugarit, obeying his commands to either act or refrain from intervening in human affairs.

They are described as being immortal spirits—bodiless, not flesh and blood—and *created* just as are the angels of both the Old and New Testaments. One long story on the Ugarit tablets is entitled "The Birth of the Gracious Gods." It tells how two angels named Shalim and Shahar were created by El, the high god of Ugarit.

Among the duties of these Ugaritian angels was to sing the praises of all the gods, but especially of El.

The Prophet of Islam

The Holy Koran contains a version of the biblical creation myth and fall. It also states:

Behold, the Lord said to the angels, 'I will create a vice-regent on earth.' They said: 'Will you place therein one who will make mischief and shed blood, while we are celebrating your praises and glorifying your name?' . . . He taught Adam the names of all things, then placed these before the angels; and he said: 'Tell me the names of these, if you are knowing.' But they answered: 'Glory be to Yourself! We have no knowledge but what you have taught us. Truly it is you who are both in knowledge and in wisdom perfect.' . . . We said to the angels: 'Bow down to Adam!' They bowed. Not so, however, Iblis, who refused.

According to Joseph Campbell:

It is obvious that in every syllable Islam is a continuation of the Zoroastrian-Jewish-Christian heritage, restored (as it is claimed) by proper sense and carried (as it is further claimed) to its ultimate formulation. The whole legend of the patriarchs . . . is rehearsed with its lessons time and time again throughout the Koran, as are, also, certain portions of the Christian myth . . . The basic Koranic origin legend is of a descent of both the Arabs and the Jews from the seed of Abraham.

In a similar manner to Zoroaster, Mohammed's revelation, or vision, came to him in a cave, in the side of Mount Hira, three miles north of Mecca, a spot to which he was accustomed to retire for peaceful contemplation, usually alone, but sometimes accompanied by his wife Khadija, who was quite a bit his senior (he was her third husband).

As the story goes, he was sitting alone in his private cave pondering the fact that humans live in corruptible flesh when he was overcome by a dazzling vision of beauty and light. So great was this effect that he lost the use of his very senses. Hearing "Proclaim!" called out, he was utterly confused and struck with terror.

However, the cry rang out again, clear and commanding: "Proclaim! Proclaim! Proclaim!" His mind cleared, and he realized in a flash that he was hearing the voice of God. In a moment, he knew exactly what to do and why. His mission was clear. God wanted to write a book, and he was to take down the dictation. This would be a great and holy book that men were to read, study, recite, and hold dear to their hearts and souls.

Upon reaching this conclusion, his own soul was filled with divine ecstasy, but, as is usual with these trance states, when he returned to the here and now, he was once again subject to a state of confusion and fright. Off he rushed to his lifemate, Khadija, for

Iblis

Iblis, known as "the Calumniator," is the Koranic counterpart of Zoroastrian Angra Mainyu. Although a later verse says of Iblis that "he was one of the jinn, and he broke the command of his Lord" (15:50), the text quoted above implies that Iblis was an angel. Iblis, therefore, can be seen either as a fallen angel or an unconverted jinni.

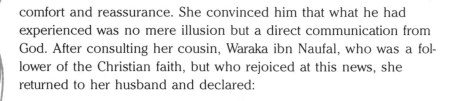

comfort and reassurance. She convinced him that what he had experienced was no mere illusion but a direct communication from God. After consulting her cousin, Waraka ibn Naufal, who was a follower of the Christian faith, but who rejoiced at this news, she returned to her husband and declared:

O Chosen One, may you be blessed. Do we not see your inner life, true and pure? Do not all see your outer life: kind and gentle, loyal to kin, hospitable to strangers? No thought of ill or malice has ever stained your mind; no word that was not true and did not quiet the passions of narrower men has ever passed your lips. Ever ready in the service of God, you are he of whom I bear witness: There is no god but God, and you are his Chosen Apostle.

Now, clearly, Mohammed had his work cut out for him, and he began at once. As the Arabs before him had recognized many gods and goddesses, including angels among them, Mohammed naturally included angels in his formulation. In fact, after being chosen, the new Prophet claimed to have had a beautiful vision of the angel Gabriel, who promised to be his guide in his new role as God's scribe: "I lay asleep in my house. It was a night in which there were thunder and lightning. No living beings could be heard, no bird journeyed. No one was awake, whereas I was not asleep; I dwelt between waking and sleeping."

Suddenly Gabriel the Archangel descended in his own form, of such beauty, of such sacred glory, of such majesty, that all my dwelling was illuminated. He is of a whiteness brighter than snow, his face is gloriously beautiful, the waves of his hair fall in long tresses, his brow is encircled as with a diadem of light on which is written "There is no god but God." He has six hundred wings set with 70,000 grains of red chrysolite.

When he had approached me, he took me in his arms, kissed me between the eyes and said, "O sleeper, how long wilt thou sleep? Arise! Tenderly will I guide thee. Fear not, for I am Gabriel thy brother."

Mohammed also had a vision of the angel Michael at a time when he went alone into the sea, only to find himself in a valley:

Over against the valley I saw an Angel in meditation, perfect in Majesty, Glory and Beauty. When he saw me he called me to him. When I had come close I asked, "What is thy name?" He said, "Michael. I am the greatest of the Angels. Whatever difficulty thou conceivest, question me; whatever thou desirest, ask of me." I said to him, "To come hither I have undergone many toils and sufferings. But my purpose was this: to attain to gnosis and the vision of truth. Show me the direction that leads to Him, so that perhaps I may attain the goal of my desire, and receive a portion of His universal Grace."

Then that Angel took me by the hand, he made me enter and led me through so many veils of light that the universe I saw had nothing in common with everything I had previously seen in these worlds.

Later visions add more colorful details about angels, such as angels made of fire and ice. And long descriptions of ranks and choirs of angels are mentioned in the Koran. Muslims believe that angels will serve as witnesses for or against people on the Day of Judgment, and that recording angels are ever present at prayer in mosques everywhere.

Mecca—where Mohammed lived and began to proselytize and which is now the holiest city of Islam—and the whole region surrounding it had been regarded as a place of sanctity long before Mohammed's time. A prosperous trading area, at its center stood a perfectly rectangular stone hut, known as the Kaaba, the Cube, which is today the central object of the entire Islamic world. The black stone (possibly a meteorite) was said to have been given to Abraham by the angel Gabriel.

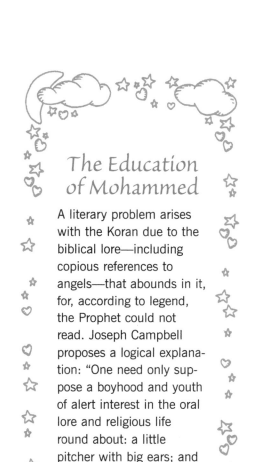

The Education of Mohammed

A literary problem arises with the Koran due to the biblical lore—including copious references to angels—that abounds in it, for, according to legend, the Prophet could not read. Joseph Campbell proposes a logical explanation: "One need only suppose a boyhood and youth of alert interest in the oral lore and religious life round about: a little pitcher with big ears; and then a youth of high intelligence, ardent religious sensibilities, and an extraordinary capacity for extended periods of auditory trance."

—*Occidental Mythology*

Are There Hindu Angels?

Angels mostly appear in strictly monotheistic religions, which require intermediaries between their far removed and distant God and their human adherents. In polytheistic religions—those with numerous gods and goddesses—angels are not as important and serve as ancillary beings.

The official Hindu view is that the Supreme Deity, a force so great and grand as to be beyond human reach or understanding, desires a relationship with humans despite his grandeur and distance. Therefore, since God cannot be perceived by humans with some kind of form to which they can relate, God takes on various bodily forms in order to relate to the worshipper or devotee. These forms are actually energies known as shaktis. (We are here again in the strange territory of quantum physics, where energy is form!)

A shakti can appear as a goddess, such as Parvati, the consort of Shiva. These energy bodies are also called devi. (It is important not to confuse the feminine form devi with the masculine form deva. A devi is a shakti, but a deva is a lowly nature spirit in Indian tradition, the same type of spirit that Zoroaster denounced as a djin, or jinn, a demon such as Iblis was called in scorn.)

There are many shaktis, or devis, all of them feminine, who are considered to be aspects of God. Of these, Lakshmi represents abundance and Surasuti, peacefulness. They aren't all nice, however; in India, good and evil are united in the Supreme Deity. Kali, for example, is a naked black-faced hag with a protruding tongue, smeared all over with blood; she holds in her four hands a sword, a shield, the head of a giant, and a noose for strangling. She is more akin to some of the Old Testament scary angel visions than to regular helping angels. One of her characteristics is that she drinks the blood of demons, no doubt helpful in the long run, once you get past her terrifying appearance.

Devi don't function as actual messengers, as do angels of the monotheistic cultures. But Hindus also acknowledge the existence of winged creatures—kinpuru'sh by name—who hover around the gods, and these kinpuru'sh could be considered angelic beings (but they don't appear to humans, at least not directly).

A Hindu Vision of Angels

Paramahansa Yogananda, in his *Autobiography of a Yogi*, tells a story of visiting a holy woman in India during the 1920s. She had had a vivid angel experience. The woman, who was the wife of the enlightened master Lahiri Mahasaya, had awakened from a dream of seeing angels in her room. The dream had had the clarity of waking consciousness. Upon awakening from this dream, the entire room radiated with brilliant light while her husband—in a meditative trance state—levitated. Her astonishment only increased when she saw that he was surrounded by angels, their palms pressed together.

When the levitation ended, the man assured his wife that she had not been dreaming, and she humbled herself before him, apologizing for her failure to recognize that he was a saint. He bade her to offer reverence to the angels, who returned her obeisance with a chorus of celestial voices. They disappeared, and the room returned to its former stage of darkness.

Alas, after this celestial encounter, the holy husband abandoned his wife's bed. Says Sophie Burnham of this story, "It reinforces all the reasons we distrust the celestial world." However, the story does prove that angels can appear to Hindus as well as to Western monotheists. However, like Christian angels, Hindu ones are not themselves to be worshiped but only revered as those who worship God.

The Findhorn Gardens

As a result of deva assistance, so it is thought by those who run these communities, both Findhorn in Scotland and Perelandra in Washington, D.C., have been able to grow amazing quantities of vegetable produce. In their view, devas manifest as "architects" of nature, and one is assigned to every living thing, including the soil. These devas design blueprints for all living things, orchestrating the energies necessary for growth and health.

According to books about Findhorn, devas dispense advice on the care of plant life—advice on fertilization, watering, soil enrichment, and general plant care. This angel-like advice has made these communities' gardens superabundant.

In *A Book of Angels*, Sophie Burnham reports a conversation with a Hindu Master teacher. She poses the question, Are there angels in ancient Hindu religious thought? To which the Master answers, "Yes." But he "could not come up with the name for them, though he mused on the Persian concept of *feresh'ta*, the winged spiritual counselors that praise and worship God both in story and art."

It is possible that these Hindu angels were post-Renaissance imports from Western cultures that traded with India and from Portuguese missionaries out to convert the "heathen" to Catholicism.

Though in traditional Indian thought, and in Zoroastrianism, devas were considered to be either lowly nature spirits or evil demons, in Sanskrit the term deva actually means "shining one." According to Harper's *Encyclopedia of Mystical and Paranormal Experience*, by Rosemary Ellen Guiley, Hinduism "distinguishes three kinds of devas: mortals who live in a higher realm than other mortals, enlightened people who have realized God, and Brahman in the form of a personal God."

Devas were rescued from their bad reputation by the founder of the Theosophical Society, Madame Helena P. Blavatsky, who lived in India for some time. It was she who introduced the concept of devas to the West, but Mme. Blavatsky conceived of them as types of angels (or gods) who were progressed entities deriving from a previous planetary period.

Again, according to Harper's *Encyclopedia,* these devas in Mme. Blavatsky's view, "arrived on earth before elementals or human beings, and would remain dormant until a certain stage of human evolution was reached. At that time the devas would integrate with elementals and help further the spiritual development of humankind."

Native American Angels

As an old man, Black Elk, who was a cousin of Crazy Horse, told his story to a white friend, John G. Neihardt, in 1931, so that his great vision would not be lost, for Black Elk believed he had a

healing mission not only for his own people but also for all the peoples of the earth. Though Black Elk considered himself a failure, Neihardt's book, *Black Elk Speaks*, and a later document, *The Sacred Pipe*, written by Black Elk with J. Epes Brown, constitute two of the most profound mystical and metaphysical records of the twentieth century. They have been a major influence in the current revival of interest in and practice of Native American religion.

At the age of nine, during an illness which was paralytic, Black Elk had a vision of ascending to heaven. Two "men" fetched the spirit of the boy and soared with him into the clouds. He says, "We three were there alone in the middle of a great white plain with snowy hills and mountains staring at us; and it was very still; but there were whispers."

At this point, the angels show the boy a preliminary vision of a mandala (a circular form) floating among the clouds. Then, a speaking bay horse points out twelve black horses coming with manes made of lightning and who snort thunder.

From the North arrive twelve white horses with manes like blowing snow; white geese overhead circle them. In the East are twelve sorrel horses wearing necklaces of elk's teeth, their manes made of dawn's light and their eyes shimmering with the bright glimmer of the morning star. At the south corner of the mandala there are twelve buckskins that have horns and with manes made of trees and grasses.

The mandala continues to grow—adding whole herds of dancing horses that change into animals and birds of every kind and description. This magnificent and enormous congregation of animal life follows Black Elk to a teepee in the clouds, crowned by a rainbow. There he meets the six "Grandfathers"—they who have summoned him from his body. He says, "They looked older than men can ever be—old like hills, like stars."

The Grandfathers rule the six directions, and he sees another mandala encompassing the entire cosmos. Each of the Grandfathers presents the young Black Elk with a gift. The eldest, representative of the West, gives a cup of water, emblematic of the power to create life, and a bow, symbol of the power to destroy. Pointing to his chest, the elder says, "Look close at him who is your spirit

A Sacred Voice

"I looked up at the clouds, and two men were coming there, headfirst like arrows slanting down; and as they came, they sang a sacred song and the thunder was like drumming. I will sing it for you. The song and the drumming were like this:

'Behold, a sacred voice is
    calling you;
All over the sky a sacred
    voice is calling.'"
                    —*Black Elk Speaks*

now, for you are his body and his name is Eagle Wing Stretches." Black Elk understands that this is his spiritual guardian, or double, and that Eagle Wing Stretches is his spiritual name.

The other Grandfathers give him various gifts, rather like the fairies at the christening of the Princess Aurore in "The Sleeping Beauty." He gets a healing herb, a peace pipe, a red stick that is the symbol for the center of the nation's circle, and power over the birds; he is told that "all the Wings of the air shall come to you, and they and the winds and the stars shall be like relatives [to you]."

The last of the six Grandfathers seems to be the most ancient, but he suddenly becomes more youthful in appearance, growing younger and younger until Black Elk discerns that "he was myself with all the years that would be mine at last."

The first and last Grandfathers are both guardian angels, and Black Elk is henceforth protected by two powerful archangels.

Once more he sees the horse-mandala form, and in this appearance, four maidens, each beautiful as the morning and all wearing robes of scarlet, precede each herd of horses. They carry the gift symbols. A black horse sings a song of renewal: "His voice was not loud, but it went all over the universe and filled it. There was nothing that did not hear, and it was so beautiful that nothing anywhere could keep from dancing." The entire universe dances to this beautiful song.

Following upon this there appears another vision. This time Black Elk stands upon a mountain top "at the center of the world." Though it was in fact Harney Peak in the Black Hills, when questioned, Black Elk answered simply, "Anywhere you are is the center of the world." In this second vision, he sees "in a sacred manner the shapes of all shapes as they must live together like one

Black Elk's Angels

Later, Black Elk painted the two figures he describes with wings and spears—they look just like one might imagine Native American angels to look!

being. And I saw that the sacred hoop of my people was one of many hoops that made one circle, wide as daylight and as starlight, and in the center grew one mighty flowering tree to shelter all the children of one mother and one father. And I say it was holy."

Finally, the two Angels return Black Elk back to his Grandfathers. "He has triumphed!" they cry in unison, all again bestowing gifts, after which they dissolve, until only the eldest is left. This last Grandfather instructs Black Elk: "Grandson, all over the universe you have seen. Now you shall go back with power to the place from whence you came, and it shall happen yonder that hundreds shall be sacred, hundreds shall be flames!"

Returning to earth to rejoin his body, the boy hears the Sun itself in song: "With visible face I appear. My day, I have made it holy." He is carried back down to earth by a spotted eagle, sees his paralyzed body lying there, re-enters it, and wakes up. He continues the narrative thus: "Then I was sitting up; and I was sad because my mother and father didn't seem to know I had been so far away."

There can be little question that angels are represented in many cultures other than the Judeo-Christian tradition of the West. The angelic experiences of these non-Christian peoples may seem quite different from the stories that Westerners have grown up with, but in their essentials, they are similar. Angels, apparently, have been with the human race from the beginning, and they have seemingly infiltrated nearly every culture of which we have any record.

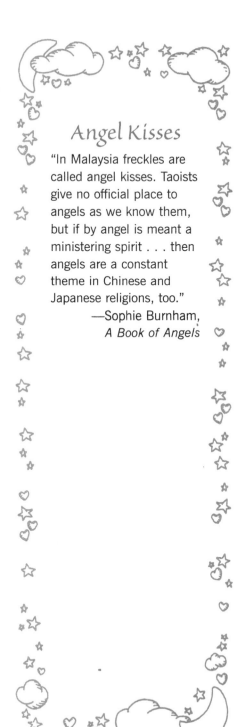

Angel Kisses

"In Malaysia freckles are called angel kisses. Taoists give no official place to angels as we know them, but if by angel is meant a ministering spirit . . . then angels are a constant theme in Chinese and Japanese religions, too."

—Sophie Burnham, *A Book of Angels*

Part Two

The World of Unseen Spirits

CHAPTER SIX

What Is an Angel?

An Author's Experience with Angels

While doing research on his angel book, G. Don Gilmore wrote many prominent religious leaders of various faiths all over the world, asking for information about angels, receiving almost entirely *negative* responses! The editor of a major Christian journal said, "I have no interest in the subject."

There are many interpretations available to answer the question, What is an angel? The narratives in early books of Scripture portray angels as mere extensions of the deity, emotionless and featureless, but later texts indicate they are capable of feelings and have individual personalities.

For example, the angel in Genesis 32:29 who wrestles with Jacob refuses to identify himself by name, perhaps because he didn't have a name? And the angel in Jude 13:18 who foretells of Samson's birth and mission also refuses to name himself. These angels lack personality and warmth; they seem more like robotic minions sent to carry out a job.

However, more personalized images of angels are available. Daniel's interaction with the angels is a good example, as are the frequent statements about Michael and his special duties. Other examples include Luke's narrative about Gabriel and Mary and the journey Tobias took with Raphael.

Looking beyond Christianity, the angel experiences of Mohammed and Black Elk seem much more personal than those of the early descriptions of angelic appearances. And then we have the idea of angels being pure energy or pure spirit. In this context, it is possible to define an angel as a "means through which the Divine is able to give expression; essences of the basal universal force of God [whatever name is used for the Supreme Deity in different cultures]; energies through which God can use as transmissions for whatever purpose He desires."

Originally, angels were not described in any one particular way, neither in form nor appearance, nor in function. Says G. Don Gilmore in *Angels, Angels, Everywhere*: "An angel is a form through which a specific essence or energy force can be transmitted for a specific purpose."

Once again, we are in the territory of leading edge scientific thought about the interaction of energy and matter. Occult philosophy shares with modern science the belief that the universe consists *only* of energy and that this energy is capable of taking different forms. Religion adds that the universal force emanates from the kingdom of the gods.

How Should We View Angels?

"St. Paul's teaching about the angels is difficult . . . if we look at St. Paul's teaching about the angels as a whole, it is particularly difficult to solve a problem . . . to what extent we should consider the teaching about the invisible world as due to the mentality of the time and possessing no supernatural guarantee, and to what extent the teaching is asserted by the author of the Scripture to be certainly divinely guaranteed. It is impossible . . . to make a neat division between two kinds of basic doctrine, especially as the Apostle only speaks occasionally about the angels, and even tries to discourage an exaggerated interest in them and a false cult of them . . . to the detriment of Christ. Nevertheless, if we look at St. Paul's fundamental idea on the subject, he will be found to do far more than merely echo the belief commonly held around him. His idea [recognizes] in the writings of scripture, however strange they may be, that which is derived from the teaching as a whole, as accepted by a simple mind, namely, the existence of messengers of god suddenly intervening in accordance with the hidden designs of him whose ways are not our ways . . . agents of a higher world which governs us. . . . Taking this view we have to try to harmonize, on the one hand that of love, grace, personal free relationships, in which the living God . . . communicates with us, his children, by personal messengers, and on the other hand, the cosmic order subject to its regular laws, in which . . . angels have a part to play . . . [and] a relationship with the 'elements of the world.'"

—Pie-Raymond Régamey, O.P.,
What Is an Angel?

Gilmore concludes that "the reason may have less to do with whether there are angels and more to do with the way angels are perceived. I believe that angels are forms, images, and expressions through which the essences and energy forces of God can be transmitted, and that, since there are an infinite number of these forms, the greatest service anyone can pay the angelic host is never to consciously limit the ways angels might appear to us."

This is good advice. The more we study angels and how they are, or were, to different cultures, the more infinitely variable they become. For example, the Gnostics, who were influenced by Persian traditions, believed that angels lived in a world of mystical light between the mundane world and the "Transcendent Causeless Cause," in other words, between heaven and earth.

Although, in the Middle Ages, angels, despite the different ideas rife about them, were part of people's everyday life, their influence upon the general populace began to wane after the great thirteenth century. With the coming of Protestantism, angels took a backseat; Protestants had no need of intermediaries between themselves and God. In fact, that was the whole idea of getting rid of Catholicism, that is, so that the individual worshipper could contact God directly, without having to go through a priest or any other intermediary, including the Virgin Mary and angels.

Although the great Renaissance painters had depicted angels as fluffy friendly winged creatures in the countless paintings of the Annunciation and as adorable little cherub babies with a tendency to float about the heads of beautiful women with cute children at their feet or on their laps, angels lost their previous importance for everyday folk. And by the time of the Enlightenment—with its emphasis on science and rational thought—angels had been relegated to the level of fairies (the stuff of poetry, romantic fancy, and children's stories).

There was, however, one powerful influence that countered the scientific materialism beginning to hold sway with the Enlightment, and that was of the eighteenth-century Swedish mystic Emanuel Swedenborg, who claimed to commune with angels in his mystical trances. Swedenborg said that all angels once lived as men and women. From his totally unorthodox, but immensely popular, point

Angel Light and Love

"Because He is love in its essence, God appears before the angels . . . as a sun. And from that sun, heat and light go forth; the heat being love and the light, wisdom. And the angels [become] love and wisdom, not from themselves but from the Lord."
—Emanuel Swedenborg, *Angelic Wisdom*

of view, Swedenborg declared that angels had all once lived as men and women on earth. Now, as angels, they are forms of affection and thought, the recipients of the Lord's love and wisdom.

Following after Swedenborg, Rudolph Steiner (1861–1925), an Austrian social philosopher and founder of the spiritualistic and mystical doctrine known as anthroposophy, developed a complex society of angels and spirits as a result of his own visionary experiences. He was influenced by Annie Besant, who took over as leader of the Theosophy movement after Mme. Blavatsky's death. Later in life, he repudiated the Theosophist system, but he continued to develop his own.

In 1924, Geoffrey Hodson, a clairvoyant and theosophist, claimed to have been contacted by an angel named Bethelda. This angel gave Hodson information, which he wrote down and later published in five books. Following is an excerpt from *The Greater Gods*:

Highest amongst the objective or fully manifested Gods are the seven Solar archangels, the seven Mighty Spirits before the Throne. These are the seven Viceroys of the threefold Solar Emperor. A planetary Scheme or Kingdom in the newborn universe is assigned to each of the Seven from the beginning. Each is a splendid figure, effulgent with solar light and power, an emanation of the sevenfold Logos, whose Power, Wisdom and Beauty no single form can manifest. These mighty Seven, standing amidst the first primordial flame, shape the Solar System according to the divine "idea." These are the seven Sephiras concerning whom and their three Superiors, the Supernal Trinity. . . . Collaborating with them, rank upon rank in a vast hierarchy of beings, are the hosts of Archangels and angels who "imbue primordial matter with the evolutionary impulse and guide its formative powers in the fashioning of its productions" (inner quotes from Madame Helena P. Blavatsky, *The Secret Doctrine*).

Hodson further believed that the whole cosmos is guided, controlled, and animated by an almost endless series of "sentient

Divisions of Angels

The angelic host, according to Hodson, is arranged into categories, or divisions:

1. *Angels of Power.* These angels teach humankind how to release spiritual energy.
2. *Angels of Healing.* These help humans avoid illness and disease, and they help heal them when they do become ill.
3. *Guardian Angels of the Home.* These protect the home and hearth against danger, disease, and ill fortune.
4. *Building Angels.* These perfect and inspire in the worlds of thought, feeling, and flesh.
5. *Angels of Nature.* These are the elemental spirits that inhabit fire, earth, air, and water.
6. *Angels of Music.* These inspire song and sing praises.
7. *Angels of Beauty and Art.* These give artists inspiration and promote the appreciation of beauty.

Angel Intelligences

"Angels . . . are hierarchical orders of intelligences, quite distinct from man in this solar system, but who either have been or will be men. They are regarded as omnipresent, superphysical agents of the creative will of the Logos, as directors of all natural forces, laws, and processes, solar, interplanetary, and planetary. Manifestations of the Logos or the One, they may be regarded as the active, creative intelligences and form-builders of all objective creation . . . ever subservient to and expressive of the One Will, the One Substance, and the One Thought."

—Geoffrey Hodson,
Clairvoyant Investigations

Beings," or angels, each having a mission to perform, and that they are "messengers" only in the sense that they are the agents of cosmic law.

Varying in degrees of consciousness and intelligence, these beings, by whatever name they are called, as they are described by Hodson, are an extremely complex organization of "perfected" or "incipient" men (and women—the term *men* is generic) and are not considered "pure Spirits." Hodson's construction of the nature of angels is a melding of several influences, of which the Bible is only one; as a theosophist, he is also influenced by Hindu concepts, such as the one of reincarnation and of perpetual cycles of birth, death, and rebirth (into new forms, whether human or not). Nonetheless, his books make interesting reading for the person interested in exploring angels and their nature.

The word *angel* is derived from the Greek *angelos*, which comes from the Hebrew *mal'akh*, translated literally as "messenger," and the Latin *angelus*, also translated as "messenger."

Other roots for the word *angel* come from *angiras* (Sanskrit), meaning "a divine spirit," and from *angaros*, a Persian word meaning "courier," another term for "messenger."

However, the image of the angel as messenger, which is the most common that we have, and which almost all of the respondents to Don Gilmore's survey thought angels were, limits angels considerably. From earliest times, angels were never seen as single-purpose beings, even though they did carry out messenger duties.

As angelology was originally developed in ancient Persia, from where it was absorbed into Judaism and Christianity, and as the medieval church was extremely disputatious as to what exactly an angel *is*, there is considerable latitude available to the modern person in answering the question, What is an angel?

Whatever **you** *think an angel is* might just be the right answer, for people today continue to experience angels through visions, dreams, and meditative states—or altered states of consciousness—just as they have throughout history.

CHAPTER SEVEN

Descriptions and Names of Angels

Angels' Wings

". . . Six wings he wore, to
shade

His lineaments Divine; the
pair that clad

Each shoulder broad,
came mantling o'er
his brest

With regal Ornament; the
middle pair

Girt like a Starrie Zone his
waste, and round

Skirted his loines and
thighes with downie
Gold

And colors dipt in Hev'n;
the third his feet

Shaddowd from either
heele with featherd
maile

Skie-tinctured grain."

—John Milton,
Paradise Lost

Descriptions of Angels

The prophet Ezekiel had an amazing vision of the wheels of God; the vision took place on the fifth day of the fourth month of the thirtieth year of the captivity of the Jews in Babylon, by the River Che'-bar. In our terms, that was about 560 B.C.E. Medieval scholars derived from Ezekiel's vision the class of angels known as wheels, or thrones, which are the most high. This is one of the most tantalizing descriptions of angels on record.

And I looked, and behold, a whirlwind came out of the north, a great cloud, and a fire infolding itself, and a brightness was about it, and out of the midst thereof as the color of amber, out of the midst of the fire.

Also out of the midst came the likeness of four living creatures. And this was their appearance; they had the likeness of a man.

And every one had four faces, and every one had four wings.

And their feet were straight feet; and the sole of their feet was like the sole of a calf's foot: and they sparkled like the color of burnished brass.

And they had the hands of a man under their wings . . .

Their wings were joined one to another; they turned not when they went; they went every one straight forward.

We have seen earlier that the first Old Testament angels appeared as ordinary men. However, as time progressed, angels took on other appearances, and we have numerous descriptions from various authors about just what the heavenly host look like.

Ezekiel's extraordinary vision—200 years after Isaiah—tells us that each of the four angels, or wheels of God, he saw had four faces—one of a man, the others of a lion, an ox, and an eagle.

Ezekiel's description of the thrones, with their four faces—one human, three animal—is apparently derivative of the griffins of Assyria from the period 600–1100 B.C.E. These winged beings are also sometimes called genii (akin to the jinn of Zoroastrianism).

In a cylinder seal at the Pierpont Morgan Library, New York, two genii are seen fertilizing the Tree of Life (700–600 B.C.E.). These figures have bearded human faces, wear helmets, and possess two wings each. However, a later depiction, from 1100–900 B.C.E. Assyria, shows a bird-headed (possibly eagle-headed) human figure with four wings, doing the same job of watering the Tree of Life. Later, in the fourteenth century C.E., an illustration for Dante's *Divine Comedy* shows a bird-headed (possibly eagle or hawk) figure with an animal body (possibly lion) at the mystic tree of Paradise.

Interestingly, there is a later rendition of a similar image to Ezekiel's, dating (it is thought) from the time of the Huns, on an Orphic ceremonial bowl known as the Pietroasa Bowl, which was recovered from its burial place in 1837, near the town of Pietroasa in Rumania. It is a complex and interesting symbolic work that contains in one area "the griffin at the god's feet [which combines] the forms of the solar bird and the solar beast, eagle and lion," as described by Joseph Campbell in *The Mythic Image*.

In an earlier biblical vision, that of the Old Testament prophet Isaiah, Seraphim are described. These angels stand above the throne of God and are awesome indeed. They have lots of wings—six of them in fact. Two they used to cover their faces. Some say against the glory of God, others for shame at human sinfulness. Another two wings were used to cover their feet in a reverential gesture (because they *stand* before the Highest Holy of Holies). The third pair of wings was used for flying, according them swiftness in delivering God's messages.

The biblical story of Adam and Eve describes the cherubims, whom God placed at the east end of the Garden of Eden to keep Adam and Eve from returning to eat the fruit of the second Tree, that of Immortal Life: "Cherubims, and a flaming sword which turned every way, to keep the way of the tree of life."

In later medieval symbolism, seraphim are shown as red, with three pairs of wings, carrying swords of fire, emblematic of their duty to inflame the hearts of humans with love of God. Clearly, the thrones, cherubim, and seraphim aren't what we imagine an angel to look like in these days.

The Angels of Emanuel Swedenborg

Emanuel Swedenborg (1688–1772) saw angels and wrote about what he saw in great detail. A well-known scientist—he was the first to use mercury for the air pump, anticipated magnetic theory, and was the father of crystallography—Swedenborg was a professor of theology at Uppsala, Sweden, and bishop of Skara. In 1747, he resigned from his position at the Swedish Board of Mines to devote himself to his clairvoyant communications from angels, learning Hebrew to enhance his studies of these beings who appeared to him. A scientist, Swedenborg wrote about his angelic encounters dryly, in a no-nonsense tone.

His position was that a spirit, or angel, was not composed of material substances and, therefore, could not be visible. As a result, the reason we see angels is because the angel assumes a material body or because our inward, spiritual "third eye" is opened. Describing angels at length, Swedenborg informs that they breathe, but it is air especially made for angelic lungs. Angels also speak, and they write. According to Swedenborg, how they speak is a marvel; they express affection with vowels, ideas with consonants, and the totality of their communication with whole words.

No single description fits all angels. Biblical accounts tell of angels appearing as ordinary men, or as radiant light, or all dressed in shining white garb. Some have wings, some don't. As we have noted earlier, angels with wings only occasionally appear in the Bible. Generally speaking, wings were a later addition, dating from the conversion of Constantine the Great.

Toward the end of the fourth century, angels acquired halos, and it wasn't long before a halo became regulation attire for angelic appearances, especially in paintings and stained glass windows in churches, even though the word *halo* doesn't even appear in the Bible, in which there is nothing at all to suggest that angels possess them. However, since the halo is a great symbol to suggest out of the ordinary beings and holiness (the Virgin Mary usually wears a halo as well), and since biblical angel appearances often involve the effect of radiant light, the halo makes sense.

Wings became standard equipment for angels especially after the Renaissance period, during which the great painter Raphael (among others) displayed angels with enormous feathery wings and benign countenances, marking the beginning of the era of the "nice" angel.

The question arises, If angels have no bodies (as is generally conceded), then are they naturally invisible? In *Angels: God's Secret Agents,* the Reverend Billy Graham speculates that "angels have a beauty and variety that surpass anything known to men." Is he speaking literally or metaphorically? Perhaps a little of both.

Names of Angels

The names of angels are as numerous as their postulated number-lessness. The least bit of research into this subject reveals not dozens but hundreds of recorded names of angels, and variations of the names of different angels.

For example, the archangel Raziel is also known as Akraziel, Saraqael, Suriel, Galisur, N'Zuriel, and Uriel. The seraph Semyaza's variations are Samiaza, Shemhazai, Amezyarak, Azael, Azaziel, and

Uzza. Metatron had a mystery name—Bizbul—but he had over a hundred other names as well.

The Seven Heavens

In Hebrew terms and lore, there are seven heavens, as well as seven archangels:

1. The first heaven is called Shamayim, and it is ruled over by Gabriel.
2. The second heaven is called Raqia, co-ruled by Zachariel and Raphael. Raphael is considered to be a great healing angel in the Near East.
3. The third heaven is called Shehaqim, whose chief ruler is Anahel. The Garden of Eden with its Tree of Life is found in the third heaven.
4. The fourth heaven is called Machonon, and its ruler is Michael. One of the oldest shrines in Turkey is dedicated to Michael, whom the Turkish people consider to be a great healer.
5. The fifth heaven is called Mathey, ruled by Sandalphon.
6. The sixth heaven is called Zebul, and it has three rulers. The main ruler is Zachiel, who has two subordinates, Zebul, who rules during the day, and Sabath, who rules the night.
7. The seventh heaven is called Araboth, and it is ruled by Cassiel.

The Seven Archangels

The earliest reference to the seven archangels is found in the Ethiopic Enoch; the order varies from what we are accustomed to:

1. Uriel
2. Raphael

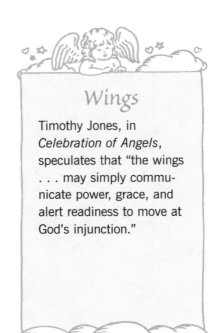

Wings

Timothy Jones, in *Celebration of Angels*, speculates that "the wings . . . may simply communicate power, grace, and alert readiness to move at God's injunction."

The Difficulty with Names of Angels

"One of the problems I ran into, in the early days of my investigations, was how to hack my way through the maze of changes in nomenclature and orthography that angels passed through in the course of their being translated from one language into another, or copied out by scribes from one manuscript to another, or by virtue of the natural deterioration that occurs with any body of writing undergoing repeated transcriptions and metathesis. For example: Uriel, "presider over Tartarus" and "regent of the sun," shows up variously as Sariel, Nuriel, Uryan, Jehoel, Owreel, Oroiael, Phanuel, Eremiel, Ramiel, Jeremiel, JacIsra'el. Derivations and/or variations of Haniel, chief of principalities and "the tallest angel in Heaven," may be set down in mathematical equations, to wit: Haniel = Anael = Anfiel = Aniyel = Anafiel = Onoel = Ariel = Simiel. The celestial *gabbai*, keeper of the treasuries of Heaven, Vretil, turns out to be the same as, or can be equated with, or is an aphetic form of, Gabriel, Radueriel, Pravuil, Seferiel, Vrevoil. In Arabic lore, Gabriel is Jibril, Jabriel, Abrael, or Abru'-el, etc. In ancient Persian lore he was Sorush and Revan-bakhsh and "the crowned Bahman," mightiest of all angels, to the Ethiopians he is Gadreel."

"Michael had a mystery name: Sabbathiel. He passed also for . . . the angel of the Lord . . . To the ancient Persians he was known as Beshter, sustainer of mankind.

"Raphael, 'christened' Labbiel when God first formed him, is interchangeable with Apharope, Raguel, Ramiel, Azrael, Raffarel, etc. And . . . operated under a pseudonym, Azariah . . . The *Zohar* equates Raphael with a king of the underworld, Bael."

—Gustav Davidson,
A Dictionary of Angels

Origins of the Seven Archangels

The number 7 is an ancient symbolic number. There were seven Akkadian elemental spirits or deities, which may have been protypical of later cultures having seven rulers or creators in their cosmological systems. These are given as An (heaven); Gula (earth); Ud (sun); Im (storm); Istar, also Ishtar (moon); Ea or Dara (ocean); and En-lil (hell). It has been suggested by some that the original models of the seven archangels were the moon and six planets (the three outer planets, Uranus, Neptune, and Pluto, were discovered only recently). All of the planets were Babylonian deities.

3. Raguel (also Ruhiel, Ruagel, Ruahel)
4. Michael
5. Zerachiel (also Araqael)
6. Gabriel
7. Remiel (also Jeremiel, Jerahmeel)

In the Hebrew Enoch 3, the angels are listed thus:

1. Mikael
2. Gabriel
3. Shatqiel
4. Baradiel
5. Shachaqiel
6. Baraqiel (also Baradiel)
7. Sidriel (or Pazriel)

The Testament of Solomon follows yet another system of names for the seven:

1. Mikael
2. Gabriel
3. Uriel
4. Sabrael
5. Arael
6. Iaoth
7. Adonael

The Christian Gnostics use the familiar order listed above for the first four, only adding Phanuel to Uriel. They then add (5) Barachiel, (6) Sealtiel, and (7) Jehudiel.

The naming system of Gregory the Great also follows the usual order for the first four of the seven: it then adds (5) Simiel, (6) Orifiel, and (7) Zachariel.

The Pseudo-Dionysius order, which was the one adopted officially by the church and which has come down to us through that channel, also duplicates the first four listed above; it adds (5) Chamuel, (6) Jophiel, and (7) Zadkiel. This system categorizes angels into three groupings according to their importance, or closeness, to God.

1. Seraphim, Cherubim, Thrones
2. Dominions, Virgues, Powers
3. Principalities, Archangels, Angels

It is to be noted that in Odeberg's edition of Enoch 3, the statement is made that each of the seven archangels is accompanied by 496,000 "myriads of ministering angels." That's a lot of angels, and one can only surmise that each had a name.

For our purposes, we will stick with the four archangels that appear at the top of the list that was handed down through the centuries from the final hierarchy of archangels decided upon and approved by the church in the Middle Ages, and the ones who are today the best known to us: Michael, Gabriel, Raphael, and Uriel.

Michael

Michael ("who is as God") ranks as the greatest of all angels, whether in Jewish, Christian, or Islamic lore and writings. His origin is Chaldean. The Chaldeans worshiped Michael as a god-like being, and it is inevitable that the later Jewish concept of Michael was influenced by that of the Chaldeans during the captivity of the Jews there (586–516 B.C.E.).

Michael is chief of the order of virtues, chief of archangels, prince of the presence (of God), angel of repentance, righteousness, mercy, and sanctification. In early times, he was also the guardian of Jacob and the conqueror of Satan, who was still alive and well and causing mischief among humans.

Michael's "mystery name" is *Sabbathiel*, and in Islamic texts, his name is Mika'il. Considered the deliverer of the faithful, he is credited with being the author of the entire Psalms 85. Also, he has been ascribed as the angel who destroyed the armies of Sennacherib (but this feat has also been credited to Gabriel, Uriel, and Ramiel, so take your choice). Michael is supposed to be the angel who stayed Abraham's knife-wielding hand at the throat of his

Angels and Astrology

Chaldea, a portion of the Mesopotamian area, was sometimes loosely used to refer to all of Babylonia. Chaldean or *Chaldee* came to be used as a general term for an astrologer or a magician because of the vast knowledge of astronomy and astrology possessed by the Chaldean Empire.

". . . late Chaldean-Hellenistic astrology . . . was to remain dominant in the Occident, one way or another, until the science of the Renaissance undid the old cosmology of a geocentric universe and opened marvels beyond anything dreamed of by the sages of the ancient mystic ways."

—Joseph Campbell, *Occidental Mythology*

young son Isaac, forbidding the sacrifice of the child. (This deliverance has also been described as the work of other angels, especially Tadhiel and Metatron.) In Jewish lore, Michael is identified as the burning bush that guided Moses in the desert. Talmudic comment Berakot 35, on Genesis 18:1–10, accords Michael as one of the three "men" who visited Sarah to announce she would have a child.

Michael has also been equated with the Holy Ghost and the third part of the Trinity; early Muslim tradition places Michael in the seventh heaven, with brilliant green wings the color of emeralds. To Christians, St. Michael is the benevolent angel of death, delivering the souls of the faithful to the immortal realm and the eternal light.

Michael was heard by Joan of Arc. According to the court testimony at her trial, Michael inspired the Maid of Orleans to raise an army and go to the aid of the dauphin of France, who became Charles VII largely due to Joan's raising the siege of Orleans.

Gabriel

Gabriel ("God is my strength") is the second highest ranking angel in the literature of all three of the major monotheistic religions—Judaism, Christianity, and Islam. The angel of annunciation, resurrection, mercy, vengeance, death, and revelation, he is an extremely busy angel with status to match.

The name Gabriel is of Chaldean origin and was not known to the Jews prior to the Captivity, but they took him up with enthusiasm. In Midrash *Eleh Ezkerah*, for example, Gabriel is a major figure in the tale of the ten martyrs (Jewish savants). One of these, Rabbi Ishmael, travels to heaven to inquire of Gabriel why they must die. He is told that they must atone for the sin of the ten sons of Jacob, who sold Joseph into slavery.

Gabriel is the only other angel, apart from Michael, who is mentioned by name in the Old Testament (except for Tobit, considered apocryphal). Gabriel, in addition to having been the angel of the annunciation to Mary of her impending pregnancy, presides over Paradise. As the ruling prince of the first heaven in Judaic lore, he

Angel of Judgment, Angel of Mercy

In the Judaic tradition, Gabriel was the Angel of Judgment, and he could be fierce indeed. However, under the aegis of Christianity, he became transformed into the Angel of Mercy! Such is the power of religious revision of history!

is said to sit on the left-hand side of God. (Presumably, Michael, who is a bit higher in importance, sits at the right-hand side of God, although this position is later given to Mary upon her assumption into heaven.)

Mohammed claimed that Gabriel—or Jibril in Islamic—who had "140 pairs of wings," was the angel who dictated the Koran to him, *sura* by *sura*. Mohammedans consider Gabriel to be the spirit of truth.

Jewish legend views Gabriel as an angel of death and destruction—to the sinful cities, naturally, Sodom and Gomorrah being especially vivid examples of this angelic fury. Talmudic lore has it that Gabriel was the angel who smote the armies of Sennacherib "with a sharpened scythe which had been ready since Creation" (Sanhedrin 95b).

Elsewhere in the Talmud, Gabriel is said to be he who stopped Queen Vashti from a nude exhibition before King Ahasuerus—and his feast guests—on behalf of Esther, who was to have taken her place. No doubt the angel intervened in this scheme because, men being men then as now, it just might have worked, and, of course, that wouldn't have done at all.

Daniel (in Daniel 8) appeals to Gabriel by flinging himself at his feet face down to learn the meaning of the encounter between the ram and the he-goat, which incident is illustrated in a woodcut in the renowned Cologne Bible. Also, in rabbinic texts, Gabriel is the prince of justice.

Mohammed apparently was in a state of some confusion between Gabriel and the Holy Ghost (the dangers of illiteracy are apparent here), but his confusion was understandable considering the conflicting accounts given in Matthew 1:20 and Luke 1:26. Matthew credits the Holy Ghost as the agent that got Mary pregnant, but Luke credits the deed to Gabriel, who "came in unto her," at the same time that he gives her the message that she "had found favor with the Lord" and "would conceive in her womb." Mohammed's interpretation makes one wonder, Could it be that Gabriel was somewhat more than a messenger angel concerning the paternity of the child? We'll never know.

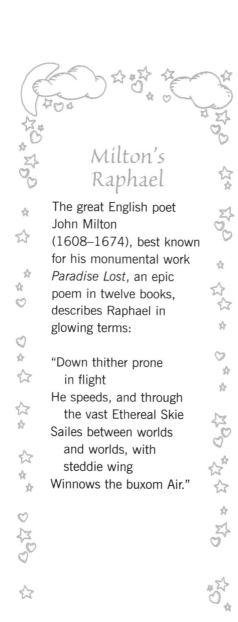

Milton's Raphael

The great English poet John Milton (1608–1674), best known for his monumental work *Paradise Lost*, an epic poem in twelve books, describes Raphael in glowing terms:

"Down thither prone
    in flight
He speeds, and through
    the vast Ethereal Skie
Sailes between worlds
    and worlds, with
    steddie wing
Winnows the buxom Air."

Raphael and the Demon Workers

The dossier of Raphael is an inexhaustible file. But one legend stands out; it is taken from the Testament of Solomon. Solomon prays to God for assistance in the building of the temple, and his prayer is answered in the gift of a magical ring, delivered to the Hebrew king personally by Raphael. This ring was engraved with a pentagram—a five-pointed star—and it had the power to summon and control demons. So it was with this God-given demon-labor (free of charge, naturally) that King Solomon completed the building of the great temple. It may be from this tale that we get the common expression, "working like a demon."

Raphael

Raphael ("God has healed") is also of Chaldean origin and was called Labbiel in that culture. Known as the healer, not only of humans but of earth itself, Raphael is one of the three great angels from post-biblical times. His first appearance is in Tobit (this text is external to the official Hebrew canon, is canonical in the Catholic Church, and is considered apocryphal in Protestant Scripture). In Tobit, Raphael guides Tobit's son Tobias on a journey from Nineveh to Media, acting as a companion. At the end of the trek, the angel reveals himself by name as one of the seven holy angels who stand at God's throne in heaven.

Raphael is a seraph who is also the head of all the guardian angels (mere angels being a lower order than archangels in heaven's hierarchy, which will be discussed in Chapter 10).

He is also known as the Angel of Providence, and in that capacity, he watches over all of humanity, which duty is an extension of his supervisory capacity of the guardian angels who each looks after only one human. He is a sort of angelic CEO of the Guardian Angel Division.

As someone who accompanies journeyers on their travels, the trip with Tobias being symbolic of all those who travel, he is related to the Greek Mercury, who is the patron god of travel and all communications. As usual, these attributes are derived from a long line of historical and mythological connotations that have come down through the ages.

As the chief travel angel, he is especially concerned with pilgrims traveling to some holy site or, metaphysically speaking, on the path toward God. Thus, he is seen walking with a staff, wearing sandals (angels often are barefooted), carrying a water gourd, and with a backpack. Raphael is a friend to the traveler as well as others.

According to the Kabbalah, Raphael was one of the three angels that visited Abraham and Sarah. Another Jewish legend credits Raphael with giving Noah a "medical book" after the flood. It is postulated that this pharmaceutical tome may have been the famous Sefer Raziel (The Book of the Angel Raziel), though this book is variously credited in a profusion of concurrences involving a number of angels and at least one demon, Rahab.

Not only is Raphael a seraph, but he also belongs to three more celestial orders, including cherubim and dominions, and powers. As such an important archangel, Raphael has many high offices, including regent of the sun, chief of the order of virtues, governor of the south and guardian of the west, ruling prince of the second heaven, overseer of the evening winds, and guardian of the Tree of Life in the Garden of Eden, to name some of the more impressive ones. He is also numbered among 10 ten holy sefiroth of the Hebrew Kabbalah.

Uriel

Uriel ("flame of God") is the last of the four top archangels of the holy seven. In Jewish legend, he was the angel of hailstorms (presumably with lightning, since he is called fire), which would relate him to the Greek Zeus, who had a habit of hurling thunderbolts of lightning when annoyed.

Moses encountered Uriel in the second heaven, and he is said to bring the light of the knowledge of God to humans. His name means "light of God," which presumably equates with fire. Milton named him a regent of the sun (along with Raphael) in *Paradise Lost*.

Uriel manifests as an eagle, and in the Book of Protection, he is described as a "spell-binding power" and is associated with Michael, Shamshiel, Seraphiel, and other powerful angels. The Zohar I says that Uriel governs the constellation of Virgo. He is said to be 300 parasangs tall and to be accompanied by a retinue of 50 myriads of angels. (A myriad is clearly uncountable. What is the total of one "myriad" times 50?) All of this multitude of attendant angels are made out of water and fire. It's not definite if some are water and some fire, or each a little of both, which seems a contradiction in terms—but, then, much of biblical lore and heavenly constructions is a contradiction in terms. Who, however, are we to question the divine?

Angel of Good News

Gabriel is the angel of good news. Djibril, the Islamic name for Gabriel, meaning "the Faithful Spirit," is credited with bringing revelation to Mohammed, in his own tongue, Arabic.

Mind you, Uriel isn't the tallest angel in heaven. His height, though quite unimaginable, is exceeded by Metatron, who is the absolutely tallest angel of all the hierarchies. He's a sort of celestial skyscraper.

According to Gnostic lore, which was thrown out by the official church for being heresy, Uriel is one of seven angels subordinate to Jehuel, known as the Prince of Fire.

Uriel is transformed from Nuriel by a strange process of transformation involving Nuriel as an eagle issuing from the side of Gebura (force) and becoming Uriel. So it is uncertain whether the two are interchangeable. But then, angels have so many different names attributed to a single one that it's nearly impossible to differentiate them clearly, as was shown earlier by the quotation from Gustav Davidson.

Uriel's Fall

After the eighth century, Uriel was demoted from the class of the archangels. According to 2 Esdras, those in charge of such matters (on earth, not in heaven) decided that he was no longer a sufficiently orthodox figure to be accepted and used as a subject for commentary.

CHAPTER EIGHT

Forms
Angels Take

ngels have a long tradition. We don't know if they appeared to prehistoric man, but when history begins to be recorded, we find images of them in many cultures around the world. These suggest that the notion of angels is embedded in our psyches.

Are Angels Real?

In *The Reenchantment of Everyday Life*, Thomas Moore describes his little daughter's matter-of-fact question to her parents. "Do you see those angels over there?" the child asks, pointing to the opposite side of the lake. "They're dressed all in white," the girl continues, as if giving a report. Moore goes on to say that he has "no doubt that my daughter saw angels and that angels are as real as anything else."

When I was a child, I held conversations with angels on a regular basis, finding the experience neither odd nor disturbing. Angels were my friends, and they have appeared to me in many different forms. As an adult, one of my most compelling experiences was being visited by a soft pink light, very diffuse but also intensely powerful. I was alone in my apartment on a summer night—a holiday weekend. The city was quiet, and I was enjoying the unusual calm and peacefulness of the usually noisy energy-driven environment of New York City.

Slowly, I became aware of a change in the atmosphere. At first I thought it was a distant fire glowing through my windows; but then it *entered* and filled up the entire space of my apartment, producing in my such a holy feeling that I spontaneously fell to my knees beside the bed.

This light communicated to me that it had traveled far, from the region of the stars, and that it was there to give me approbation for the course on which I was about to embark, which included the study of astrology. There is no way for me to adequately describe the feeling that this pink glowing light produced in me. It was a deep sense of peace and happiness—perhaps similar to the way a baby feels when bathed and powdered and held in its mother's arms. We

know that angels are messengers, and in this respect, they may be like Mercury, who is related to communication of all kinds, or like Hermes, who is a guide as well as a companion for humans.

What Are Angels?

No one knows for sure, but I believe that they are celestial intelligences—some say beings of pure light—who vibrate at a very high rate, which makes them invisible to us. However, unlike humans, they have the ability to change their vibrations at will and assume material form. When they lower their vibrations to the approximate rate of humans, they become visible to us.

They also can assume other forms and appear as people or even as thoughts and experiences. My own first clear memory of angelic interfacing with my life came at the age of 19.

At the time, I was sharing a house with two other girls. The living room was graced by a piano and a Persian rug. On one fall afternoon, I was alone in the house with nothing to occupy me. I lay down on the living room rug in front of the piano for no particular reason, except that I liked the feel of the rug. I wasn't accustomed to lying on the floor, and I wasn't sleepy. What happened was extraordinary, but, perhaps due to my earlier experience with angels, it did not seem so to me.

First, I heard music, as if someone were softly playing the piano, or as if the piano were playing itself, which my logical mind knew to be impossible. Next, I had what today would be described as an out-of-body experience. I had the sensation of being lifted up, up, up, and away; I flew out into the stratosphere, carried by an angel, who held me upside down, by the feet. I knew nothing of symbolism then, but the feet are related to Pisces, which is ruled by Neptune, the planet of higher love and mystical experience.

The angel told me I was about to see my future. We soared on until we reached outer space. The Milky Way was so close that I could have reached out and touched it; it was like a thick carpet of shining stars. From my vantage position, I could see all the stars and planets, and—believe it or not—I saw Earth exactly as it was

Recognizing Angels

Angels, then, come in many forms. In *Sacred Space*, Denise Linn says:

Right now angels are bridging our physical reality with their pure spiritual energy. Like a leaf falling softly on the still pool of our consciousness, we recognize their presence. As we trust in them, they will pour their blessings on us. . . . And as you become aware of angels they will be more and more drawn into your life.

Expect a Miracle

"Angels are *there*. You might not see them, but you can always sense them, and when you begin to have contact with your own Higher Self you are likely to have contact with higher beings and infinite energies. The more alert and open you are to these extraordinary experiences, the more likely it is you will find them in your life.

Be on the alert—if you feel the presence of an angel become still and wait for a message. As you become more and more aware of their presence when they visit, you will draw them closer and experience them more often. Many of them are coming closer to the human realm in this period of the ending of an old, outworn, millennium and the birth of a new age."

—M. J. Abadie, *Awaken to Your Spiritual Self*

later photographed by the astronauts. I distinctly remember the shock of recognition when years later I first saw the actual pictures of our beautiful blue-and-white planet photographed from space. *I knew I had already seen it*—just as it appeared in the NASA photographs! This experience would be called déjà vu, or a sense that one has been somewhere one could not logically have been before.

Who Sees Angels?

There are many factors in who sees angels. The old virtue of "purity of heart" may be the deciding factor, but there are stories of evildoers who, confronted by an angel, gave up their wrongful ways. Certainly children can see angels, and this may be simply because they have not been taught that angels are mere superstition. A child's eyes are open wide to the wonders of life on earth, until adult admonitions and restrictive "teachings" cause them to close tight against the miraculous.

What Do Angels Look Like?

They seem to take a form that the person who is receiving their message can relate to. No angel speaks English to someone whose native and only tongue is French or Spanish. Sometimes angels appear without form, as a sense of being given unerring direction. Angels can manifest as a thought in your mind, an urge of your body, or a surge of intuition.

In *Care of the Soul*, Thomas Moore says:

When a summer breeze blows through the open window as we sit reading in a rare half-hour of quiet, we might recall one of the hundreds of annunciations painters have given us, reminding us that it is the habit of angels to visit in moments of silent reading.

We tend to see our angels as we have had them represented to us through our culture. This variability of angelic presences may

account for the ease with which skeptics dismiss angel "sightings" or other evidence of these messengers. But would consistency of form be an appropriate characteristic for a divine messenger?

Angelic presences, or spirits, do not necessarily exist separately from the humans around us. How often do we say to a child, "You little angel!" or to a loved one, "What an angel you are!" How are we to approach angels if they are so variable and mysterious? The answer is *with belief and total trust,* as did the great painters of the past who have left us with so many representations of angels—with wings and without, grand and small, fierce or benign, male and female, adult and child, serene or active, speaking, singing, flying, standing, enfolding, defending, praying, announcing, and playing a variety of musical instruments from harps to trumpets. We must take their reality and their powers seriously and with respect to invoke it in our lives. Thomas Moore says, "Angels . . . are all we have left in our desire to connect with ultimacy and divinity. Without the flutter of their wings in the background of experience, we have only the grinding and purring of machines or the white noise and hum of our own ceaseless thought."

As has been said, angels can appear in many different forms, visible and invisible. Mostly the Christian West associates angels with white-robed, winged, humanlike figures. However, this popular conception of the angel rarely appears to our perception. Often, angels come in human or animal form, or they operate through the agency of a real human.

There is still another way the angelic realm interfaces with us. This is when a celestial energy superimposes itself on someone, who then *acts in the angel's stead*, without knowing the person being helped or why he or she came to be there. When this happens, a person is unwittingly called upon to render assistance and does so as a matter of course, just being "the right person in the right place at the right time." Such an occurrence marked a life-saving rescue mission undertaken for me.

It was on a sailing excursion when I was 22. I couldn't swim, but I liked being on and in the water, and I was a skilled sailor. My friend Harry, divorced and with a little boy, owned a lovely boat with a ketch rig and liked to use it for weekend parties, with me

The Psychology of Sight Perception

Experimental psychologist Mary Orser cites this example of the gap between what actually happened and what is *perceived* (or "seen"): Teachers of psychology have staged events in which, for instance, several people burst into a classroom making a great racket and much commotion. One points a banana at different people. Another sets off a firecracker, making a loud bang and smoke. After the intruders rush out, each class member reports what he or she has seen. A large percentage report the banana as a gun; many think the firecracker was a gunshot. Descriptions of what the "bandits" wore, their number, their sex, and so forth, vary widely.

serving as hostess. As he didn't like to be bothered with the details of getting a party together, he left everything to me, including which guests to invite and what food to prepare and bring. One Sunday, I invited a couple who asked if they could bring their houseguest, a single man. None of these three knew how to sail, and Harry liked to have extra crew on board, so I also invited a man named John, who was an experienced boat person. A stranger showed up at the last minute to take John's place.

When my hostess chores were finished, I wanted to get in the water and be towed by the boat. Harry indulged me by tying a 20-foot line around my wrist so that I could play porpoise in the sea. I was shallow diving and enjoying the *whoosh* of being pulled through the water when the rope slipped from my wrist and I found myself suddenly untethered in the open sea. The boat shot forward at an alarming speed when relieved of my weight drag, and I watched helplessly as it grew smaller and almost disappeared. I remember little else, except that, under the water, I was very happy, even ecstatic. I saw visions of light and could communicate with the fish and other marine animals. This underwater world seemed a wondrous place. All was beauty and serenity, with a wonderful luminosity.

The next thing I knew I was flat on my back on the deck being given artificial respiration by strong arms and vomiting a lot of sea water. Harry, at the tiller, had known immediately that I was no longer tethered to the boat. But under full sail and with a brisk wind, the boat had traveled a considerable distance before the crew could tack and come around and return using power. But, in the open sea, with no markers, how had they managed to find the precise spot where I had vanished?

The extra man brought by the couple was a strong swimmer, as was Gary, who had replaced John. These two had dived into the water and—miraculously—found me. When we returned to the Houston Yacht Club's dock and disembarked, Gary took me aside while the others went into the clubhouse.

He was older—mid-30s or so—and he looked at me intently. I can still remember the clear green color of his eyes, like peridot flecked with spots of amber. Taking my hand in his strong, tanned one, he said gravely, "You lead a charmed life. Did you know that?"

Not knowing what he meant, I shook my head in the negative, but his tone impressed me with its seriousness. Oddly—or perhaps not, given my history—the incident had not seemed to me particularly extraordinary. Being close to death had not made much of an impression on me. Looking into my eyes penetratingly, he continued, "I was the one who found you. And I wasn't supposed to be on this boat today. I'm supposed to be in San Francisco right now. I don't even know Harry. I only came because my flight was canceled and John wasn't feeling well. And I'm the *only* other friend John has who knows how to sail. I came because of *you.*"

Without understanding this, I accepted it as fact because of the way he said it with total conviction. I never saw Gary again, and he never sailed with Harry again. Later, John told me he was a professional diver who traveled all over the world guiding searches for lost treasure.

Although he did not say it in so many words, I sensed that uncanny guidance had led this man to be on the boat and to find me in the sea. Considering the time lag and the open ocean, he knew the odds were against them finding me alive, or at all. Clearly the experience had impressed him deeply. I also sensed that he was a man of extraordinary sensibilities. Perhaps spending so much time under the water does that to a man.

Why didn't I drown? Why didn't I sink? I can only say that while I was under water, I felt buoyed up by a force of light, like resting on an air mattress. That I floated was a major factor in the rescue. Did an angel hold me up until they found me? Did an angel cause Gary—just the person needed—to be on the scene? Was there some lesson for me in the near-death experience? For me, the answer is yes to all three questions.

Angels are less often seen than they are felt—as presences, as thoughts, as ideas, as guidance. Often when I am searching for a reference, a book will catch my eye, and when I pick it up, it will fall open to precisely the information I need. The well-known writer

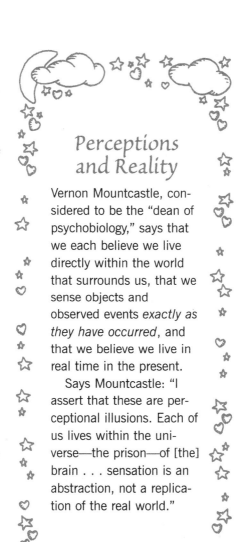

Perceptions and Reality

Vernon Mountcastle, considered to be the "dean of psychobiology," says that we each believe we live directly within the world that surrounds us, that we sense objects and observed events *exactly as they have occurred*, and that we believe we live in real time in the present.

Says Mountcastle: "I assert that these are perceptional illusions. Each of us lives within the universe—the prison—of [the] brain . . . sensation is an abstraction, not a replication of the real world."

Perception and Memory

"It takes time to learn a meaning for our sensa- tions, and different people learn different lessons. Perception turns out to be a part of memory. We per- ceive what we have experi- enced and understood in the past. It never occurs to us that . . . sight is a way of thinking . . . "
—Edmund Blair Boles, *A Second Way of Knowing: The Riddle of Human Perception*

Arthur Koestler named this phenomenon the Library Angel, and many writers and students experience it frequently.

In *Angels, Angels Everywhere*, G. Don Gilmore says that he believes that "angels are forms, images, and expressions through which the essences and energy forces of God can be transmitted," and that "since there are an infinite number of these forms, the greatest service anyone can pay the angelic host is never con- sciously to limit the ways angels might appear to us."

Angels, then, come in many forms. How we perceive them will depend on our personal belief systems and what images we have received as children. The classic picture most of have of an angel is a being with a serene face, wearing flowing white robes, borne on big, beautiful feathered wings, and radiating brilliant light.

This child's version of the ideal was imprinted early on most Christian children, but as we have seen earlier, the Old Testament angels often arrived disguised as ordinary men. However, in their visions, which seem to have been extraordinary out-of-body experi- ences or else the product of a vivid and complex ability to receive images or information in a trance state, the prophets and later reli- gious philosophers, such as Swedenborg, "saw" angels as almost unbelievably glorious beings.

When we read the proliferating accounts of people, both in our own time and in past history, we find that there are many descrip- tions of the form in which an angel can be seen, felt, or in some other manner experienced.

Angel stories in our times are so varied that it is impossible to come to any conclusion. Just as witnesses to an accident will describe different versions of what they saw—or thought they saw— happen (as any law officer can confirm), so recipients of angel experiences will recount surprisingly, even contradictory, versions of the event.

Our perceptions of angels are ordinarily accompanied by positive feelings. But whether they are perceived as being beneficial or threatening, we tend to accept what we see as being the true reality.

This is what the philosopher Immanuel Kant realized when he wrote of phenomena as the product of "things in themselves," which we input as sensations and then later organize into forms, categories, ideas, and the like. Kant called the "things in themselves" *noumena*, and our perceptions of them are the *phenomena*. As the noumena energy seeks to express itself in a form, the angel form is always an *appearance*, which can differ in different times, places, circumstances, and to human observers. Therefore, we should not try to create a concept of a single definite form in which an angel is always supposed to appear. To do so limits our ability to perceive and interact with these marvelous celestial energies who sometimes visit us.

Who Sees Angels the Most Easily?

Clearly the deeply religious or those especially inclined to seeing visions may be the most frequent recipients of angel visitations. However, as stated previously, the angels appear in forms that are familiar to the person who receives the vision. For example, a devout Hindu wouldn't likely see the standard feather-winged white-gowned Christian angelic form; nor would a person who speaks only French receive a message from an angel speaking another tongue. Angels for the most part appear in both the cultural norm and the religious format to which the person is accustomed.

Angels can appear as animals, as they did when Elijah was fed in the wilderness by ravens (those birds flying to him morning and evening with sustenance were angels in disguise). But Elijah, as a desert inhabitant, would not have found ravens unusual. Birds—quite possibly because they are naturally winged creatures and have the gift of flight that humans yearn for—are often thought of as angels.

A gentleman I once knew fairly closely, who was a blind massage therapist to whom I went for treatments, was at a particularly difficult time in his life. Born sighted, he had lost his vision in his early twenties from an illness, and the adjustment was intense and difficult. One fine spring day, just after he had opened his massage offices in Manhattan, he had all the windows open, and a pair of beautiful birds—brightly colored songbirds—flew in the window and around his head in a circle. He, of course, could not see them, but

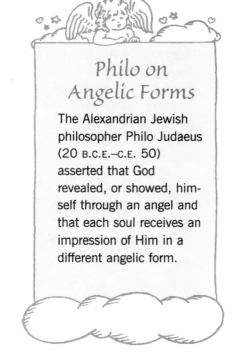

Philo on Angelic Forms

The Alexandrian Jewish philosopher Philo Judaeus (20 B.C.E.–C.E. 50) asserted that God revealed, or showed, himself through an angel and that each soul receives an impression of Him in a different angelic form.

Saint Augustine on Angels

"Angels are spirits, but it is not because they are spirits that they are angels. They become Angels when they are sent. For the name Angel refers to their office, not their nature. You ask the name of this nature, it is *spirit*; you ask its office, it is that of an *Angel*, which is a messenger."

—Saint Augustine

he could sense them. He called to his wife, who was also his receptionist, to come into the room and tell him what was happening. To her utter astonishment, she saw the pair of birds flying in circles above his head. They both interpreted this extremely unusual appearance as angelic, as a message that his new massage business would prosper. And it did. Later, he claimed to be glad of his blindness, as it gave him special feeling senses with which to diagnose and treat his patients.

There are many passages in Scripture that describe angels in one or another bodily form, human or otherwise. However, there are those who believe that angels *never* assume bodies, that all the so-called angelic appearances cited in the Bible were *visions*, divinely inspired perhaps, but taking place in the imagination of the prophet or person who had the vision. Contradicting this are the cases in which the Scriptures speak of angels appearing visibly to several people simultaneously, such as Abraham's servants and the populace of Sodom, who saw the angels who visited Lot—and lusted after them as well!

Therefore, it is probably safe to say that angels are incorporeal beings who are capable of assuming bodies in order to present themselves to humans for whatever deed needs doing. Father Walter Farrell, O.P., a twentieth-century Aquinas scholar, observes that an angel assuming a body is analogous to a man renting a tuxedo to wear to a wedding. He puts the garb on for the special occasion and then takes it off again and returns to the natural angel state. If this is so—and it seems a likely construct—then the bodies angels assume for their earthly tasks do not operate in the same manner as human bodies—in terms of the usual bodily needs and functions, such as eating, drinking, the digestive and elimination processes, sleep, and so on. The angel Raphael makes this clear in Tobias. Just before rising up and disappearing into thin air, he said, "You thought you saw me eating, but that was merely an appearance and no more."

It seems clear to me that *angels can function in any medium*, be it human or animal forms, intuitions, feelings, apparitions, or—especially—dreams. (There is more information on angels and dreams in Chapter 17.)

Angels and Clairvoyance

Clairvoyant Nick Bunick claims to have had "over fifty angelic experiences," in many forms, "ranging from signs such as the '444,' by celestial voice, and by claircognizance." In *In God's Truth,* Bunick says:

> I am often asked if angels are able to take human form? I have not experienced an angel in human form. . . .We have all heard stories of how a person was helped during an incredible moment of danger or need and that the person providing the help usually came out of absolutely nowhere and then immediately disappeared into thin air following the event. We are then led to believe that the person who provided the help, in reality, was an angel disguised in human form. . . . I have no personal knowledge of such an event. . . . But God does perform miracles.
>
> An angel normally does not have a corporeal body, but instead is translucent. . . . If you have seen an angel, you literally would be able to see through the angel, just as if you held a flimsy nightgown in front of a flood light. Even though you could see the gown, you could also see what was behind the gown in the background.
>
> Also, you cannot tell the gender of an angel. . . . Although I am told they do have a gender, you cannot tell if you are looking at a beautiful young woman or a beautiful young man. And, yes, they do have wings.

Contradicting Bunick, C. Leslie Miller, in *All About Angels*, flatly states that "angels have appeared in human form upon many occasions." He says:

> Someone has suggested that angels are visible, but our eyes are not made to see them. Human sight is adjusted to only a small portion of the light waves and is far from being perfect or complete. Animals and birds see and hear things beyond our range of sight and hearing.
>
> But there have been many times in the past when God permitted human eyes to focus in on heaven's light rays and actually see the heavenly bodies of angels. At other times the Holy Ones assumed human form and were seen in the physical appearance and dress of the culture of the person who was the object of the divine visitation.

CHAPTER NINE
Fallen Angels

*A*s you probably know, the war between God and the Fallen Angels, which can be interpreted as the conflict between good and evil, began when Lucifer—most beautiful and wise of all the beings created by the divine artificer and prince of the entire angelic order—decided to no longer bow to the authority of his sovereign Lord. In short, he rebelled against the highest authority. Isaiah describes that treasonable action most dramatically:

> *How you have fallen from heaven, O star of the morning, son of the dawn! . . . You said in your heart, "I will ascend to heaven; I will raise my throne above the stars of God, and I will sit on the mount of assembly in the recesses of the north. I will ascend above the heights of the clouds; I will make myself like the Most High."*
>
> —Isaiah 14:12–14

It reads like the pilot plot for a new TV drama. Not only did the exquisitely beautiful and glamorously grand Lucifer decide to be entrepreneurial and go it on his own—like some rebellious VP who has been passed over for promotion—but rumor has it that he took at least a third of the angelic population along with him in the insurrection.

As Scripture often refers to angels as "stars," Lucifer (the name means "bringer of light") was called "the star of the morning," which would relate him to the planet Venus, which rises as the morning star during part of her cycle and as the evening star at other times. Venus is the planet of love—earthly love, not divine love. She represents the principle of beauty, which includes vanity. Her Greek predecessor was Aphrodite—the most beautiful of the goddesses (at least *she* thought so), who, bribing the youth Paris to make sure she got the beauty queen title, started the Trojan War by promising Helen, the Elizabeth Taylor of her time, to Paris in return for naming her (Aphrodite) the most beautiful of the goddesses. Unfortunately, Helen was already married, and her husband caused quite a ruckus over the deal.

God's Description of Lucifer

Ezekiel delivers this message from God to Lucifer, the most famous of all the "fallen," or bad angels in Ezekiel 28:12–17:

You had the seal of perfection, full of wisdom and perfect in beauty. You were in Eden, the garden of god; every precious stone was your covering: the ruby, the topaz, and the diamond; the beryl, the onyx, and the jasper; the lapis lazuli, the turquoise, and the emerald; and the gold, the workmanship of your settings and sockets was in you. On the day that you were created they were prepared. You were the anointed . . . and I placed you there. You were on the holy mountain of god; you walked in the midst of the stones of fire. You were blameless in your ways from the day you were created, until unrighteousness was found in you.

By the abundance of your trade you were internally filled with violence, and you sinned; therefore I have cast you as profane from the mountain of God. And I have destroyed you, O [guardian] cherub, from the midst of the stones of fire.

Your heart was lifted up because of your beauty; you corrupted your wisdom by reason of your splendor.

Actually, Isaiah, in writing about Lucifer was referring to the king of Babylon, but his text was misunderstood as a reference to the fallen angel. Hence, the name Lucifer became synonymous with Satan, also known as the Devil. Interestingly, in Greek, Lucifer was Phosphorus.

In Hebrew, Satan means "adversary," and as a name, it was applied to the principle of evil, which was conceived by Judaism, Christianity, and Islam, as a person-like being. The word *devil* is derived from the Greek word for "accuser."

In the heavenly cosmologies of all three of these monotheistic religions—following the ideas of Zoroaster (remember Iblis, who wouldn't bow down?)—Satan was originally an angel who rebelled against God, fell from heaven, and was condemned to eternal damnation. Remember the first Commandment? "I am the Lord thy God. Thy shall have no other Gods before me." Yahweh, or Jehovah, was well known as a jealous god. He even declared it.

This fallen angel, by whatever name you choose, presides over Hell (on earth as well as in the nether regions) and is served by a coterie of minor angels, the ones who chose his side against God and fell along with him, to become devils (not with a capital *D* like "the Devil," a term reserved for Satan himself, once Prince of Light, now Prince of Darkness). (Note that the Devil has many names: Abaddon, Apollyon, Dragon, Serpent, Asmodeus, Beelzebub or Baalzebub, and Belial.)

Nowhere in Scripture are we told just *why* Lucifer/Satan rebelled against God's authority. Ezekiel suggests that it was sheer vanity—pride in his own splendiferous gorgeous self, not to mention his possession of great wisdom.

Images of War

We see many warlike images in both Scripture and in Christian contemporary writing—always, as is to be expected, with the accompanying certainty of victory over evil forces. Consider this passage from Christian writer Timothy Jones:

The battles we face, the temptations we withstand or submit to, the good we accomplish, and the evil we leave unchallenged, are all ultimately part of a larger battlefield, one that, for now, stretches across creation into our daily lives and even our momentary thoughts. And God sends his appointed helpers to enter our own battlefields. . . . Until recently, I found that I rarely thought of angels being at work in the battles of my life. . . . I know that whatever the specifics of the battle that takes place between the angels and demons, it has to do ultimately with the powerful presence of the Lord of the Universe. That means it is never a futile fight.

Under the subtitle *Destined to Win*, Jones continues this imagery of war:

If we share in the battle waged by armies of good and evil, a second truth needs forceful statement: God and his angels of light are more powerful than Satan and the forces of darkness . . . we need not fear. We tread paths "covered by shields of angels." . . . We cannot avoid the effects of living in a battle zone. Human life—and the Christian's life in particular—entail elements of vigorous struggle.

Jones's conception of the warlike stance of opposing forces on the "battlefield(s)" of humanity's struggles, as well as his confidence, is fully backed up by Scriptures that, sometimes in extremely strong language, reassure the believer that all will be well—eventually. Always, even when the wrongdoers seem to be profiting from their evil, God's battle against the Evil One and his minions continues, as is demonstrated in this passage from Isaiah 24:21–24:

On that day the LORD will punish
the host of heaven in heaven,
and on earth the kings of the earth.
They will be gathered together like prisoners in a pit;
they will be shut up in a prison,
and after many days they will be punished.

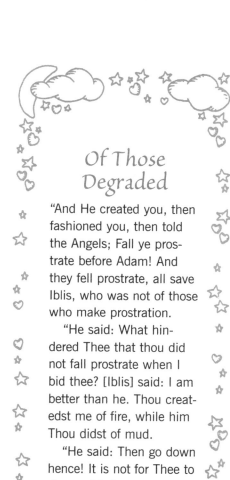

Of Those Degraded

"And He created you, then fashioned you, then told the Angels; Fall ye prostrate before Adam! And they fell prostrate, all save Iblis, who was not of those who make prostration.

"He said: What hindered Thee that thou did not fall prostrate when I bid thee? [Iblis] said: I am better than he. Thou createdst me of fire, while him Thou didst of mud.

"He said: Then go down hence! It is not for Thee to show pride here, so go forth! Lo! Thou art of Those degraded."

—Koran, VIII

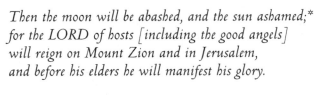

Then the moon will be abashed, and the sun ashamed;*
for the LORD of hosts [including the good angels]
will reign on Mount Zion and in Jerusalem,
and before his elders he will manifest his glory.

The imagery of a great war is seen also in the last book of the Bible. Revelation 12:7–12 contains this passage: "And war broke out in heaven; Michael and his angels fought against the dragon. The dragon and his angels fought back, but they were defeated, and there was no longer any place for them in heaven."

Oddly enough, there are more references to the fall of the evil angels, which confirms the goodness of the good angels, than there are references to the creation of the angels. In 2 Peter we learn that "God did not spare the angels when they sinned, but cast them into hell and committed them to pits of nether gloom to be kept until the judgment."

The Angelic Sin

Clearly, the early Fathers were uncertain about the precise nature of the angelic sin and just when it had taken place. Timothy Jones comments, in *Celebration of Angels*, that "the Bible does not tell us a great deal about the Devil, the chief of fallen angels. He receives mention a number of times in the Old Testament, but we nowhere find an exhaustive account of what went wrong."

And John Calvin, the reformist French theologian who experienced a "sudden conversion" and left the Catholic Church, fleeing to Switzerland to defend Protestantism, chastised those who "grumble that Scripture does not in numerous passages set forth systematically and clearly the fall of the devils, its cause, manner, time, and character" (*Institutes*, Vol. I, 164).

But this the early church fathers knew: God created the demons, but He did not create them evil. This feat they accomplished by

---

*This line evidently refers to fallen angels as stars—or planets. Remember, Lucifer was the morning star.

themselves. The problem here is that if God created all things to be *good*, then where do bad things originate, if not with God? That's a big, baffling question. Answer: devils—or fallen angels.

It is remarkable that the equation of sin with sex was in place during biblical times—and it is with us still. When we speak of immorality, we aren't usually referring to stealing, murder, or inside trading. We are talking about sexual peccadilloes. Early interpretations of Genesis 6:2–4 reveal that the sin of the angels consisted in sexual relations—with human women.

Genesis tells us that "the sons of God saw that the daughters of men were fair; and they took to wife such of them as they chose," producing thereby a race of giants called the Nephilim. What happened to these creatures isn't reported.

Further on, in exploring the nature of demons (a popular theological pastime), medieval scholars discovered, in Genesis 6, a confirmation of their suspicions that demons could have sexual intercourse with women. Hurrah! Now we have those nasty succubi and incubi who sneak into the beds of innocent humans and corrupt them by sexual means.

Unfortunately, there was a serious problem with this interpretation: Lucifer and his followers had fallen *before* the creation of Adam and Eve, who, since they were the first humans, hadn't been around, nor produced any human progeny, for the fallen angels to have sex with. Unable to resolve this thorny issue, St. Augustine, the early Christian church father and prolific writer of orthodox Christian texts, decided that what really caused the angels' sin and consequent fall was their pride—their desire to be God's equal—and that this event took place *before* the creation of the world! Any port in a storm!

This consensus view of the fallen angels took deep root in subsequent Christianity. Question: To where did the fallen angels fall, if not to earth to have sex with human women? Answer: Into the middle air between heaven and earth. From there it was a short trip to Hell, where they engage in torturing the souls of the damned.

This argument, torturous in itself, holds that because the angels had the ability to *choose*, they can never be redeemed. The issue

Angels in the Dead Sea Scrolls

Among the recently discovered Dead Sea Scrolls is one entitled *War of the Sons of Light Against the Sons of Darkness*. In this text, Michael is called the Prince of Light. He leads the angels of light in battle against the legions of the angels of darkness, who are commanded by the demon Belial.

of free will is an important one in this debate because the very nature of the angelic intellect and will is designed so that their first (and only) free choice forever determined their orientation toward good or evil.

Insofar as the angels' free will was concerned, they were supposed to have had sufficient knowledge of their alternatives instantly upon being created. So the angels' freedom, knowledge, and responsibility are inseparable and sufficient to make what today we would call "an informed decision." Thus it was that the angels fell, and became demons or devils, through their own choice, heavily influenced by their willful pride. No one has answered the question of just where the angels—created good, all of them—came by the vices of pride and willfulness. Did they invent them in that split second available to them to make such a far-reaching life decision? Not a smart career move.

The fall of Satan was a burning topic for medieval Christians, for it gave them lots of scope for argument and opinion. Anselm of Canterbury devotes an entire treatise to the subject. Aquinas considers whether Satan was originally a cherub or a seraph. Cherubim are characterized by their knowledge and wisdom, but that alone does not make them immune to mortal sin. On the other hand, Seraphim are characterized by their burning love of God, which would preclude sinning against such an all encompassing feeling. A spouse does not cheat on a spouse that is really and truly loved, and a seraph couldn't possibly deny God's ultimate authority and superiority. But in one of those quick turnarounds for which Aquinas was famous, he flips the coin and declares that Satan had to be a seraph (the seraphim are the highest order of angels) for the simple, but hardly logical, reason that no angel but one of the most exalted would suffer the sin of pride. Aquinas wriggles out of this incompatibility between seraphic love and mortal sin by saying that Satan "is called a cherub." What's in a name? A rose by any other name would still be a rose, but is a cherub who is called a cherub really a seraph? Try reading Aquinas and see what *you* think.

Demons and Devils

The result of all this doctrine of fallen angels turning into demons and devils—think of all the variations on the word *devil*, such as devilment, which is a lighthearted word, or expressions such as "beating the devil out of" someone, or "Oh, you little devil!" which is a compliment of sorts—was the creation of the belief, which we hold to this day (despite our modern world), that somewhere, either "out there" or active on earth, there is an actual force of evil, a vast and powerful kingdom of darkness.

The apostle Paul was a great propounder of this notion, calling Satan "the prince of the power of the air . . . the spirit that is now working in the sons of disobedience," in his sermons to the Ephesians (2:2). There's no truer believer than the convert, that's for sure. And Paul's conversion on the road to Damascus was dramatic as well as sudden. True to Joseph Campbell's description of the patriarchal mentality as being of "fire and sword," Paul writes to the Ephesian Christians warning them to "put on the full armor of God, that you may be able to stand firm against the schemes of the devil," referring to an organized kingdom of Satan, much as we refer to organized crime, as a dangerous and powerful force, "For our struggle is not against flesh and blood, but against . . . the powers."

The Need for Fallen Angels

The fall of the evil angels in this era had important implications for humans as well as for heaven, because the heavenly thrones vacated by the falling angels (or perhaps abdicated) were up for grabs. Who was going to fill them? As with all things, the church provided the answer: holy saints, to be canonized by the church authorities after due consideration and investigation of their good works and performance of miracles. Now, mere humans could aspire to be—not angels exactly—but saints who could sit in the seats of former angels. Did not Jesus promise that men and women will be "like angels in heaven" (Matthew 22:30)? The angel personnel problem was solved. Humans made saints would fill

The Importance of Calvinism

"Calvinism differs basically from Catholicism in holding that redemption is for elect alone, the free gift of God not to be won by good works. Calvinism characterized the Covenanters in Scotland, the Puritans in England and in New England, and the Huguenots in France. The extension of Calvinism to all spheres of human activity was extremely important in a world emerging from an agrarian, medieval economy into a commercial, industrial era because the development of a successful industrial economy was stimulated by the Christian virtues of thrift, industry, sobriety, and responsibility that Calvin preached as essential to the achievement of God's reign on earth."
—*The Columbia Viking Desk Encyclopedia*, 1968

those empty chairs. Without those vacancies, where would humans be in terms of heaven?

Now you can see why fallen angels were a necessity, for without them, how were humans to get a place in heaven? Bonaventure, in presenting the life of Francis as a model for human sanctity, had a vision of Francis, as Saint Francis, occupying a celestial seat that once belonged to an angel, now fallen. It was a very well-decorated throne, encrusted with precious jewels and glowing with radiance. A thoughtful person might wonder of what use are expensive baubles such as diamonds, rubies, and emeralds in heaven, but Bonaventure never broached that consideration. Heaven, after all, was supposed to be pure bliss. And how could one interpret bliss except by earthly standards—great wealth and social position being among the most desirable of human conditions.

There were other problems, too, with the seats left vacant by the fallen angels. For example, would humans join the angels who had remained true to God as their equals, or would they form a minor, lower, order of saints—the lowest, beneath the angels and their replacement saints?

Aquinas took the position that such a two-story arrangement would violate Augustine, who was a revered church father. Augustine had held that in heavenly society, saints and angels would be one. But had he factored in the population explosion? Surely there weren't as many fallen angels as there were humans, and if all humans were to be given sainthood and thereby be eligible for an angel chair, there might have to be a "standing room only" policy instituted for latecomers. Or maybe they could rotate, like a game of angelic musical chairs. On the other hand, it has now been scientifically proven that we live in an expanding universe—so why not postulate an expandable heaven? The thing is: How many empty chairs were there to begin with, and are there any left?

Going against Aquinas, as he often was wont to do, Bonaventure preferred to disallow human mingling with the heavenly host. Angels were to excel in dignity—none of this equality business for him. However, Bonaventure interprets the rejoicing of angels over the repentance of sinners as a sign that the angels are happy to have their diminished numbers restored via salvation of human souls.

Another hot theological argument was whether humans had specifically been created to fill the seats of the fallen angels (which was a possibility if the angels fell before humans were created, thus leaving their chairs vacant whilst no humans yet existed to be turned into future saints). Augustine argued for this view, but the common belief was that humans had been created for other reasons, that is, to love, revere, and serve God for His greater glorification.

Whatever view was taken, the general consensus, which holds to this day, is that the angels and the demons are in constant battle for either the salvation or the damnation of humanity. Christians don't worry on this point, for it is promised in the last book of the Bible that the good will be victorious. These words from the Eastern Orthodox liturgy confirm the prediction, also in military terms:

> *Rank on rank the host of heaven spreads its vanguard on the way*
> *As the Light of light descendeth from the realms of an endless day*
> *That the powers of hell may vanish as the darkness clears away*
> —*Liturgy of St. James*

Perhaps one reason that a precise explanation of just why the angels fell is missing from the Bible—to the chagrin of Calvin and others whose responsibility it is to interpret Scripture for the lay people of their churchly communities—is that the church elders succeeded in barring the book of Enoch from the accepted canon of the Bible, and also from the accepted Apocrypha (added books).

In Medieval Times

Medieval dramatic productions, such as the York Cycle's *Creation and the Fall of Lucifer*, which were popular entertainment, created opportunities for good angels to sing the *Te Deum* and the *Sanctus*—Lucifer only gets a monologue!

Enoch and the Watchers

As a result, the First Book of Enoch, which is a strange and wondrous story of a troop of fallen angels called the Watchers, was suppressed by the canonical authorities and would have sunk into

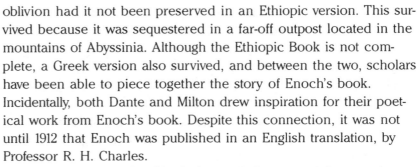

oblivion had it not been preserved in an Ethiopic version. This survived because it was sequestered in a far-off outpost located in the mountains of Abyssinia. Although the Ethiopic Book is not complete, a Greek version also survived, and between the two, scholars have been able to piece together the story of Enoch's book. Incidentally, both Dante and Milton drew inspiration for their poetical work from Enoch's book. Despite this connection, it was not until 1912 that Enoch was published in an English translation, by Professor R. H. Charles.

Forty years after Dr. Charles's translation, material supporting the story Enoch tells of the Watchers was found among the writings of the Dead Sea Scrolls.

Says Emily Hahn, author of *Breath of God*:

Reading Enoch we can see why the elders rejected his Book. If they had accepted it (literally) as Gospel, they would have been faced with the dangerous idea that angels of God are not infallible, and there was . . . quite enough trouble . . . over the question of why God should have invented Evil in the first place, *if* He did. And if He didn't, who did? A disturbing question whichever way one pursues it.

The story Enoch tells is this (according to the 1912 translation):

Two hundred angels, called the Watchers, or the Awake Ones, or Those Who Sleep Not, rebelled against God because they had become enamored by human women and were experiencing a shocking vulnerability to human passions.

Needless to say, the church fathers didn't approve of such goings on—angels consorting with human women! Angels were supposed to be pure beings who were beyond "sin," and as I have pointed out before, sin early on got linked to sex, until the two became almost inseparable, except under certain prescribed conditions, such as marriage and exclusive use for the reproduction of human beings. Otherwise, it was an ecclesiastical no-no.

Enoch, in fact, hearkened back to the pagan mythology—quite replete with sex. (Zeus, for example, turned himself into a myriad of disguises, such as a swan and a shower of gold in order to consort with human women and propagate half-divine, half-mortal babies. One might even argue that Christ himself was half divine and half mortal, considering that he was "born of woman.")

Now, as the Jews were working mightily hard to replace this sexually robust pagan mythology with their own version of how things should be, sexually as well as otherwise, and since Enoch's narrative bears a strong resemblance to a pre-Zoroastrian, pre-monotheism, Persian myth that relates a tale of demons marrying human women and thereby corrupting earth's population, they took extreme exception to his story and declared it unacceptable.

Although Enoch did not aver that he had traced evil to its original root, he seems to believe that it was already lurking around long before any angels fell from heaven. By the lights of the new monotheism, as it was taken up by the Jews, this idea just wouldn't wash. So they rejected Enoch out of hand. This excerpt from Enoch will explain why:

> And it came to pass, when the children of men had multiplied that in those days were born unto them beautiful and comely daughters. And the angels, the children of the Heaven, saw and lusted after them, and said to one another: "Come, let us choose wives from among the children of men and beget us children." And Semjaza, who was their leader, said unto them: "I fear ye will not indeed agree to do this deed, and I alone shall have to pay the penalty of a great sin."

But Semjaza needn't have feared: The other angels were glad to accompany him and begin to consort with human women. So, according to Enoch, they—all two hundred—descended to earth and landed on the peak of Mount Hermon, which was still quite a distance up from actual human women. Later they descended from the mountain top and found themselves smack in the middle of a human community, after a nine-day trip.

Having achieved their first goal, that of coming to earth in search of human wives, the Watchers each set forth to take unto himself a wife with whom, as Enoch puts it most delicately but with

The Devil's Power

"The Devil . . . has the power to make you see things and think things as he wants you to see and think them. The natural mode of converse between spiritual beings is by the direct communication of ideas. The Devil, being a spirit, can so act upon the souls of men. It is quite evident [to Merton] that God can make use of other intelligences—his angels—to act in the same way upon the minds of men and make them see visions."

—Thomas Merton, *The Ascent to Truth*

firm disapproval, "he defiled himself." As if this sexual sinning wasn't bad enough, the Watchers began to teach their wives the secrets of heaven. "They taught them charms and enchantments, and the cutting of roots, and made them acquainted with plants."

It requires only a bit of reflection on the previous agrarian, mother-right cultures to realize that women had always known these things, that it had *always* been women who were responsible for the planting in the agrarian cultures, as opposed to the hunting cultures dominated by males. But since patriarchy in the form of Judaism was attempting to stamp out all remnants of the old pagan Mother Goddess religion, it named this kind of knowledge "divine" and took the position that since the knowledge belonged to God alone, the women who received it were guilty of witchcraft. And we know where that line of thinking led a few hundred years later in Christian Europe, when millions of women who practiced herbalism and healing were burned at the stake, accused of being witches.

(In another context, Yahweh had declared, "I thy God am a jealous God," and the action of the elders in declaring the possession of knowledge of nature to be witchcraft was a reflection of that jealousy.)

Another of the Watchers was Azazel, who is named by Enoch as the leader, even though he previously called Semjaza the leader. Maybe Semjaza was just the instigator of the idea of going down to earth and having human wives. In any case, Azazel taught humankind to do metal work "and [make] bracelets, and ornaments, and the use of antimony [most likely for cosmetics], and the beautifying of the eyelids, and all kinds of costly stones, and all coloring tinctures. And there arose much godlessness [apparently the result of face-painting and personal adornment which the elders abhorred in humans], and they [human men] committed fornication, and they were led astray, and became corrupt in all their ways."

Enoch goes on to list all of the arts that the Watcher angels taught humans, along with the names of the teachers. Semjaza taught root cuttings and enchantments; Armaros, in a neat turn-around, taught the breaking of enchantments; Baraqijal was an astrology teacher; and Kokabel was the astronomy teacher. Weather, or knowledge of the clouds, was taught by Ezeqiel, and so forth.

The Watchers quite naturally endured the wrath of God, who wasn't going to put up with all this disobedience and leaking of heaven's secrets to unauthorized recipients. According to Enoch, all this knowledge given to humans was having bad effects on them, and they weren't at all happy. In fact, they were miserable, for knowledge can do that to a person. It makes you think, and thinking can be extremely painful. Innocence is bliss, as the saying goes. And with the acquisition of knowledge, humans had lost that blissful innocence and now cried out to God for help. God responded, and the Watchers came to a dreadful end, which resulted in such destruction upon earth that Uriel was sent with a message to Noah to build an ark against the coming deluge that would wipe out all the Watchers had done.

God's judgment against the Watchers was extremely harsh and makes for painful reading, as this excerpt of God's command to the good angel Gabriel shows:

Proceed against the bastards and reprobates, and against the children of fornication and the children of the Watchers from amongst men: and cause them to go forth: send them one against the other that they may destroy each other in battle: for length of days they shall not have.

Enoch continues this awful pronouncement of God:

Inasmuch as they delight themselves in their children, the murder of their beloved ones shall they see, and over the destruction of their children shall they lament, and shall make supplication unto eternity.

Enoch himself proceeds to heaven to ask God to have mercy on the Watchers, but the answer is a decisive NO. And God reproaches Enoch for interceding, saying that as a man, he had no

Fallen Angels

We don't know the names of all of the fallen angels, for there were a multitude of them—one-third of all the heavenly host—and they came from all the angelic ranks of principalities, virtues, cherubim, seraphim, and thrones. It was the poet John Milton who finally listed those few who where named.

◇ Satan, the original Foul Fiend, a.k.a. the Devil himself
◇ Beelzebub, the second in command, a.k.a. the Lord of Flies
◇ Moloch, a nasty bit of business smeared with human blood
◇ Chemosh, a.k.a. Peor
◇ Baalim, a male spirit
◇ Ashtaroth, a female spirit
◇ Astoreth, another female spirit, who wore crescent horns
  (She is derived from Astarte, Queen of Heaven, a Phoenician goddess of fertility, beauty and love, who corresponds to Babylonian Ishtar and Greek Aphrodite, all versions of the Great Mother Goddess. Note also that Hathor, the Egyptian mother goddess, wears crescent horns that represent the moon, and that all of these goddesses are Moon goddesses, emblematic of the feminine principle.)
◇ Azazel, a cherub of extraordinary height
◇ Mammon
◇ Thammuz
◇ Dagon
◇ Rimmon
◇ Belial, emblematic of lewdness

In Milton's version, all of these fallen angels lie together in Hell alongside the gods of the old pagan religions that predate the Bible—Egyptian Osiris and Isis and the entire Greek pantheon.

business trying to intercede for angels, who were, fallen or not, above his state.

Many were the horrible punishments God decreed for the Watchers, and Enoch describes them vividly. I haven't even scratched the surface of all the ghastly tortures God devised to avenge Himself upon the Watchers; it would take a Stephen Spielberg or a George Lucas with their legions of special effects experts to do justice to Enoch's horror story of God's revenge on the Watchers who lusted after human women. So grim are these depictions that I wonder whether Enoch served as an inspiration to those who devised the torture chambers of Medieval Europe and those exquisitely painful contraptions used by the Grand Inquisitor of Catholic Spain to ferret out witches and heretics.

There is one bright spot in this terrible narrative, or you would not be reading this book today: A Watcher named Penemue "taught the children of men the bitter and the sweet, and he taught them all the secrets of their wisdom. And he instructed mankind in writing with ink and paper, and thereby many sinned from eternity to eternity and until this day," which tells us what God thinks of writers!

Evidently, Enoch didn't have much historical background or formal learning himself, for those detested pagan religions had attributed the gifts of knowledge, including writing and planting, to the Goddess in her various forms, such as Isis and Athena, the Greek goddess of wisdom. And, clearly, books had been written long before there were any theories of fallen angels corrupting humans by teaching them the arts of putting pen to paper and making marks that could be understood. We aren't told specifically whether the Watchers also taught humans to read, but one must suppose so, for the ability to write without the ability to read what is written is a self-defeating proposition.

Eventually, in the Book of Jubilees, the story of the Watchers got whitewashed, giving the pursuit of knowledge a clean reputation. The author of Jubilees declared: "The angels of the Lord descended on the earth, those that were named Watchers, that they should instruct the children of men, and that they should do judgment and uprightness on the earth."

Six centuries later, in the Book of Adam and Eve, the whole thing had been neatly resolved. In Adam and Eve, the Watchers aren't genuine angels but the sons of Seth (the name of an Egyptian god, and a later name for the Devil), neither supernatural nor human but somewhere in between. They are allowed to be called "angels of God," but only so long as they remain righteously pure and innocent and keep their hands off human women.

Retelling this tale, I am reminded of a story that Joseph Campbell liked to tell. D. Z. Suzuki, the bringer of Zen to this country, was lecturing, comparing Zen to the Judeo-Christian tradition. He said: "Man against God. God against man. Man against Nature. Nature against man. Very funny religion."

Part Three

The Knowledge of Angels

CHAPTER TEN
The Hierarchy of Angels

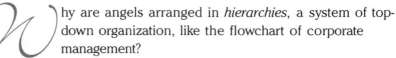

St. Augustine and Angels

"Augustine could think . . . that 'every visible thing in this world is put under the charge of an angel' (*Book on the Eighty-Three Questions*). He did not hesitate to write: 'The angels manage natural things, as the natural order requires, according to the will of him to whom all is subject."

Such a view was neither illogical nor foolish for St. Augustine. It was deeply thought out, and flowed from his conviction of a danger of failure, inherent in created natures. This notion was religious and emphasized personality to the point of supposing a multitude of personal providences by which was exercised the Providence of the heavenly Father. These saw that everything should work together for the glory of God, and the salvation of the elect.

—Pie-Raymond Régamey, O.P., *What Is an Angel?*

hy are angels arranged in *hierarchies*, a system of top-down organization, like the flowchart of corporate management?

There are several reasons why the various religions found this hierarchical arrangement necessary. One was the sheer number of angels. The Jewish patriarchs produced angels swiftly and vigorously. Their method of naming them was simple: Scramble the Hebrew alphabet and add *el* and *iel*. Such angels came to be known as suffix angels, of which there are thousands. The Catholic Church did its best to disband this trafficking in angels, but with little success, as it also named more and more angels. Even the great St. Augustine complained that angels "breed like flies."

Finally, there were so many angels that someone had to get them in some kind of sequential order to manage the total confusion about what kinds of angels did what and which ones were closest to the high throne of God. Since the Bible already had put in place the sense of angels as armies (which is what the word *host* means, as in "a host of angels"), the military scheme was employed, and the angels became arranged in ranks (in the same way that an army has generals, majors, captains, and lieutenants of various grades, and lower ranks from sergeant to buck privates. Mere angels, in this system, are analogous to privates.

Where it all got started was the result of a bit of literary fraud. There had been a famous Athenian named Dionysius, who later became St. Dionysius the Areopagite after his conversion, by none other than St. Paul, in the town of Areopagite, Greece, during the first century.

This Dionysius became the first bishop of Athens and a martyr and church hero. Then, in the fifth or sixth century (no one is exactly sure when), along came a Syrian monk from Palestine who produced a series of obtuse mystical books replete with literary allusions and scriptural references. One of these was called *De Hierarchia Celesti*. It discussed in excruciating detail the nature and properties of angels.

However, the Syrian, who wrote in Greek, passed his work off (successfully) as having been penned by the first-century Dionysius who was famous for having been converted by Saint Paul. He called himself "Dionysius the Areopagite" and duped the church authorities.

Later, around 1450, he was discovered to be a fraud (and came to be known as Pseudo-Dionysius). But by then it was too late, for none other than the great Thomas Aquinas had already put his seal of approval on the hierarchal system that Pseudo-Dionysius had created (as had Pope Gregory the Great, though he made a few minor changes).

Despite his fraudulent identity and the hoax he perpetrated, Pseudo-Dionysius was later sainted! In addition, his angelic hierarchy system endures to this day. (No one has ever suggested that change comes easily to the church; consider that it pardoned Galileo just a few years ago. Galileo, as you probably know, was tried by the Inquisition in 1632 for writing a treatise in which he asserted, correctly, that the sun is the central body around which the planets revolve. The official church position had been that the earth was the center of the universe.)

Though the Syrian monk hadn't been around to hear Paul's actual words, he picked up on them and named the three highest angels, from the Old Testament, as follows:

1. Seraphim
2. Cherubim
3. Thrones

Still using Paul's list, Pseudo-Dionysius further put the angels into three groupings:

1. Seraphim, cherubim, thrones
2. Dominions, virtues, powers
3. Principalities, archangels, angels (the privates)

The ruling Princes of the Nine Celestial Orders as designed by Pseudo-Dionysius are as follows:

Seraphim. Michael, Seraphiel, Jehoel, Uriel, Kemuel (Shemuel), Metatron, Nathanael, and Satan (before his fall). Seraphim is

Angel Prayer

The venerable *Book of Common Prayer*, used for centuries by Christians, includes this prayer:

Everlasting God, you have ordained and constituted in a wonderful order the ministries of angels and mortals; mercifully grant that, as your holy angels always serve and worship you in heaven, so by your appointment they may help and defend us here on earth.

Ranking the Angels

In all of this, there were many ideas of how the hierarchy should work and much disputation as to the ranking of the various classes of angels, as if angels were the same as the British class system of aristocrats and all the rest of the population. St. Thomas Aquinas finally settled the matter during his copious discourses on angels, and 70 years later, around 1320, this was followed up by the Florentine politician and poet Dante Alighieri, who in his *Divine Comedy* definitively ranked all creatures, the good and the bad.

the highest order of angels. They surround the throne of God, ceaselessly singing his holy praises. They are the angels of love, light, and fire.

Cherubim. Gabriel, Cherubiel, Ophaniel, Raphael, Uriel, Zophiel, and Satan (before his fall). Cherubim are the guardians of the fixed stars, keepers of the heavenly records, and bestowers of knowledge. In the Talmud, cherubim are also related to the order of wheels, also called ophanim. Chief rulers are Opaniel, Rikbiel, Zophiel, and Satan (before his fall).

Thrones. Orifiel, Zaphkiel, Zabkiel, Jolhiel (or Zophiel), and Raziel. Thrones bring God's justice to earth. They are often called wheels or (in the Jewish Kabbalah) Chariots or the Merrabah. Zohar the occult book, ranks thrones above seraphim, but other sources place them as cherubim, thus the whole thing becomes confused. The ruling prince is Oriphiel or Zabkiel or Zaphiel.

Dominions (Dominations). Zadkiel, Hashmal, Zacharael (Yahriel), and Muriel. Dominions or Dominations regulate the angels' duties. The majesty of God is manifested through them. Dominations carry an orb or a sceptre as an emblem of authority, and in Jewish lore, the chief of this order is called Hashmal or Zadkiel.

Virtues. Uzziel, Gabriel, Michael, Peliel, Barbiel, Sabriel, Haniel, Hamaliel, and Tarshish. Virtues are sent to earth to work miracles. They are bestowers of grace and valor.

Powers. Camael, Cabriel, Verchiel, and Satan (before his fall). Powers keep demons from overthrowing the world, otherwise they preside over demons or (according to St. Paul) are themselves evil. Ertosi, Sammael, or Camael (depending on the source) is chief of the Powers.

Principalities. Nisroc, Naniel, Requel, Cerviel, and Amael. Principalities protect religion. Nisroc, in Milton, is "of principalities the prime," and others include Requel, Anael, and Cerviel.

Archangels. Metatron, Raphael, Michael, Gabriel, Barbiel, Jehudiel, Barachiel, and Satan (before his fall).
Angels. Phaleg, Adnachiel (Advachiel), Gabriel, and Chayyliel.

As Scripture gives very little support to angels, let alone hierarchical arrangements of them, some modern religionists have taken issue with the very idea of angelic hierarchies. One, philosopher Mortimer Adler, finds such speculation "highly entertaining." And Christian evangelist writer Timothy Jones, in *Celebration of Angels*, states flatly:

Dionysius simply had no way to determine if his nine-fold ordering was literally true. Nor do we. Even Paul the apostle, who claimed to have been caught up into the "third heaven" (2 Corinthians 12:2), hinted that such things are not to be told. . . . Indeed, in Scripture, we gain only glimpses and fragments of how the angels might be organized. . . . However tantalizing the recorded glimpses of angels in Scripture are, they are ultimately just that: glimpses. We can take great comfort, however, in knowing that populating the heavenly spheres are creatures so great they boggle and frustrate our every attempt to pin them down.

Names of Angels

By the fifth century, there were so many angels' names that a riot of confusion set in, causing the church to declare that only seven angels, the archangels, are known by name. In line with the usual disputation about angels, only four of these—Raphael, Michael, Gabriel, and Uriel—remain constant throughout all the various systems.

Finally, at the Ad Lateran Synod of 745, the active practice of giving names to angels was condemned. The good fathers worried that if angels *all* had names, angel worship would become a problem (it might hearken back to the pagan way of naming all sorts of spirits, both celestial and nature), so they decreed "no more naming of angels," in order that only God would be worshiped.

Pseudo-Dionysius Ranks the Angels

1. Seraphim
2. Cherubim
3. Thrones
4. Dominations
5. Virtues
6. Powers
7. Principalities
8. Archangels
9. Angels
   —*Celestial Hierarchy*; Thomas Aquinas,
   Summa Theologica

The Orders of the Celestial Hierarchy

1. Seraphim
2. Cherubim
3. Thrones
4. Dominations
5. Principalities
6. Powers
7. Virtues
8. Archangels
9. Angels
   —Gregory the Great, *Homilia*

1. Seraphim
2. Cherubim
3. Powers
4. Dominions (Dominations)
5. Thrones
6. Archangels
7. Angels
   —St. Jerome

1. Seraphim
2. Cherubim
3. Dominations
4. Thrones
5. Principalities
6. Potentates (Powers)
7. Virtues
8. Archangels
9. Angels
   —St. Ambrose, *Apologia Prophet David*, 5

The Jewish Hierarchal Systems

1. Chaioth ha-qadesh
2. Auphanim
3. Aralim (Erelim)
4. Chashmalim
5. Seraphim
6. Malachim
7. Elohim
8. Bene Elohim
9. Kerubim
10. Ishim

—Moses Maimonides, *Mishne Torah*

1. Malachim
2. Erelim
3. Seraphim
4. Hayyoth
5. Ophanim
6. Hamshalim
7. Elim
8. Elohim
9. Bene Elohim
10. Ishim

—*The Zohar,* Exodus 43a

Constitutions of the Apostles

1. Seraphim
2. Cherubim
3. Aeons
4. Hosts
5. Powers
6. Authorities
7. Principalities
8. Thrones
9. Archangels
10. Angels
11. Dominions

—*Clementine Liturgy of the Mass*

Dante's Celestial Hierarchy

1. Seraphim
2. Cherubim
3. Thrones
4. Dominations
5. Virtues
6. Powers
7. Archangels
8. Principalities
9. Angels

CHAPTER ELEVEN

Functions
of Angels

*A*ngels perform a multiplicity of tasks, some greater and some lesser, depending on the hierarchical rank from which they derive. Their primary duty is to serve God and, by extension, carry out His commands. A main heavenly function is the constant and ceaseless chanting of "glory, glory, glory," as they march in a circle around the throne of God. It is inferred from various sources that the higher orders of angels—seraphim, cherubim, thrones, dominions—are the ones who constantly praise God and do not leave heaven to perform His chores on earth.

Other duties fall to the five lesser orders, messenger and guardian angels being the foremost among them, and these duties are manifold.

Angels also serve humans as counselors (or comforters), guides, interpreters, and healing agents, at birth and death, and they give warnings, rescue people, and console those who are suffering loss or bereavement. Angels also function to protect our homes, to interact with the natural environment in which we live, to protect different places (*genius loci*), and to participate in ceremonial services. They can even act as matchmakers, cooks, judges, and interpreters. The list is long, but these are the major categories in which angels are known to have a hand.

Occult lore holds that angels can be conjured by the adept for various purposes: to strengthen faith, heal afflictions, locate lost articles, increase prosperity, bring fertility, and vanquish enemies. Angels are said to be responsive to invocations when these are performed correctly and properly formulated under auspicious conditions.

Instances of angels performing some of these services have already been seen in the story of Hagar, when she was lost in the desert, and in the story of Daniel's rescue from the lion's den, as well as in other biblical tales and legends.

Rudolph Steiner

An interesting variation on the hierarchical scheme that came down from Pseudo-Dionysius and was scrambled into several other

Leaders and Guides

"The Angels are . . . actually the leaders of men, their guides, preparing them, and there exists an intimate connection between what gradually develops in man and the task of these Angel Beings."

—Rudolph Steiner

The Mission of Angels on Earth

"With regard to the mission of angels, the theologian raises four questions.

1. Are any angels sent forth on missions?
2. Are all angels sent forth?
3. Do those who are sent forth remain in God's presence?
4. From what angelic orders are they sent forth?

"In answering the first question, the theologian [cites] Exodus 23:20—'Behold, I will send my angels to go before thee.'

"A minister . . . 'is an instrument with intelligence.' The ministry performed by angels at God's behest is instrumental in the Divine government of the corporeal world, especially in manifesting God's providence with respect to the human race.

"Angels not only carry messages from God to man. They also influence human action . . . and they act directly on the physical environment . . . on which human action takes place.

"It would appear from a question asked by St. Paul in his *Epistles to the Hebrews* (1:14)—'Are not all the ministering spirits sent forth?'—that the answer to the second question should turn out to be affirmative. But . . . St. Gregory the Great [approves of] a statement by Dionysius declaring 'the higher ranks of angels perform no exterior service.'

"The exterior service referred to is the angelic ministry that is performed on earth with respect to human beings and their environment. Such angelic activity falls mainly, but not exclusively, to the two lowest orders of angels. 'Those who announce the highest things . . . are called archangels,' . . . Below archangels, the lowest order, simply called angels, perform lesser ministries.

"Considering the nine orders in the three-tiered hierarchy . . . the earthly ministry of the celestial spirits is carried out only by the lower five. The upper four . . . never leave heaven on errands or missions [of] the Divine will."

—Mortimer J. Adler, *The Angels and Us*

Biblical References to Angels' Duties

The "living creatures" to which Revelation frequently refers were likely cherubim. The Bible's only mention of another form of angel is in Isaiah 6:2: He speaks of the six-winged seraphim as distinct from cherubim. God is said to be seated *above* the cherubim in I Samuel 4:4, Psalm 80:1, and Psalm 99:1. However, in Isaiah's vision, the seraphim stood *above* God. Evidently, the duties of these two orders differ: Cherubim are the guardians of the throne of God and act as God's elite corps of ambassadors; seraphim are charged with the ceaseless worship of God, as well as the purification of His other servants.

formats over the centuries is one much closer to us in time. Rudolph Steiner, a German-speaking Czechoslovakian, was born in 1861, when what is now the Czech Republic was part of the Austro-Hungarian Empire.

Steiner, who was educated in many fields—natural history, mathematics, philosophy, the arts, architecture, medicine, education, and agriculture—was a brilliant and charismatic man who, by the age of eight, had discovered himself to be a clairvoyant. He refrained from relating his visions—which included the seeing of other worlds—until about age forty after which he began to write about what he had clairvoyantly perceived.

Steiner's résumé is impressive: he wrote his Ph.D. thesis on truth and knowledge, and when in his late 30s began to teach in the Waldorf Astoria Tobacco Company school in Stuttgart, Germany. While doing this work, he developed an unusual system of education that is still used today in the Waldorf Schools around the world.

Not a mystic but a methodical thinker, Steiner became a member of the Theosophical Society but became disillusioned with it and created a spin-off called "anthroposophy ("the wisdom of man"). He saw his mission in life as one of differentiation and sought to understand the world of physical substance in order to develop a consciously discrete model of the spiritual world. In doing this, he thought of himself as a scientist, not a religionist, and he believed that the human race stood on the verge of a new age—a time when the mysteries of spiritual life were to be freely available to all and not confined to the hands of a spiritual elite of priests and other spiritual authorities. In this, he was prophetic and were he alive today the often-made accusation that he was "a nut" would be disproved.

Steiner created his own system of the angelic hierarchy. Accordingly, in descending order, seraphim, cherubim, and thrones form the first hierarchy. Seraphim receive information about the cosmic system's ideas and aims from the Trinity (as opposed to God alone). The work of cherubim is to translate these ideas into practical plans for humans. It is then the job of the thrones to, "figuratively speaking," as he puts it, work closely with humans to help them put the whole schema into practice here on earth. (This is another top-down corporate-type flowchart; the Trinity provides the ideas to the seraphim, who transmit them to the cherubim, who then work them over—much like a contractor interprets an architect's blueprints—to make a practical plan, after which the thrones deliver the plan to humans and help them put it into action.)

In developing his system, Steiner elaborated on angelic functions not specifically described elsewhere. Because he based his epistemology on rational thought backed up by his scientific background, Steiner's system is unusual in that it does not rely on experiential data, or actual encounters with angelic beings. Though Steiner regularly was in the company of nature spirits and was surrounded by angels of every description, his careful methodology is a hierarchy of a different color (to paraphrase a common saying) in that it is unlike both what went before and what came after.

Following the first hierarchy of three orders, Steiner placed the dominions, mights, and powers in the next tier, with archai, archangels, and angels on the bottom tier. He also calls angels *angeloi.*

Steiner believed that every individual human being has his or her own angel, an idea similar to the regular and popular concept of the guardian angel, which the Catholic Church promulgates. However, as Steiner believed strongly in reincarnation, in his view this personal angel accompanies and guides the person to whom it is assigned through many lifetimes, incarnation after incarnation. At a certain point in the process, not specified, the person can ask his angel for information about prior incarnations.

The personal angel—one from the lowest ranking (coinciding with the Pseudo-Dionysius hierarchical scheme)—sticks close to the person from birth until between the ages of 25 and 40, when it retreats to allow the person to develop his or her own sense of identity and get on with a career and the founding of a family. Then, in mid-life, the angel rejoins the human to help guide her or him into the spiritual dimension appropriate to the aging person.

Further, according to Steiner, angels are water spirits who rule the space between earth and the moon, and archangels are fire spirits concerned with the evolution of what might be called

Archangels Help Society

Archangels do not restrict their inspirations to politicians; they also inspire artists, writers, philosophers, professors, and other individuals whose work serves a purpose beyond the individual's personal interest.

Guardian Angel Advice

"In whatever place you may be, in whatever secret recess you may hide, think of your Guardian Angel. . . . If we truly love our Guardian Angel, we cannot fail to have boundless confidence in his powerful intercession with God and firm faith in his willingness to help us. . . . Many of the saints made it a practice never to undertake anything without first seeking the advice of their Guardian Angel."

—St. Bernard of Clairveaux

multi-souls, what Brinton has referred to as the oversoul, a soul that contains within its jurisdiction many individual souls. The archangels look after the relationship between the individual and the collective human race. Their reach of influence stretches from earth to the planet Mercury.

Archangels are believed to carry within their consciousness everything related to the destiny of an entire people. The archangel helps a nation to achieve its goals and inspires groups and individuals to cooperate in that process so that what they accomplish is part of the overall plan for the development of the entire nation or people.

The highest beings in this final triad, the archai ("spirits of personality"), have governance over the relationships of the human species in general, living in waves of time and changing their spiritual selves from age to age, which relates them to time itself. Their rule extends from earth to Venus.

The archai, though not concerned with the development of individuals, are the angelic force that makes people fully human. Their function is to integrate the unique individual with the world community and to advance humanity as a whole as it stretches over time and different lands.

In Steiner's sense of the personal, or guardian, angel, this angel is closer to us than we can ever know. It is said they participate in our feelings, thoughts, and behavior impulses. They live right next to us, so to speak, "an angel at your shoulder," and not in the remote heavenly heights. There are those who believe our guardian angels suffer along with us, but that belief is of modern origin.

Steiner's belief that the guardian angel carries the person through many lifetimes echoes the teaching of the Roman Catholic doctrine. From earliest times the church taught that every human is given an individual guardian angel at birth. The guardian angel is assigned to look after the person's spiritual and physical welfare and guards not only the body but also the soul. St. Ambrose went so far as to advise believers to "pray to the angel who is our Guardian."

The Gnostic View of Messenger Angels

In the Gnostic view, this messengership is carried out by the hierarchies of benevolent angels in a dual manner: First, they convey impulses to humans to receive revelation and to fan the spark of their spirits into the flame of knowledge. Secondly, the messenger angels serve to unite the human soul with its angelic "twin" or guardian angel. In this view, Jesus—as a messenger of the transcendental father—was called angel, and the biblical references to the "Angel of the Lord" are taken to refer to Jesus in advance of his arrival on the scene.

A Gnostic text from the Gospel of Thomas says:

Jesus said to them: When you make the two one, and when you make the inner as the outer and the outer as the inner and above as the below, and when you make the male and the female into a single one, so that the male will not be only male and the female not be only female, when you make eyes in the place of an eye, and a hand in the place of a hand, and a foot in the place of a foot, and an image in the place of an image, then shall you enter the Kingdom.

Our Angel Companions

"I believe . . . from the very beginning of our race, angels were appointed as our guardians, to watch over us constantly, from conception until we leave this world and enter the dimension where they live, which is called heaven or paradise or the Kingdom of God. Part of their reason for existence is to help us grow and be healed.

"The angels are our companions on the journey—guides, aides, even nurses. I think there's a special connection between nursing and what the angels do; I don't think it's coincidental that nurses are referred to as 'angels of mercy'. . . . The angels want to help. Behind the scenes, they ceaselessly carry out their divinely assigned tasks, watching over us and all life on Earth."

—Eileen Elias Freeman, *Angelic Healing*

Angels as Messengers

It is a commonplace belief that angels are messengers, that the primary meaning of the word *angelos*, from the Latin, means "messenger." And we have seen earlier in this book references to messengers (of the gods) as angels and angels (of the Lord) as messengers. The two terms would seem to be interchangeable.

Angels as Guardians

That modern Roman Catholic authorities emphasize the role of the guardian angel is powerfully expressed in a poem by John Henry Cardinal Newman, who penned it to express the angel's words of consolation to a soul in purgatory:

> *Farewell, but not forever, brother dear,*
> *Be brave and patient on thy bed of sorrow;*
> *Swiftly shall pass thy night of trial here,*
> *And I will come and wake thee on the morrow.*

The Archangel Raphael

The Archangel Raphael is known as the Healer of God, and he is the quintessential medical specialist. Raphael's history as a healer shines like a ray of light all the way back to the ancient Near East. As one of the magnificent seven, Raphael is known to have a special healing relationship with human beings, a unique relationship that transcends the ordinarily thought of work of angels as mere messengers.

In Hebrew, the name Raphael (*rapha'* = "heals" + *'el* = God) means "to heal." This word root, however, covers more territory than just physical healing of the sick. It includes all sorts of "fixing" of things as well as people. Other translations of the name Raphael include "to stitch together," "repair," "strengthen," and "pacify." Essentially, Raphael's name implies changing something to better its condition, whether that be a sick human being or a nonfunctioning vehicle. In a spiritual sense, the idea is to restore to the original (pure and innocent) state of being.

In addition, Raphael is said to be the healer of the planet Earth itself, and today his ministrations are much needed in our environment. We should all be praying to Raphael constantly for help with the enormous task of restoring our environment—our earth—to its original condition!

Other Work of Angels

For thousands of years, the great religious and philosophic traditions have held that God works through the angels to prosper and protect our planet. The angel makers of early Judaism felt so strongly about this issue that they created literally thousands of angel names to signify the angels that looked after earth. For example, Baradiel is called "the angel of hail," because in Hebrew *barad* means "hail." We have already commented on the making of angels by the "suffix" method.

Because some angelic presences relate to nature, some people believe that the recent increase in angel appearances and interest in angels is an attempt by the angels to raise our level of consciousness regarding the current troubled state of our environment.

Angels, as the landscape architects and gardeners of God, watch out for plant and animal life as well as human life. They also take care of our mountains, oceans, rivers, lakes, rainfall, cloud formations, and the atmosphere in general. And, it is said by some, they cause volcanic activity and earthquakes, which serve as either warnings ("You shouldn't be building houses on this site") or regulators of the planet.

Denise Linn, author of *Sacred Space* and a practitioner of *feng shui*, says that there are house angels who serve to protect the home. She says: "I believe that the most powerful guardian for your home is an angel. Calling upon the angels to be your house guardians for protection and spiritual rejuvenation can bring a wonderful feeling of peace, harmony and safety to your home."

"My Father gave
In charge to me
This child of earth
E'en from his birth.
To serve and save.
Alleluia,
And saved is he.

This child of clay
To me was given
To rear and train
By sorrow and pain
In the narrow way
Alleluia,
From earth to heaven."
—John Henry
Cardinal Newman

Angels in Nature

In *A Book of Angels*, Sophie Burnham says: "To people who live close to the earth, spirits live everywhere—in rocks and stones and trees and rivers and desert scrub. Divinity shines forth everywhere."

Angels also deliver messages of warning to people. There are many angel stories in which someone was about to board an airplane and was somehow prevented from doing so, only to find out later that the plane crashed. Why *all* the people on the plane weren't warned remains a mystery, as does much else in life.

Angels also serve as guides and protectors, as this story told by writer Hope MacDonald demonstrates: A young girl, homeward bound on a bus, found herself being followed by a suspicious-looking man. Terrified, she began to pray. When the bus drew up to her stop, there stood a large white dog, a Great Pyrenees, waiting for her to disembark. As she stepped down, the huge dog put its head under her hand and together they walked the distance to her house. The stalker, apparently wary of the dog's size and presence, took another route. When the girl reached her own door, the dog disappeared. MacDonald has no doubt the dog was a manifestation of an angelic presence, perhaps even the girl's own guardian angel, who transformed itself into a form that would get the job done.

Linn, who insists that "angels are real," suggests using an *animal* house guardian, an idea that is related to the MacDonald story of the little girl and the dog. She believes that when we use house guardians, what we actually do is place a protective energy field around our home. I have personally done this many times and find it works well.

This same idea can be applied to *places*, for each particular place has its own angel, and we can call upon these *genius loci*, or "local angels," anywhere we happen to be, especially in places we have designed as sacred spaces or in traditional holy spots, such as any of the great henges (e.g., Stonehenge) or sacred burial grounds.

Angels also attend death. The eighteenth-century Swedish scientist-turned-mystic Emanuel Swedenborg, who wrote prolifically about angels, gives an account of how he first encountered "some of the kindest and most profoundly loving of all angels," in what we would today call a near-death experience. He explains that people "wake up" after dying, gradually becoming aware of angels at their heads. These "death angels" are apparently able to communicate with persons who have just died and make them feel peaceful, safe, and happily welcomed to their new state. The transition period, whether it is easy for the dead one or difficult (for some resist believing they are dead), is supervised by these special angels.

As a natural corollary, angels also attend the birth of an infant. Many people believe that the just-born infant is born with an "angel twin," the guardian angel, that accompanies it throughout life. Others believe that there are special "birth angels," who attend the birth to make sure that all is well and then depart for other birthings. A friend of mine who is an experienced midwife has told me that frequently, just when it seems the laboring mother might have to be transferred to a hospital for a Caesarean section, the room fills with a new energy, the woman's contractions become normal, and the child is delivered without difficulty.

After experiencing this phenomenon several times, my friend began to ask other midwives of their encounters with what at first seemed difficult births, and she discovered that many other midwives have had *exactly* the same experience. In a few cases like

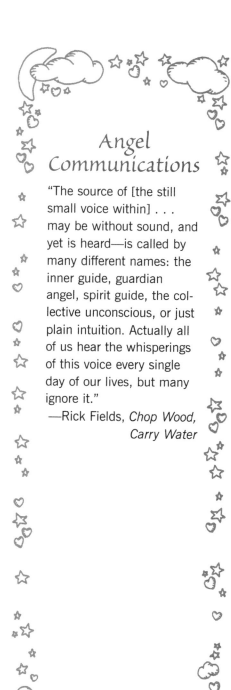

Angel Communications

"The source of [the still small voice within] . . . may be without sound, and yet is heard—is called by many different names: the inner guide, guardian angel, spirit guide, the collective unconscious, or just plain intuition. Actually all of us hear the whisperings of this voice every single day of our lives, but many ignore it."
—Rick Fields, *Chop Wood, Carry Water*

this, the energy was seen as a suffused light—not bright or glaring, just a comforting glow such as comes from a fireplace or a candle.

The author of *Angels in Action*, Robert H. Kirven, asserts that "spiritual protection of infants is typical of angelic occupations in that it is a kind of service [and that] angels have a special affection for newborn children."

Kirven goes on to say that other angels and spirits replace these earliest guardians when infants grow out of infancy and into childhood; it is a position also held by others, as I have mentioned earlier. The question as to whether the *first* angel assigned to a child is the lifetime guardian angel has never been definitively answered. Kirven bases his opinion on his extensive study of the works of Emanuel Swedenborg.

Angels help with ceremonial occasions, from formal celebrations (such as the Catholic mass) to informal ones (such as weddings and birthdays). Often the receipt of good news, the resolution of a thorny problem, a promotion at work, or confirmation of a much wanted pregnancy is accompanied by the feeling that an angel presence is near and is joyfully celebrating along with the humans involved.

When I am working well, for example, I always get the feeling that "my angel is with me," and when I have a problem to solve, I always ask for help from a specific angel.

One of my special angels, which I share with friends who travel frequently, is the Angel of the First Class Upgrade, who makes sure that we get bumped up from coach into first class anytime we fly. And then there is the Clear Away the Traffic angel, who I send along in front of me to make sure that there aren't any traffic jams—even in rush hour!—to impede my progress.

There's no sensible reason why we cannot create angels for our own purposes. The wonderful news is that it works! Praying to angels for specific purposes almost always guarantees a good result.

It's also effective to create ceremonies for any purpose you require and invite angels to attend and participate with you. I do prayer circles at which I invoke angelic presence (I'll tell you more about them in Chapter 17).

Ministering Angels

In the opinion of some Talmudists, the ministering angels are the highest order in the celestial hierarchy. The *Mekilta of Rabbi Ishmael* calls them the "hosts of the Lord." Yet, in the judgment of others, the ministering angels are of an inferior order, or rank, because they are so numerous, which, in this view, makes them expendable.

Angels All Year-Round

The Governing Angels of the Twelve Months of the Year:

January	Gabriel
February	Barchiel
March	Machidiel
April	Asmodel
May	Ambriel
June	Muriel
July	Verchiel
August	Hamaliel
September	Uriel
October	Barbiel
November	Adnachiel
December	Hanael

There are four angels of the spring: Amatiel, Caracasa, Core, and Commissoros. In addition, Spugliguel is the ruler of the sign of spring, and Mikiel is the ruling angel.

Gargatel, Gaviel, and Tariel are the serving angels of summer. And Tubiel is head of the sign of summer.

The serving angels of autumn are Tarquam and Guabarel. And the governing angel is Torquaret, head of the sign of autumn.

Amabael and Cetarari are the serving angels of winter. And Attarib is the governing angel and head of the sign of winter.

CHAPTER TWELVE

The Heavenly Chorus: Angels' Music

The Hallelujah Chorus

Humans are most familiar with the third stanza of that heavenly chorus engaged in song: The holy ones came to earth to sing it in the shepherds' fields near Bethlehem, 2000 years ago, at the birth of the Christ child. Luke has given us the words:

"And suddenly there appeared with the angel a multitude of the heavenly host praising God, and saying, 'Glory to God in the highest, and on earth peace among men with whom he is pleased.'"
—Luke 2:13–14

The Liturgy of Paradise

The holy ones are always engaged in the singing of praise. Both in heaven and on earth, angel choruses abound. When the apostle John was teleported into the presence of the most high, he had the privilege of witnessing the angelic hosts engaged in the function of giving glory to God.

And I looked, and I heard the voice of many angels around the throne and the living creatures and the elders; and the number of them was myriads of myriads, and thousands of thousands: saying with a loud voice,
"Worthy is the Lamb that was slain to receive power and riches and wisdom and might and honor and glory and blessing."
—Revelation 5:11–12

But that was only the first stanza of the great "Hallelujah Chorus" that John heard all the angels around the throne singing, apparently at the top of their voices. He continues his description of the heavenly host in song:

Around the throne and around the elders and the four living creatures; and they fell on their faces before the throne and worshiped God, saying,
"Amen, blessing and glory and wisdom, and thanksgiving and honor and power and might, be to our God forever and ever. Amen."
—Revelation 7:11–12

According to John's account, the "four living creatures" were a heavenly music group that chanted their praise. (Chant singing has become a part of the regular liturgy of the Christian church, especially Gregorian chant in monasteries during the Middle Ages). John continues his narrative:

Day and night they do not cease to say, "Holy, holy, holy, is the Lord God, the Almighty, who was and who is and

who is to come." And . . . the living creatures give glory and honor and thanks to Him who sits on the throne, to Him who lives forever and ever.

—Revelation 4:8–9

Apparently, singing is an integral part of what angels do. They ceaselessly sing the praises of God. But do they sing to humans, and if they do, can we hear them? That is the question.

St. Bernard, in his Sermon 1 for the Feast of St. Michael, tells us this:

> The angels act for God, for us, and for themselves. For God: they reflect the great mercy with which he encompasses us: our likeness to them arouses their pity. Then for themselves: they eagerly desire to see us fill the places made empty in their ranks, for the lips of children, but lately fed with milk and not with solid food, *ought to perfect the choir destined to celebrate divine majesty.* [emphasis added] The angels have made a beginning, and in these first fruits they already enjoy a wonderful happiness. But they wait for us with a great eagerness, and the desire to see this choir perfected urges them forward.

I deduce from this passage that humans are supposed to learn to sing in the heavenly choir, to learn to praise God's glory through song, as do the angelic host. However, instances of angels actually *singing* to humans seem to be rare, except for the appearance in the shepherd's fields with which we are so familiar.

Yet, there are many tellers of angel stories who claim to have heard angels in song; whether they were singing for themselves, or as a way of announcing their presence, is debatable. Of course, all liturgy in the Middle Ages was sung, not merely spoken, and those of us who attend church generally sing hymns that praise the Lord. Do angels join in when we sing? Or do we just add our voices to theirs, since they are constantly singing? The celebration of the liturgy seems to answer the question.

Joyous Song

"Every creature in heaven and on earth and under the earth and in the sea [sing to the Father on the throne and to his Son the Lamb] blessing and honor and glory and might forever and ever" (Revelation 5:13). This "eternal and joyous song" is the singing silence that sang the creation into being.

But what about humans hearing angels when they are not performing liturgy? Does this happen? Mark Lewis of Washington, D.C., tells this story, quoted by Sophie Burnham in *A Book of Angels:*

This happened to my great-great uncle, Calvin Jones, and it was instrumental in making me choose the ministry, because we've always been close, and I think I'm the only person he told this story to.

Calvin will be 96 this year, 1989. He's always lived in Boswell, in Izard County, Arkansas, in the northern Ozarks. It's the most remote inhabited place in the United States, without even a road into his farm. He has river frontage but no road frontage. So he has lived there in isolation and great stability, with no radio and no TV, unpoisoned by what's going on in this country, and as a result, he trusts in what he sees and hears. His experience is limited to his own experience. He's lived alone since his wife died 10 years ago. They were married in 1912. That isolation affects everything. He's always been a faithful Christian. But mountain people never have community worship; it's not a community-oriented religion.

The Voices happened from late fall to early spring of 1984–85, from first frost to first thaw, the nonworking time. And I heard about it in the summer of '85. Calvin began hearing songs, music playing. There were the voices of women, men, and children, singing both sacred and secular songs, but when he started listing the songs, Calvin remembered only a few. One was "The Little Rosewood Casket" and another "After the Ball"—parlor songs; and then some gospel, like "Whispering Hope." The singing was repeated daily every dawn, always with the same characters, so he came to recognize their voices, and "one of the men," he said, "had the coarsest voice I ever heard."

He never saw anything, but he heard it: a Singing Procession in the sky, about thirty-five degrees above the horizon and moving from south to west—not with the voices

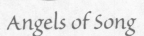

Angels of Song

The angel Radueriel (also Vretil) is the choirmaster of the muses, those spirits that provide inspiration to composers and artists. The great angel Metatron—he of the hundred names—is, in rabbinic lore, called Master of Heavenly Song. The Koran names Israfel, or Uriel, as the angel of song. The color of the music angels is always white.

moving, but *extending*, actually, like the mercury in a thermometer, until it filled the whole southwestern horizon.

He lives in a hollow, ringed by mountains, so the procession followed round a ridge, at the front of the house, window to window, following the path of the White River.

He was never self-conscious about angels. He never interpreted them as such, never said, "Oh, boy! I'm hearing angels!" He reached instead for natural explanations, and without revealing what he'd heard, he would ask questions of people: "It's awful cold. Are there campers nearby with radios?" Was it water that he heard? But he never asked, "Was it supernatural?"

One day he was visited by a university professor doing an oral-history project with a tape recorder. He thought, "Here's my chance," because he has great respect for a university education. The Voices began to sing. Calvin said, "Can you hear them?"

"No," answered the historian.

"Turn on the tape recorder, then," said Calvin.

"You sing along with them," said the professor, and Calvin began to sing "After the Ball."

After the choir faded and stopped, they turned on the tape recorder and to Calvin's astonishment he heard only himself. He was mystified. To his ears the whole of creation was singing, and on the tape it was one old man.

He found he enjoyed singing with them.

At no point did he go looking for these people or address them. Neither did he assume he was crazy. People spared the twentieth century never think they're crazy. And to him nature is so wondrous that it's no miracle nature would sing.

One day as the weather warmed enough to open a window, and when it was still dark, for the first time ever Calvin used his voice.

"Who are you?" he asked. He hadn't thought to ask it before.

The Psalmist's Song

"I will bless the Lord at all times, His praise shall continually be in my mouth. My soul shall make its boast in the Lord; the humble shall hear it and rejoice. O magnify the Lord with me, and let us exalt His name together.

"I sought the Lord, and He answered me, and delivered me from all my fears. They looked to Him and were radiant, and their faces shall never be ashamed. This poor man cried and the Lord heard him; and saved him out of all his troubles. The angel of the lord encamps around those who fear Him, and rescues them."

—Psalms 34:1–7

Pure Spirits Sing the Glory of God

"There are different kinds of glory. . . . The 'heavens,' made up of the countless numbers of angels, sing his glory in a different way from the stars, the immense galaxies, or our souls here on earth, for the angels, like the saints of paradise, *see* the glory praised by their song.

"What can we say, or imagine, or think, which will give any notion of paradise? Yet we need such a notion if we are to have any idea of the principle office of the angels. For it is certainly their principal office to sing the glory of God."
—Pie-Raymond Régamey, O.P., *What Is an Angel?*

The man with the coarse voice answered, and in Calvin's own Ozark dialect: "This yer's from heaven. Cain't everbudy hear it."

That satisfied him. The voices continued to sing off and on, but not as frequently. And now that it's satisfactorily explained, Calvin takes it for granted. He notices it now and again but doesn't dwell on it.

But it changed my life.

"There are seven countries in heaven," Calvin told me. "We know all kinds of history. We know the history of America, and we know the history of Arkansas. And these angels tell you the history of heaven." Then he said farewell: "If I don't see you in this world, I'll try to see you in the next one."

What did Calvin hear? Surely it was a chorus of angels—humans, who turned into angels to replace those who left their chairs vacant.

Angels are often depicted carrying musical instruments. In nineteenth century America, a popular outdoor art form was a weathervane in the shape of an angel blowing a trumpet.

Renaissance artists depicted many angels as musicians, some singing in huge choirs, others singly with a lyre or a lute. One of the most well known of these is a large canvas by Fra Angelico (1417–55) entitled *Christ in the Court of Heaven*, which shows a crowned and haloed center figure surrounded by row upon row of angels, some with trumpets, others with stringed instruments of various sorts—all singing in praise of the resurrected Christ.

Many of these angel paintings—some by the great masters like Raphael and others by lesser-known artists—are particularly charming. One of my personal favorites is the altarpiece at Champagny in Savoy, which pictures a throng of musical cherubs—little naked babies floating about in a crowd with all sorts of musical instruments. Angelic rock 'n' roll perhaps? These darling toddlers are descended from unlikely ancestors—those fearsome many-winged terrifying cherubim of the Old Testament. But they have metamorphosed into a lovely angelic children's choir.

Not Just a Christmas Song

See how the heavens proclaim God's glory.

—Psalms 19:2

Usually we sing the Hallelujah Chorus as part of the Christmas songfest, but it can be sung all year. Since the angels are singing all the time, why not join in?

Praise the Lord

The Psalmist David, the "sweet singer of Israel," called attention to the angelic activity of singing praise, and in his ecstasy of discovery of this wondrous activity in heaven, he, too, cried out, "Praise the Lord!"

Psalm

Praise the Lord from the heavens;
Praise Him in the heights!
Praise Him, all His angels;
Praise Him, all His hosts!
Praise Him, sun and moon;
Praise Him, all stars of light!
Praise Him, highest heavens,
And the waters that are above the heavens!
Let them praise the name of the Lord,
For He commanded and they were created.

—Psalms 148:1–5

CHAPTER THIRTEEN

Angels in Art and Literature

Angels have a long tradition in art and literature. However, depictions of them in stone are the first forms of angel art we know. As history begins to be recorded we find images of them in many cultures around the world. These suggest that the notion of angels is embedded in our psyches.

Milton's Paradise Lost

In literature, the English poet John Milton (1608–74) gave the world the incomparable epic poems *Paradise Lost* and *Paradise Regained*, in which he undertook the daunting task of attempting to unravel the truth of the fallen angels and their impact on humanity. This is Milton's description of Raphael (from *Paradise Lost*):

> *Down thither prone in flight*
> *He speeds, and through the vast Ethereal Skie*
> *Sailes between worlds and worlds, with steddie wing*
> *Now on the polar windes, then with quick Fann*
> *Winnows the buxom air*

Milton built much of this epic poem around the unremitting heavenly warfare between the angels and their fallen brethren. Consider these lines:

> *The discord which befell, and War in Heav'n*
> *Among th' Angelic Powers, and the deep fall*
> *Of those too high aspiring, who rebell'd*
> *With Satan.*

Gothic Design

As Europe emerged from the Dark Ages and the great Gothic cathedrals began to rise during the twelfth through fifteenth centuries, the Gothic form dominated art and architecture. It was notable for its use of the high, pointed arch and ribbed vault with

Direct Communication?

The Jewish authors of the primary Kabbalistic text, the Zohar, though pictorial images were forbidden, provide instructions for attaining states of mystical consciousness in which it is possible to converse directly with angels. The information is not easily accessible to the uninitiated.

flying buttresses, which gave a flowing, soaring effect, the hallmark of Gothic architecture.

Much sculpture and stained glass windows were part of the Gothic design, and these magnificent cathedrals that seem to rise up into the very heavens were graced with beautiful depictions of the entire Christian story and included a plenitude of angels and angelic hosts. (It is important to remember that in this era, before Gutenberg's invention of the printing press, the populace was largely illiterate, and the stained glass windows were there not only for aesthetic reasons, but also to educate believers in the story of their faith.) For example, the angels surrounding the main portal of the cathedral at Chartres, France, are there to express the sense of perfection of God's creation as well as the sense humans had developed of angels being their protectors and guides or guardians.

Halos in Christian Art

In Christian art from the twelfth century onward (that with which we are most familiar), angels almost always wear halos, though halos are not mentioned in Scripture as being part of standard angel gear. The halo is found in ancient Buddhist art and was also used in Greco-Roman art to indicate gods and heroes. In the fourth century, Christian artists adopted the use of a halo to float over the heads of Jesus, angels, and saints, presumably to indicate that these were supernatural beings, different from humans.

Russian and Greek Orthodox Icons

Not only Christian Europe but also the Russian and Greek orthodox forms of Christianity contributed to great artistic renditions of angels (and saints). These brilliantly executed paintings, mostly on wood instead of canvas, are called icons. Their jewel-like mystical quality is riveting to the beholder's eye, and they are intended to be visual meditations for the purpose of direct contact with the image portrayed.

Michael

Michael, the Prince of the Heavenly Hosts, is always pictured in Renaissance paintings as young, strong, handsome, and wearing armor. He is supposed to be God's champion or chief warrior as well as the protector general of the Roman Catholic Church. Michael is also known as the patron saint of the Hebrew nation, but the Jewish tradition forbids images or icons, so there's no Jewish religious art. The same is true of Islam, which forbids idolatry of images and which, therefore, has developed astonishingly beautiful geometric art forms to be viewed symbolically rather than literally.

A Collection of Angels from Literature

The man who has seen the rising moon break out of the clouds at midnight, has been present like an archangel at the creation of light and of the world.
—Ralph Waldo Emerson

And the angel said, 'I have learned that every man lives, not through care for himself, by by love.'
—Leo Tolstoy

They buried him, but all through the night of mourning, in the lighted windows, his books arranged there by three kept watch like angels with outspread wings and seemed, for him who was no more, the symbol of his resurrection.
—Marcel Proust

Around our pillows, golden ladders rise,
And up and down the skies,
With winged sandals shod,
The angels come and go, the messengers of God!
—R.H. Stoddard, *Hymn to the Beautiful*

The German lyric poet and writer Rainer Maria Rilke, author of the lyrical prayer book *Stundenbuch* (1905), among his many poetic and prose works, did not neglect the angels. The following is a quotation from *Duino Elegies* (9):

Praise this world to the angel . . .
show him
something simple which, formed over
generations,
lives as our own, near our hand and within our
gaze.
Tell him of Things . . . .

To My Friend on the Death of His Sister
With silence only as their benediction
God's angels come
Where, in the shadow of a great affliction,
The soul sits dumb.
—John Greenleaf Whittier

The Other World
Sweet souls around us watch us still,
Press nearer to our side;
Into our thought, into our prayers,
With gentle helpings glide.
—Harriet Beecher Stowe

Angels in Islamic Culture

Half a world away, during the time of the Crusades, when the concept of ideal beauty was beginning to be developed, alongside the idealization of romantic love (which is to say the lady beloved was unavailable and the knight's love was intense but unconsummated) that was being popularized by the wandering troubadours during the twelfth century, especially in France, the great Sufi poet, Ibn Arabi, claimed that his major prose work, *The Meccan Revelations*, was dictated to him by the Angel of Inspiration. Another Sufi, Suhrawardi, left two major works, *The Crimson Archangel* and *The Rustling of Gabriel's Wing*, which are the richest documentation of angelic encounters in the Islamic culture.

Angels' Wings

The question of wings is still a matter of debate, as we have seen earlier. Few of us today would imagine a wingless angel—unless, of course, it appeared in human or animal form—because the image of the winged angel has been burned into our consciousness by centuries of beautiful and compelling art, much of it painted or sculpted by great masters, who represented angels with wings most magnificent. Curiously, however, even though Scripture speaks of angels flying—in Daniel 9:21, Gabriel is said to come to Daniel "in swift flight," and in Revelation 14:6–7, Gabriel flies again—there is no specific mention of *wings* per se.

Dante's Bird of God

Dante Alighieri's classic epic, *The Divine Comedy* (*Purgatory*), gives a vivid description of an angel at the helm of a boat, his wings flared upward, acting as sails, ferrying souls to their destination. Dante calls the angel "the Bird of God." By now, angels and wings go together like coffee and cream, or Christmas and decorations. For this, we have primarily the great artist of the Renaissance, Raphael (no doubt named for the great archangel), to thank. He painted countless canvases (a great many of them in the Vatican) of ethereal

Islamic Literary Angelic Descriptions

Though we have no *pictures* of angels, the Koran abounds in vivid verbal descriptions of angels. For example, Raphael, who is Azarel to the Muslims, is said to be veiled with a million veils. He has four faces—one in the usual place, another on top of his head, a third at the back of his head, and the fourth under his feet. In addition to this configuration of four faces, he possesses no less than 74,000 wings, and his body is covered with eyes, an idea with roots in ancient Buddhist art.

looking angels with fluffy, feathery wings. These rather blurry representations are quite dreamlike, as befits the angelic realm.

Are Wings Necessary?

Other painters have shown angels with wings that seem less than impressive—but wings are the norm. However, I've never seen a picture of an angel with six wings, as described in Isaiah, nor four wings, as Ezekiel envisioned.

At least one Christian writer has noted with some asperity that wings are not necessary for angel work. He states that they may be "a concession to us on God's part," by which he means that "angels are always ready to help with incredible swiftness," when the situation demands speed.

Clairvoyants' Visions of Angels

Clairvoyants who claim to have seen angels report that the wings appear to be light streaming from two "chakra centers" in the shoulders. In the Indian chakra system, the chakras are energy points all along the body.

Rembrandt

In *Paradise Lost,* John Milton equates the archangel Gabriel with the chief of the angelic guards placed over Paradise. Gabriel is credited as the angel in the famous wrestling encounter with Jacob (though different sources credit Michael, Uriel, Metatron, Samael, and Chamuel with the role of the "dark antagonist"). No matter which angel was responsible for the fight, the famous scene was immortalized for all time in a canvas by Rembrandt.

Rembrandt was continually inspired to paint angels, many of which appear in his larger canvases; there are also glimpses of angels in his multitude of sketches (most of which repose in the Dutch national museum in Amsterdam). In these, the angels are more informal, charming, and approachable, especially the rendering of the archangel Raphael with Tobit, as companion on the journey.

Dante's Divine Comedy

Dante constructed such a towering spire in mere words that it would take an entire volume just to examine and discuss it. One part of the great cathedral in words that Dante created is his

More Angels from Literature

This is what you are to hold fast to yourself—*the sympathy and companionship of the unseen worlds*. No doubt it is best for us now that they should be unseen. It cultivates in us that higher perception that we call 'faith.' But who can say that time will not come when, even to those who live here upon earth, the unseen worlds shall no longer be unseen?

—Phillips Brooks

Who does the best [her] circumstance allows
Does well, acts nobly; angels could do no more.
—Edward Young, *Night Thoughts*

The contemporary poet Francis Thompson, in his "The Kingdom of Heaven," from his book *Francis Thompson: Poems and Essays*, writes:

The angels keep their ancient places,
Turn but a stone and start a wing,
'Tis ye, 'tis your estranged faces,
That miss the many splendoured thing.

Here is my own contribution to angel poetry:

Gift of Iris*
Sudden rainbow in evening's misty sky
Tossed off by an angel passing by—
Purpose: none but delight for eye.
Ventured I to admire it more,
And found Enchantment's hidden Door.
For in that glowéd air, all mixed with
Rain, shewed the ancient mystery plain:
And then knew I of olden dreams, wondrous
Tales of pots of gold; for that arching
Faery bow, gleaming color all unsound,
Reached it down and touched the solid
    ground!

—M. J. Abadie
Two Birds with One Stone

---

*Iris, goddess of the rainbow, daughter of Zeus, is called angelo, or messenger of the gods.

Angel Art Books and Quotations

Angels: An Endangered Species, Malcolm Godwin, Simon and Schuster. A beautiful picture book about angels.

Angels, Caroline Johnson, Barnes and Noble. Twenty-six full-color plates of angels by great artists, including data on the paintings, reproduced in a small volume.

The Angel Tree, Lynn Howard and Mary Jane Poole, Knopf. A history with photographs of the angel tree at the Metropolitan Museum of Art, New York City.

A Host of Angels, Gail Harvey, Gramercy Books. Quotations from a wide variety of literature accompanied by angel art.

Angels and Cupids, Sylvia Lawrence, Rizzoli. A picture book with quotations as captions.

Angels: A Book to Keep and Fifteen Postcards to Send, Chronicle Books. A set of fifteen angel postcards packaged with a small book.

"Angelic Orders," derived from the work of Dionysius (or Pseudo-Dionysius) the Areopagite (see Chapter 10).

Dante's *Celestial Hierarchies* compares God to a ray of cosmic light that, although it will always remain the "One," "becomes a manyness," dispersing itself and proceeding into the manifestation of the myriad universe and all in it from largest to tiniest.

This primal ray of light, according to Dante's interpretation of the angelic hierarchies, must be so arranged "that we might be led, each according to his capacity, from the most holy imagery to formless, unific, elevative principles and assimilations." Thus, everything is "delivered in a supermundane manner to Celestial Natures [Angels] . . . given to us in symbols," so that we may attain "our due measure of deification."

In Dante's concept, theophany, which is "a beholding of God which shows the divine likeness, figured in itself as a likeness in form of that which is formless [through which] a divine light is shed upon the seers . . . and they are initiated into some participation of divine things."

In this theological system, the angels are the most potent of theophanies, who, in a top-down manner, pass along God to humanity through all their ranks, from highest to lowest (angels), until it reaches humans via the angels. Thus, one could say that every angelic appearance is in fact an appearance of God in disguise; rather like the Greek Zeus, who appeared as a swan or a shower of gold because his full glory would incinerate the beholder, the Divine Light must be dimmed for human consumption.

Several centuries later, the French illustrator and painter Paul Gustave Doré (1833–83) would be inspired to create illustrations for Dante's *Divine Comedy*—magnificent, brooding etchings of demons writhing in the pits of hell and gloriously rendered angels—the entire heavenly host spiraling off into the infinite region of the most high.

William Blake

At the time of his death, the English mystic-poet-engraver William Blake (1757–1827) was engaged in designing etchings to illustrate

the *Divine Comedy*. Previously, Blake, who etched his own designs on copper plates, using a newly developed technique, had executed and engraved many religious designs for his own lyrical poems. He wrote volumes about his experiences with angels and had great influence upon many of the major thinkers of his time. His munificent legacy bequeathed to the world includes some of the most impassioned drawings of angels to ever come from the hand of an artist. Here is an excerpt from one of his texts:

> It is not because angels are holier than men or devils that makes them angels, but because they do not expect holiness from one another, but from God alone.

The Pre-Raphaelites

Blake was followed by a group of artists and writers who named themselves the Pre-Raphaelites. They formed a brotherhood of painters and poets in 1848 in protest against both the prevailing standards of British art and the oncoming rush of the Industrial Revolution, which threatened all handicrafts. They chose the name because their inspiration came from the work of Italian painters that predated Raphael. In ethereal tones, the Pre-Raphaelites depicted angels and angelic-like portraits of humans. But they were fated to fade away before the end of the nineteenth century, and with their passing, angels were eclipsed by the onset of technological "progress" and the new scientific materialism, neither of which needed them, pictorially or otherwise.

Yet, angels remained, carved in stone, etched on copper, painted on canvas; their images can be seen in nearly every city and town of the Western Hemisphere. They grace railway stations and libraries. They are seen on murals and friezes. They decorate war memorials and museum façades and are cast in bronze atop skyscrapers. They float gracefully on the domes of town halls. They are even seen on the walls of department stores, hospitals, and movie theaters. They stand in marble in the middle of park fountains or set upon pedestals in public squares. Wherever you look, you'll see an angel.

Richard Crashaw

There exist innumerable paintings, by both masters and lesser artists, of the Annunciation scene, with Gabriel pictured as the angel who brings Mary the "glad tidings." Though pictorial representations of this momentous event abound, verse versions are rare. There is one by the seventeenth-century English poet Richard Crashaw in his *Steps to the Temple*:

> *Heavens Golden-winged Herald, late hee saw*
> *To a poor Galilean virgin sent.*
> *How low the Bright Youth bow'd, and with what awe*
> *Immortall flowers to her faire hand present.*

John Donne

Angels are as well represented in both prose and poetry. The English poet John Donne (1573–1631) wrote of angels in his *Sermons on the Psalms and Gospels*: "I throw myself down in my Chamber and I . . . invite God and his angels thither, and when they are there, I neglect God and his angels for the noise of a fly, for the rattling of a coach, for the whining of a door."

In his *Devotions*, Donne says, "I consider thy plentiful goodness, O my God, in employing angels more than one, in so many of thy remarkable works." Detailing the many instances in Scripture in which not a single angel but a whole chorus (or crowd in the case of those ascending and descending Jacob's ladder) are seen, Donne continues: "From the first to their last, are angels, angels in the plural, in every service angels associated with angels."

Angel Books

There is a mail-order business specializing in books about angels. For information, write to John Ronner, Mamre Press, 107-AK South Second Avenue, Murfreesboro, TN 37130. Most angel books can be ordered through New Age bookstores, and regular bookstores stock angel books from major publishers.

Israfel

In Heaven a spirit doth dwell
    'Whose heart-strings are a lute';
None sing so wildly well
As the angel Israfel,
And the giddy stars (so legends tell),
Ceasing their hymns, attend the spell
    Of his voice, all mute.

And they say (the starry choir
    And the other listening things)
That Israfeili's fire
Is owing to that lyre
    By which he sits and sings—
The trembling living wire
    Of those unusual strings.

If I could dwell
Where Israfel
    Hath dwelt, and he where I,
He might not sing so wildly well
    A mortal melody,
While a bolder note than this might swell
    From my lyre within the sky.
                    —Edgar Allan Poe

Part Four
Angels and Human Interactions

CHAPTER FOURTEEN

Do Angels Exist?

*W*hy should we bother ourselves by trying to prove the actual existence of angels? Certainly we have all heard enough stories of people's actual experience to believe that they aren't "just whistlin' Dixie," as a Southern saying goes. No matter which way you turn on this question, the answer remains moot. Maybe they do, maybe they don't. Yet, for some unexplained reason, the human mind always wants to *know*—absolutely, always, and for certain.

Naturally, it's difficult to accept the *unseen* as being *real*—unless you practice quantum science which does this very thing on a daily basis and calls it scientific. Ah, but scientific logic is different from ordinary logic—especially when it comes to angels. We can accept that invisible particles called quarks exist because we are told they do by a phalanx of serious-faced, white-coated, highly educated Ph.D.s, equipped with all the latest technological gadgets, working in pristine laboratories funded by the government and foundations. But neither the Rockefeller nor Ford Foundations have ever contributed a cent toward determining whether angels exist. Nor has the government—which of course has more serious things to fund, such as in-depth studies of the mating behavior of grasshoppers.

Once upon a time, the question Do angels exist? would simply never have been asked; the answer was too obvious—"*Of course they do; the Bible says so.*" And that was that, until science came along and a vast amount of skepticism set in—and Aquinas and his ilk went out.

The great theologian St. Thomas Aquinas wrote a great treatise, *Summa Theologica*—a vast summing up of all the theological knowledge up to his time. It contained an entire tract on angels, which the masterful chronicler of angels considered were bodiless, exceeding humans in number, and spiritually perfect. And the contemporaneous German mystic poet, Meister Eckhart, had quite a number of personal encounters with angels, which he described in fine detail.

For intellects such as these, the question was never moot; it was always a given that angels exist. Religious belief in angels is based on three things:

1. Sacred Scriptures attest to the existence of angels on earth. As they perform their mission as messengers from

Do Angels Really Exist?

"Of prime importance is *whether angels or devas actually exist* . . . . We find a diversity of views. Intellect-scientists of the old school would categorically say that they do not. More modern ones, less dogmatic, might be a little more open; though the tendency is today to think in more general and impersonal terms, of a 'life-stream' behind biological forms rather than of intelligent and more personalized entities.

"Depth psychology offers us a viewpoint which in some ways is two-edged. For analysts of the non-materialistic schools know that, at a certain point in individual self-discovery, they will dream and see visions of angelic and other mythological figures, which are of great importance to them. These convey 'messages' from some-where beyond the ordinary personal mind. They tell us about our-selves and the state we are in, and in that sense they are 'divine messengers.' But it is usually assumed that these images are cre-ated by the mind of the dreamer, emanate from within, not that they represent self-existent entities of any kind. . . . The more intel-ligent psychologist allows for the point of view of clairvoyants who tell us of angels or devas in terms of independent beings which . . . 'visit' them and teach them."

—Laurence J. Bendit, "The Incarnation of the Angels,"
in *Angels and Mortals*

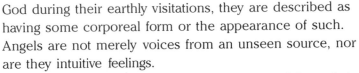

God during their earthly visitations, they are described as having some corporeal form or the appearance of such. Angels are not merely voices from an unseen source, nor are they intuitive feelings.

2. The word "heaven" in the opening sentence of Genesis is interpreted to attest the existence of an incorporeal realm, invisible but nonetheless real, as well as the existence of the visible, material world in which humans live.

3. Angels, despite whether they assume human form (usually as men) or other forms, belong to the nonmaterial world; they come from heaven to earth. Thus, the scripture-based religious belief in angels is a belief in the existence of angels not as solid material entities but as purely spiritual beings.

As soon as science became God—with the scientific revolution that began 300 years ago—and drastically changed the meaning of the word *existence*, belief in angels bottomed out like the stock market did in 1929. Belief in angels crashed, and anyone who stubbornly insisted they were real was considered mildly nutty or just plain crazy, at least in the advanced Western developed cultures.

No doubt, alongside this new Western skepticism regarding angels, there remained certainty of their existence in other parts of the world that had not as yet been touched by the new science and its attendant rejection of the invisible realm of life. Traditional cultures all over the world, in places where shamanism was a way of life, had no problems with the question, for it was never asked and therefore never had to be answered.

However, we have chosen to both ask and attempt to answer this question that refuses to go away. So, do angels exist?

The dictionary isn't helpful—Webster's unabridged edition of 1989—fairly recent—defines *exist* thusly:

1. to have actual being; be.
2. to have life or animation.

Going further, if we look up the word *actual*, we find:

1. existing in act or fact; real.

Now, let's look at *real*, and see what we find there:

1. true; not merely ostensible, nominal or apparent.
2. existing or occurring as fact; actual rather than imaginary, ideal, or fictitious.

Investigating *imaginary*, we learn:

1. the action of imagining, or of forming mental images or concepts of what is not actually present to the senses.

"The Day We Saw the Angels"

Do you feel as though you're going around in circles? Let's look at an interesting little story, reprinted many times in various publications, including *Guideposts* and *Spiritual Frontiers Fellowship*. The story, entitled "The Day We Saw the Angels," is by Professor S. Ralph Harlow of Northampton, Massachusetts. It took place during the 1930s.

It was not Christmas, it was not even wintertime, when the event occurred that for me threw sudden new light on the ancient angel tale. It was a glorious spring morning and we were walking, my wife and I, through the newly budded birches and maples near Ballardvale, Massachusetts.

Now I realize that this, like any account of personal experience, is only as valid as the good sense and honesty of the person relating it. What can I say about myself? That I am a scholar who shuns guesswork and admires scientific investigation? That I have a B.A. from Harvard, an M.A. from Columbia, a Ph.D. from Hartford Theological Seminary? That I have never been subject to hallucinations? That attorneys have solicited my testimony, and I have testified in the courts, regarded by judge and jury as a faithful, reliable witness? All this is true and yet I doubt that any amount of such credentials can influence the belief or disbelief of another.

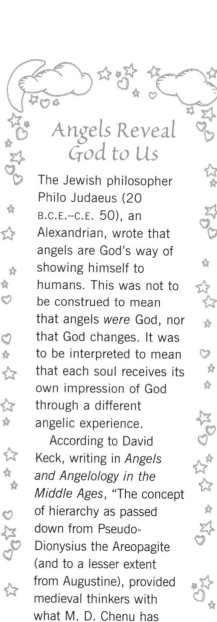

Angels Reveal God to Us

The Jewish philosopher Philo Judaeus (20 B.C.E.–C.E. 50), an Alexandrian, wrote that angels are God's way of showing himself to humans. This was not to be construed to mean that angels *were* God, nor that God changes. It was to be interpreted to mean that each soul receives its own impression of God through a different angelic experience.

According to David Keck, writing in *Angels and Angelology in the Middle Ages*, "The concept of hierarchy as passed down from Pseudo-Dionysius the Areopagite (and to a lesser extent from Augustine), provided medieval thinkers with what M. D. Chenu has called a 'total hypothesis,' a framework for understanding everything, a framework comparable to evolution today."

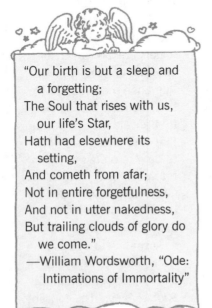

"Our birth is but a sleep and
   a forgetting;
The Soul that rises with us,
   our life's Star,
Hath had elsewhere its
   setting,
And cometh from afar;
Not in entire forgetfulness,
And not in utter nakedness,
But trailing clouds of glory do
   we come."
—William Wordsworth, "Ode:
   Intimations of Immortality"

In the long run, each of us must sift what comes to us from others through his own life experience, his view of the universe, his understanding. And so I will simply tell my story.

The little path on which Marion and I walked that morning was spongy to our steps and we held hands with the sheer delight of life as we strolled near a lovely brook. It was May, and because it was the examination reading period for students at Smith College where I was a professor, we were able to get away for a few days to visit Marion's parents.

We frequently took walks in the country, and we especially loved the spring after a hard New England winter, for it is then that the fields and the woods are radiant and calm yet show new life bursting from the earth. This day we were especially happy and peaceful; we chatted sporadically, with great gaps of satisfying silence between our sentences.

Then from behind us we heard the murmur of muted voices in the distance, and I said to Marion, "We have company in the woods this morning."

Marion nodded and turned to look. We saw nothing, but the voices were coming nearer—at a faster pace than we were walking—and then we knew that the strangers would soon overtake us. Then we perceived that the sounds were not only behind us but above us, and we looked up.

How can I describe what we felt? Is it possible to tell of the surge of exaltation that ran through us? Is it possible to record this phenomenon in objective accuracy and yet be credible?

For about ten feet above us, and slightly to our left, was a floating group of glorious, beautiful creatures that glowed with spiritual beauty. We stopped and stared as they passed above us.

There were six of them, young beautiful women dressed in flowing white garments and engaged in earnest conversation. If they were aware of our existence they gave no indication of it. Their faces were perfectly clear to us, and one woman, slightly older than the rest, was especially beautiful. Her dark hair was pulled back in what today we would call a ponytail, and, although I cannot say it was bound at the back of her head, it appeared to be. She was talking intently to a younger spirit whose back was toward us and who looked up into the face of the woman who was talking.

Neither Marion nor I could understand their words, although their voices were clearly heard. The sound was somewhat like hearing but being unable to understand a group of people talking outside a house with all the windows and doors shut.

They seemed to float past us, and their graceful motion seemed natural—as gentle and peaceful as the morning itself. As they passed, their conversation grew fainter and fainter until it faded out entirely, and we stood transfixed on the spot, still holding hands and still with the vision before our eyes.

It would be an understatement to say that we were astounded. Then we looked at each other, each wondering if the other also had seen.

There was a fallen birch tree just there beside the path. We sat down on it and I said, "Marion, what did you see? Tell me exactly in precise detail. And tell me what you heard."

She knew my intent—to test my own eyes and ears to see if I had been the victim of hallucination or imagination. And her reply was identical in every respect to what my own senses had reported to me.

I have related this story with the same faithfulness and respect for truth and accuracy as I would tell it on the witness stand. But even as I record it I know how incredible it sounds.

Perhaps I can claim no more for it than it has had a deep effect on our own lives. For this experience of almost 30 years ago greatly altered our thinking.

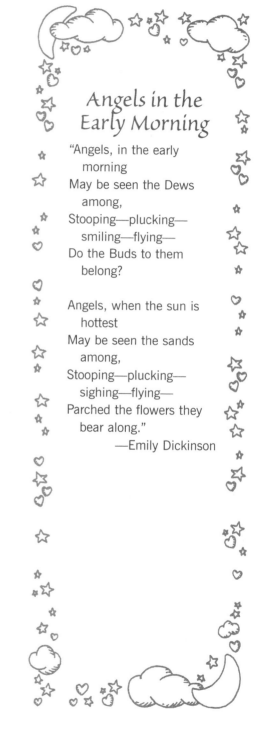

Angels in the Early Morning

"Angels, in the early morning
May be seen the Dews among,
Stooping—plucking—smiling—flying—
Do the Buds to them belong?

Angels, when the sun is hottest
May be seen the sands among,
Stooping—plucking—sighing—flying—
Parched the flowers they bear along."
—Emily Dickinson

Neurolinguistics and Astrology

Do angels exist? In my quest to answer this vexing question, I turned to Mary Orser. The author of several books, Mary is a professional astrologer who holds a master's degree in experimental psychology and who, having studied the relatively new science of neurolinguistics extensively, coauthored *Changing Your Destiny* (Harper and Row), a fascinating book linking neurolinguistics with astrology. She has kindly allowed me to reprint the following essay from her (unpublished) book, *Reality: What Is It?*

The scientific revolution was a reaction against the naive acceptance of practically anything that anyone might report, or believing simply because some "authority" has decreed that it was so. Scientists rightly questioned the "truths" that had become accepted simply because somebody important had asserted that such-and-such was Truth (usually Church authorities).

Scientists insisted upon testing "objective reality" themselves, and "objective reality" came more and more to be defined as something *all* observers could see, or hear, or smell, or taste, or touch—in other words, something that could be perceived through the five physical senses, something with a *physical* reality that could be weighed and/or measured.

At the height of the reign of scientific materialism, whatever didn't meet these "scientific" requirements was declared incontrovertibly as "imagination," "hallucination," "unreal," "not existing." And, because science and its hallowed methods had achieved such wonders—especially in medicine and technology—the general publics of the Western world accepted the statements of scientists as Authority.

With this shift from ecclesiastical to secular authority, most people stopped believing in anything that wasn't able to be apprehended through the five physical senses—if it didn't have a physical body you could weigh and measure, or stick pins in and hear it yelp, it wasn't real. Out the window of "existence" went whatever was invisible, or bodiless—angels, fairies, elves, spirits (of the dead), spirits that animate other life than that of humans (such as Nature spirits)—simply ceased to exist. This shift occurred despite the fact that people in all cultures in all nations all over the world had for centuries uncountable reported interactions with such beings. Never mind the witnesses through the ages: in the new world view of scientific materialism, such things were mere whiffs of air borne on imagination's fancy.

Now, clearly science as a *method* is a legitimate way to seek certain kinds of "truth," but the conclusions of scientists are based on *theory*—evidence that doesn't fit the theory is simply discarded. There is an entire body of discounted theories that subsequent research has found unsupportable. The problem with this system is that the fact that some theories have been proved incorrect does not always filter down to the lay populace.

It took Albert Einstein's advent upon the scientific world to lay the ghost of the theoretical foundation that matter is the only reality. With very little fanfare, Einstein burst the scientific bubble, pulling the rug out from under the theory that matter is the fundamental reality.

Thus began the revolution that has totally changed our understanding of how the world works. This "revolution" was based on the equating of *matter and energy*, and the development of quantum physics abetted and continued it. Recent discoveries have turned our previous understanding of reality on its head, to the extent that leading-edge scientific thinkers are beginning to sound like mystics!

Consider this statement from the eminent physicist John Wheeler: "The universe does not exist out there independent of us. We are inescapably involved in bringing about that which appears to be happening. We are not only

The Familiar Becomes New

"One of life's most fulfilling moments occurs in that split-second when the familiar is suddenly transformed into the dazzling aura of the profoundly new."

—Edward B. Lindaman, *Thinking in the Future Tense*

An Angel Saves a Child

Writer Hope MacDonald, who wrote about the young girl and the dog, in Chapter 11, relates a tale about her sister, Marilyn. At the time, Hope was four, Marilyn eight. One day, after leaving to take Marilyn to school, her parents returned carrying the child—all bruised and bloodied—and laid her on a sofa while awaiting the doctor's arrival. They explained that Marilyn, while crossing the street to the school, had been hit by a car and that upon impacting the pavement, she had begun to roll very fast toward a large open sewer at the bottom of an incline. But Marilyn's swift progress had halted abruptly at the sewer's edge. How, they wondered aloud, could she possibly have stopped when she was rolling so fast?

Marilyn piped up from the couch, "But didn't you see that huge, beautiful angel standing in the sewer, holding up her hands to keep me from falling in?"

observers. We are participators. In some strange sense this is a *participatory universe*."

The new physics has opened the door for acceptance of all kinds of manifestations that Newtonian physics considered "impossible." And that includes "beings" whose form is not composed of the material solids, liquids, and gasses that we have always associated with form.

Teachings of the wisdom traditions from many parts of the world have asserted that there are different levels of matter, of various degrees of density. These, sometimes called the "planes of nature," are considered to *interpenetrate* each other, much in the matter that a drop of dye interpenetrates a glass of water, or a spoon of sugar a cup of coffee.

In this view, everything with a physical body also has bodies in each of these subtle—or non-material—planes, and our physical senses perceive only the densest plane. However, we also possess subtle senses that allow us to experience these other realms. Unfortunately, these "extra" senses (extrasensory, as it were) are usually obliterated by the information coming in from the gross, physical senses, and we aren't accustomed to paying attention to our subtle senses. Unless we make a special and conscious effort, we miss the information they provide us. It is like being inside a brightly lit room prevents you from seeing what is going on outside a window when it is dark. Turn off the bright lights and your eyes grow accustomed to the darkness and you begin to see what before was "invisible," because you were blocked from observing it.

Clairvoyance is the ability to consciously receive impressions from these subtler levels of manifestation—the clairvoyant bypasses the physical senses and "tunes in" to the other "planes." Clairvoyance can be a gift, like perfect pitch, or it can be developed like any other skill. There is evidence that *everyone* has some degree of clairvoyance built in, and this can be demonstrated by the observation of children, many of whom are clairvoyant when still quite young, before they have been told that what they are experiencing is their imagination. It is a great pity that this wonderful gift is stamped out in our children by the strength of the still prevalent materialistic world view. If adults would take seriously and be attentive to the invisible playmates and other non-physical beings, like fairies, that children see naturally, we would all benefit.

Each of the physical senses has a counterpart on the subtle planes: clairvoyance = seeing; clairaudience = hearing; clairsentience = feeling (touch) and smell. Apparently, more people are *clairsentient* than *clairvoyant*: most of us seem capable of sensing atmospheres of a place or sensing if someone behind us is staring at us.

According to worldwide traditions, many beings live in bodies on the more subtle planes but do not have bodies on the physical plane. For centuries, clairvoyants in many different cultures have reported sightings of "nature spirits"—fairies, elves, and the like. Angels dwell on the more subtle planes as do recently deceased humans who retain their subtle plane bodies after having left their physical bodies by dying.

Numerous books have been published by medical doctors and other near-death experience researchers, reporting on the experiences of those people certified as dead who were then revived. Many such people tell extremely similar stories of what happened during the period they were "dead," or not breathing. They knew they were out of their physical bodies—some saw themselves lying on the operating table—and they met relatives and friends no longer alive; they also met loving beings of light—angels.

Some clairvoyants have claimed to have seen the auras of angels—a glowing energy flow that streams outward and upward from the shoulders, resembling wings. It may be that subtle plane manifestations are a type of energy field. We already have instrumentation that can photograph different energy fields, from X rays

Life After Life

Raymond Moody wrote *Life After Life*, a collection of near-death experiences. An example is that of Dr. Hugh Hildesby, who was on an operating table, when he was expelled from his body.

I was washed in light. I felt the absence of weight, and this pulsing, flowing light of incredible brilliance—gold and white, but with a white so pure and scintillating it was alive. . . . Around the light were "angels," but they were not angels as we conceive of them. They were spirits without form. . . . There was no anxiety. I was totally protected, and the angels are part of that . . . you are one of the angels. You have found your identity.

First-Person Accounts

Angel Letters, Sophie Burnham, Ballantine

Angels Among Us, A Guideposts Book

Angels Among Us, Don Fearheiley, Avon

Angels of Mercy, Rosemary Ellen Guiley

Answers from the Angels, Terry Lynn Taylor, H. J. Kramer

A Rustle of Angels, Marilynn and Bill Webber, Zondervan

Brush of an Angel's Wing, Charles Shedd, Servans

In the Presence of Angels: Stories from New Research on Angels, Robert C. Smith, A.R.E., Edgar Cayce

Meetings with Angels, H. C. Moolenburgh, C. W. Daniel Co., Ltd. (translated from the Dutch)

Touched by Angels, Eileen Elias Freeman, Warner Books

Where Angels Walk: True Stories of Heavenly Visitors, Joan Wester Anderson, Ballantine

to Kirlian photography. Perhaps the day will come when an energy field video camera will enable a computer user to project the presence of an angel on the monitor screen. Angels on the Internet? Could be.

Now that recent scientific theory has opened the door to the existence of forms other than the dense physical one of our bodies, there can be no denying the possibility that beings without physical bodies do exist. Though the existence of subtle-plane beings cannot be "proved" through the means presently available, there is no reason not to expect that these means will one day be discovered. Then, we will be able to translate superphysical sensory impressions into a form with which our ordinary physical senses can relate. Until that happens, we can rely on the actual experiences of all of those who have given vividly detailed descriptions of angelic beings.

To the question of whether angels exist, we can answer in the affirmative. Yes! The weight of evidence is in favor of the existence of angels.

CHAPTER FIFTEEN

Angel Stories:
The Evidence

Angel Stories

Writer Joan Wester Anderson asked her readers to send her their angel stories. She received thousands of replies!

"The letters were a joy to read . . . magazines printed my [angel story] invitation . . . many strangers shared their 'special event.' . . . My files began to grow.

"I found it fascinating that, although angel incidents varied, the *reaction* of those involved was almost always the same, and twofold: first, a hesitancy about sharing; then . . . an awe that, even years later, was still powerfully aroused by the memory of the incident. . . . None wanted to lose that precious conviction that they had been especially blessed, permitted . . . to look into a world they . . . usually accept on faith . . . . The emotional response seemed universal too."

—Joan Wester Anderson, *Where Angels Walk*

The many books being written about angels today attest to a renewed and burgeoning interest in them and people's faith that angels are real and are concerned about us. Angels are everywhere we look, not just in angel books, but on TV, represented as dolls, pictured on greeting cards, written about in angel newsletters, and even in gift shops devoted entirely to angel products. This angel explosion is a certain indication that even if our faith in other matters is often in doubt, our faith in angels is having a resurgence—a renaissance one might say—for many are those who have angel stories to tell.

Why are angels such a popular topic now? Why are so many angel stories being told and written about—not only those already published many times, such as the story of the angels at Mons, Belgium, during World War I (which is told later in this chapter), but also brand-new stories that are coming forth every day, in books, magazines, on TV programs, and in private personal reports.

In pondering this phenomenon, I can only surmise that the angels are manifesting to our consciousness in response to the heartfelt prayers of many people. The angels seem to recognize our urgent need for their intervention and interaction in our lives.

Another reason I think that angels are suddenly so much with us is to serve as an antidote to our wired society with all its technological gadgets. As Marshall McLuhan pointed out in *The Medium Is the Message*, these technologies are "cold." When abused or relied upon too heavily, they can separate us from ourselves, from human companionship, from spontaneous warmth and loving kindness. The angels are launching a backlash against our almost total immersion in nonhuman devices that serve to alienate us not only from our fellow beings but also from our deepest innermost selves as well. The fact that we have managed to turn angels from the fierce and fiery multi-winged, multiple-eyed creatures of history and biblical visions of prophets into gentle, fluffy, "touchy-feely" creations of our

What Is Faith?

"Faith is the touching of a mystery," according to Russian Orthodox priest Alexander Schmemann. He writes: "It is to perceive another dimension to absolutely everything in the world. In faith, the mysterious meaning of life comes through. . . . To speak in the simplest possible terms: faith sees, knows, senses the presence of God [and His angels] in the world."

Protestant theologian Paul Tillich defines faith this way: "Faith means being grasped by a power that is greater than we are, a power that shakes us and turns us, and transforms and heals us."

"Faith is not a momentary feeling but a struggle against the discouragement that threatens us every time we meet resistance," says Bakole wa Ilunga, the Catholic archbishop of Zaire.

Protestant minister Samuel H. Miller asserts that "Faith faces everything that makes the world uncomfortable . . . and acts with a compassion by which these things are transformed, even exalted."

Kenneth Leech, an Anglican priest, declares that "true faith can only grow and mature if it includes the elements of paradox and creative doubt is . . . an essential element of it. For faith in God does not bring the false peace of answered questions and resolved paradoxes."

Rabbi Abraham Joshua Heschel says faith is "to bring God back into the world, into our lives. . . . To have faith in God is to reveal what is concealed."

"To choose what is difficult all one's days as if it were easy, that is faith," says English poet W. H. Auden.

longing is a hint to the new role angels are playing in our lives in answer to our prayerful needs.

We have come a long way from the quiet messenger men who visited Abraham and Sarah to inform the old couple they would have a child, from Isaiah's awesome vision of gloriously terrifying creatures with four faces who put a hot coal to his lips to purify him, from Lot's angel visitors who destroyed the city of Sodom, from Jacob's unnamed angelic adversary, from Ezekiel's ox-faced beings, and from the angelic destruction of the troops of King Sennacherib during the time of David.

Angels have become *nice*—some say vapid and sentimental, but that may be mere caviling. If we remember that all the universe is thronged with hosts of angels, who are at a higher level of evolution than we have achieved, and who have the responsibility for guiding and controlling the manifold processes of nature, including ourselves, it makes sense that angels are coming in the way we need them *now*, rather than in the way they did 2000 or more years ago to a world that was so different from ours.

What do angels look like? Whatever pleases them or suits their purpose. They seem to take a form that the person who is receiving their message can relate to. No angel speaks English to someone whose native and only tongue is French or Spanish, as is amply illustrated in the story of the Angels of Mons, perhaps the most compelling story ever told about angels and certainly one of the most famous.

The Angels of Mons

During World War II, there were many who believed that the angels were fighting on the side of the Allied forces, and that their help was instrumental in the victorious result.

However, the most dramatic story of angels fighting on the winning side comes from another war—World War I. This is the story of the angels at Mons, Belgium, which occurred between August 26–28, 1914.

The battered troops of the French and British forces were in retreat toward Paris having been overpowered by the massive artillery of the German army occupying Belgium. Although this was not the most disastrous loss of that bloody and murderous war—the average life expectancy of a British officer was said to be twenty minutes—in which massive carnage was a daily occurrence, it was still a sad and inglorious retreat for those gallant fighting men who were attempting to free Europe from the German yoke.

Gradually, as the soldiers and their officers regrouped and the wounded were hospitalized, peculiar tales began to be circulated about the retreat from Mons, which had been successfully accomplished to the surprise of the entire cadre. One nurse in a hospital caring for the wounded men reported that she and her fellow nurses had heard the same tale, in slightly different versions, from many of the men who had survived the retreat from Mons.

French soldiers reported seeing the archangel Saint Michael—some said they saw Saint Joan of Arc—all clad in golden armor, riding a magnificent white charger whose mane flowed like wings in the wind. The angel (or whatever it was), whose uncovered head was crowned with locks of a golden hue, brandished a shining sword of great heft.

The British soldiers saw Saint George emerging out of a shining golden mist, also seated on a great rearing white

Celestial Visitants

"Angels are not etherealized human beings . . . they are celestial visitants . . . pure thoughts from God, winged with Truth and Love. . . . Human conjecture confers upon angels its own forms of thought, marked with superstitious outlines, making them creatures with suggestive feathers; but this is only fancy. . . .

"Angels are God's representatives. These upward-soaring beings . . . guide to the divine principle of all good. . . . By giving earnest heed to these spiritual guides they tarry with us."

—Mary Baker Eddy, *Science and Health*

Personal Stories

Marilynn Carlson Webber and William D. Webber, authors of *A Rustle of Angels*, which relates true angel stories, ask, "If people keep these angel experiences to themselves, how did such experiences find their way into this book?"

By way of answer, they say, "We did not find them—they found us. Marilynn wrote a moving true-life story about a woman whose life had been changed by an angel. The story was published [*Guideposts*, October, 1992]. David Briggs of the Associated Press, writing an article on the explosion of interest in angels, interviewed Marilynn."

Briggs's story was picked up by numerous papers and appeared in the *Ladies' Home Journal* (December 1992).

"We were unprepared for the response. . . . People began to call, usually long distance. . . . Frequently the caller would say, 'I've never felt so compelled to call someone in my life, but after reading your story I know that you would understand.' . . . Thousands of letters began to arrive. Hundreds had first-person accounts of angels [often saying] 'I've never told this to anyone before.'"

The authors say that "many whose personal experiences are recounted in this book, the events . . . treasured and held close to the heart [had] . . . a secret longing to disclose the occurrence, but at the right time, in the right way, to the right person . . . . When the staff of the television series *Unsolved Mysteries* asked us to open our files and give them stories for their program, we turned them down. Angels are not 'unsolved mysteries' to be placed in the same context as . . . paranormal activity."

horse, "a tall man with yellow hair in golden armor, on a white horse, holding his sword up, and his mouth open, crying *Victory!*" as the newspaper report told it.

And it was not just a single man, or two or three, who told the stories: it was many, many of the wounded of both French and British nationalities. They asked for medallions or colored prints of Saint Michael or Saint George, respectively.

One patient reported that just when they feared the retreat would be overrun by the German forces he saw "an angel with outstretched wings, like a luminous cloud," between the rapidly oncoming Germans and the retreating troops. At that moment, the German onslaught slowed.

Another patient told of "a strange light, which seemed to be quite distinctly outlined and was not a reflection of the moon. . . . [It] became brighter and I could see quite distinctly three shapes, one in the centre having what looked like outspread wings, the other two were not so large, but were quite plainly distinct from the centre one. They appeared to have a long, loose-hanging garment of a golden tint, and they were about the German line facing us."

Back in London, hearing about the retreat from Mons on the radio, an English journalist, Arthur Machen, was moved to write a short story entitled, "The Bowmen," which appeared in the *London Evening News* on September 14, 1914, three weeks after the Mons retreat had taken place. The story—which Machen claimed was pure fiction—told of how the retreating soldiers had seen an apparition of "shining" medieval knights in armor, "phantom bowmen" supposedly from the battlefield of Agincourt—quite near to Mons—where King Henry V of England had routed the French on October 25, 1415. As the stories continued to flow in, Machen thought his fictional account was the source of the tales and tried to dissuade people from believing that any "angels" appeared at Mons—unsuccessfully.

Fearsome Angels

Biblical angels can be fearsome. The first picture of angels given in the Bible includes a fiery sword: "At the east of the Garden of Eden he placed the cherubim, and a sword flaming and turning to guard the way to the tree of life."
—Genesis 3:24

Because, a year later, the German side began to tell a remarkably similar story: at the critical moment, just as they were about to overtake the retreating troops, the Germans found themselves "absolutely powerless to proceed . . . their horses turned sharply round and fled . . . and nothing could stop them." The German regiment involved was sharply chastised by its superiors, but they nonetheless held to their claim, saying that they saw "thousands" of troops holding the Allied lines even though the reality was that there were but two regiments, severely decimated, which made but a thin line, the men standing fifteen yards apart or in a straggle along the road in hasty and disorderly retreat.

What really happened at Mons? We will never know for sure. What is most interesting is the French saw a French angel, or St. Joan, while the British troops saw St. George, the patron saint of England! The Germans, on the other hand, saw *troops* of "Allied soldiers," which might be interpreted as the angelic host referred to in the Bible's many references to angels as militants.

Unfortunately, many of the wounded men were beyond saving, but the nurses reported that those who were dying had about them a curious aura of serenity and peace, an air of joy and exaltation.

Some skeptics dismissed the stories as mass hysteria of defeated men who had departed only four days earlier as an army of a hundred thousand expecting a quick rout of the Germans but instead suffering the stunning loss of fifteen thousand of their number in the first engagement of the battle.

Other nay-sayers claimed that the nurses—suffering from fever and fatigue, working forty-five hours straight without sleep, incredibly overworked and daily experiencing the horror of having to pull live wounded men out from underneath cold dead corpses as the horse-drawn wagons pulled into the hospital grounds—were having hallucinations.

Whatever the "truth," it is clear that *something* happened at Mons—something extraordinary. And to this day there are many people who believe there were angels at Mons.

The Cosmonaut's Encounter with Angels

An amazing story that was reported in the newspapers during the 1980s was told by a Russian scientist who defected to the United States early in 1985. If true, it sheds amazing light on angels in our world today.

According to the scientist, on the 155th day on board the orbiting Russian space station Soyuz 7, three cosmonauts—Vladimir Solevev, Oleg Atkov, and Leonid Kizim—were in the process of doing some medical experiments when suddenly they were blinded by a brilliant orange glow.

Stunned, the scientists feared a disaster of some sort. But then, when their eyes adjusted to the bright orange light, they saw "seven giant figures in the form of humans, but with wings and mist-like halos as in the classic depiction of angels. They appeared to be hundreds of feet tall with a wingspan as great as a jetliner."

According to the cosmonauts who witnessed this almost incredible sight, their faces were cherubic, round, and smiling, and they were all identical! The band of figures—were they angels?—followed the space capsule for several minutes and then disappeared.

That, however, was not the end of the sighting. Twelve days later, they reappeared, all seven, all identical; on this second visit, other scientists saw them too. Says Svetlana Savistskaya, the only woman scientist on board: "We were truly overwhelmed. There was a great orange light and through it we could see the figures of seven angels. They were smiling as though they shared a glorious secret."

One cannot help but remember that there are *seven* archangels!

Stories of Supernatural Light

Bright light, whether white or colored, seems to be a constant with the presence of angels. Malcolm Muggeridge in *Something Beautiful for God*, tells a story about Mother Teresa of Calcutta, India.

George Washington's Angelic Vision

George Washington wrote about an angel he saw at Valley Forge; it visited him three times. The angel told him that there would be three great conflicts and that, after a time, the United States of America, when it seemed that it would be eclipsed on the world stage, would emerged not only victorious but the absolute leader of the entire world. This message gave the future first president of the United States the courage to carry on the battle, and the prophecy seems to have come true, as this country is now the sole surviving superpower.

Muggeridge describes an experience involving filming a documentary about her by the British Broadcasting Company. The script required some scenes inside the Home for the Dying, which was but dimly lit and had only some small windows high up on the walls. The photo crew was not sure whether they could film in this light-deprived atmosphere [why they didn't have flashes or strobes is unexplained; maybe there wasn't any electricity available in this poor section of Calcutta], but they decided to give it the old college try—so that the trip wouldn't be a complete waste. As a backup, the film crew took some outside footage in a sunny courtyard of the home.

Later, back in London, when the film was processed, the footage taken *outside* in the sun was disappointingly dull, but the film from the dimly lit inside room was "bathed in a beautiful glow." Technicians examined the film and found it to be in perfect condition; they could offer no explanation for this reverse effect that broke all the rules.

Says Muggeridge of the event: "I am convinced that the technically unaccountable light is, in fact, supernatural. Mother Teresa's Home for the Dying is overflowing with a luminous love, like the haloes artists have seen and made visible. . . . I find it not at all surprising that the luminosity should register on a photographic film."

An Archangel of Creative Light

In *Clairvoyant Investigations*, Geoffrey Hodson relates this story about a vacation taken at Onerahi, Whangarei, North Auckland, New Zealand:

> Suddenly there appeared in the sky beyond our hotel window a number of great and brilliantly shining Devas. One of these approached us more closely and flashed the following communication into my mind: "With yourself, we members of the devic hierarchy are veritable manifestations of the great procedures of external creation ema-

nating from the most deeply interior Source of the out-
wardly 'knowable,' objectively existent universe, all nature
at every level."

Never before do I remember having perceived so great
a being . . . an individualized archangelic center of creative
light. Shining forth from and through the angel, as if from
star-shaped centers of force, were radiations of form-pro-
ducing ideas, forces, and light. This Devaraja would seem
to be carrying out individually—but with cosmically
expanded consciousness—the procedures of the formation
and preservation of the universe. Some of the white, five-
pointed, four-dimensional stars were apparently permanent
in the upper portion of the extensive shining aura. Yet,
strangely, they also appeared to be constantly flashing forth
and transmitting their light, thereafter disappearing as if the
source of the light had completed its manifestation. This
continued throughout the upper portion of the aura, not
only at the front but also at the sides and behind the great
and shining being.

The predominating color of the lower half of the aura,
which spread downwards from a region corresponding to
the solar plexus in man, was leaf-green with touches of
gold and white, somewhat like rays shining within it.
Wing-like radiations, sky-blue and gold in color, shone
above the "shoulders" high into the air. The "eyes" were
more like great centers of light than our human organs . .
. and the color gold was seen to be glowing both within
the "head" and radiating upwards beyond. The auric
activity of this great being was definitely wing-like and
wing-shaped.

Personally, I have heard many angel stories that I was able to
verify, often because I was there at the time. Other reasons are that
the person telling the story was accompanied by witnesses or
because the person is known to me as a reliable and honest
source of information.

Devas

Today, devas are popular
as beneficent nature
spirits who can choose to
help humans. Usually,
they are not visible, but
clairvoyants can see them,
and they are said to com-
municate through clairau-
dience and meditation.

The Angel of My Twenty-First Birthday

On three separate occasions, angels have saved my life. My second encounter with an angel was dramatic. It occurred on my twenty-first birthday. I was living in Houston, and my housemate, Nancy, had arranged a surprise birthday party for me aboard a Holland-America Lines ship, which was docked in the Houston ship channel. This was a major treat, as no one was allowed aboard cargo ships without an invitation from the captain. As it happened, Nancy was friends with the local manager of the shipping line, and he did the honors.

When we started out in our car, with Nancy driving, I had no idea where we were going. I'd never been to the dock area, which was ugly and very different from the beautifully manicured part of town where I lived, which was off Houston's broad and tree-lined Main Street. We stopped at a sleazy looking bar and there met the manager and his wife, who then led the way along a bleak industrial road, known as Navigation Road to the dock itself. Nancy had never been there either, and the way was complex and dark.

The long confusing trip was well worth taking, however, as aboard ship we were placed in the lap of festive luxury. The Scandinavian captain and his officers were all in their dress-blue brass-buttoned and gold-braided uniforms, a resplendent sight. First, we were entertained with cocktails and delicious hors d'oeuvres in the salon. I thought this was the entire party, until a steward announced that dinner was served.

We then entered a formal dining room, the table set with snowy double cloths and an array of silverware that foretold many courses to come. I had never before nor since seen such a display of elegant food. We had been instructed by the manager, in the customs of the country, that you did not drink the aquavit, which was on the table at all times, until the captain stood and raised his glass. Then you downed the contents of your glass in one gulp, followed by a beer chaser. A steward stood behind each chair making sure the aquavit glasses were kept full at all times. After several of these toasts, I was more than tipsy. But that was not all. Different wines were served with each course and, at the end, after cheeses and a huge sparkling bowl of fresh strawberries (in January!) served with champagne. Then, a dessert of English trifle was served, followed by coffee and cognac in the salon.

It was a marvelous evening. No 21-year-old could wish for a more splendid birthday celebration. We disembarked clutching an assortment of gifts, including a five-pound wheel of French Roquefort cheese that the captain had insisted I take because I appreciated it so much. Navigating the narrow, swaying gangplank over the dark harbor water below, I lost my balance and nearly dropped my treasure in the oil-slicked water.

Our guides lived off in another direction and, assuming we could find our way, had left us to our own devices to get home. As we climbed into our used car, the sky was lightening slightly from the ink dark of night to the pale gray of predawn. Nancy took the wheel, but as the old car had an unreliable starter, she had trouble starting the engine. Finally, it sputtered to life. I hoped it would not stall on us, but it did, quite often, and it usually took 20 minutes to start it again.

Shortly after we began the long and unfamiliar drive along deserted roads, I promptly passed out in the passenger seat. Suddenly, I woke and found myself in an unmoving car that sat astride a railroad track. Nancy was slumped over the wheel. As I took in the situation, I saw the glaring eye of an oncoming train. Immediately cold sober and with no aftereffects from the night's imbibing, I assessed my options with lightning speed and utter clarity, as if some directing force had taken over my brain. There was no time for me to get out of the car, run around it, open the door, shove her into the passenger seat, get back in, and try to start the car. Also, Nancy was a tall girl, heavier than I, and I knew I could neither move her body nor drag her to safety. The only possible solution was to get the car started *immediately*. But how?

Despite the gravity of the circumstances, I remained absolutely calm and coolly collected. With the train bearing down, only minutes away, I knew precisely what to do. Shoving the double seat

Angel Definition

According to Harper's *Encyclopedia of Mystical and Paranormal Experience*, by Rosemary Ellen Guiley, an angel is "an immortal being who lives in the spirit world and serves as an intermediary between God and humanity."

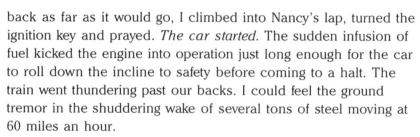

back as far as it would go, I climbed into Nancy's lap, turned the ignition key and prayed. *The car started.* The sudden infusion of fuel kicked the engine into operation just long enough for the car to roll down the incline to safety before coming to a halt. The train went thundering past our backs. I could feel the ground tremor in the shuddering wake of several tons of steel moving at 60 miles an hour.

At the bottom of the incline, only a few feet from what might have been the disaster scene, I looked back and saw a glowing light hovering about the track.

After 20 minutes of pushing and shoving the still unconscious Nancy, I finally got her into the passenger seat and climbed into the driver's seat. At that point I realized I hadn't the faintest idea of where we were or of how to get home. The pale pink rim of dawn was staining the horizon by the time I got the car started. I drove unerringly, rather like a homing pigeon, through a maze of unknown territory—in the bleak, deserted industrial dock district—for more than an hour, without once getting lost or having to retrack, until I reached familiar ground. Somehow I just *knew* the correct route, although I am known for poor sense of direction. Friends would say I could get lost in a phone booth. Angels, apparently, can function like global positioning satellites.

Exactly *what* angels are, no one knows for sure, but I believe they are celestial intelligences. Some say they are beings of pure light who connect with us through our own intuition—our subtle senses.

Sometimes angels appear without form. Angels can manifest as a thought in your mind, an urge of your body, or a sudden, spontaneous surge of intuitive insight. In what form they manifest is not important. That you perceive the angelic presence and receive the angel's message—and are properly grateful for the beneficence you receive—is what counts.

The Motel Angel

Here is a wonderful and mysterious story that happened recently to a close friend, who for many years has been the sole caretaker of his mother. His mother had moved to Arizona in 1966, after her divorce. Although she had grown up on Long Island and lived her married life in Westchester, New York, she felt that Arizona was her true home and wanted to remain there.

This devoted son uprooted himself from a full life in New York and moved to Arizona, where his mother was her happiest. Time passed, and other illnesses plagued her, including a skin cancer that required extensive facial reconstruction. At times he was barely hanging on, but being an extremely spiritual person, he never gave up hope that she would improve. Eventually, things did get better, but as she grew older she began to miss her old life and all her friends back in New York and thought that she'd never see any of them again.

Secretly, he began putting together plans for a trip—knowing it would be the last chance for a reunion for her. He began calling on the angels for help. (He hadn't really believed in the angels until he and I took a road trip together in 1987 that lasted a week: I'll tell that story later.) He *knew* the angels were there, because he'd begun having angel experiences frequently during the last few years (after our trip).

With hardly the rustle of a wing and nary a feather to be seen, each part of his carefully planned scheme quietly fell into place. First, he wanted everything to be first class for her; she'd never flown first class in her life. Money was scarce, but what we've come to call the Angel of the First Class Upgrade came through for him in an unusual way (miraculous?). He'd recently switched long-distance phone companies, and his old company called to woo him back, offering 10,000 frequent flier miles as a lure. Right there was the upgrade from coach to first class! Thanking the first-class angel profusely, he continued his quest to make everything perfect for his mother's sake.

To accommodate their luggage and her mobility vehicle, they needed a large car, but when he checked rental prices, he found

Angels in Many Shapes

The Pharisees believed in angels, but the Sadducees thought angels were mere human fantasies. Jewish mysticism had this to say: "Angels, who are God's messengers, turn themselves into different shapes, being sometimes female and sometimes male."

—*The Zohar*

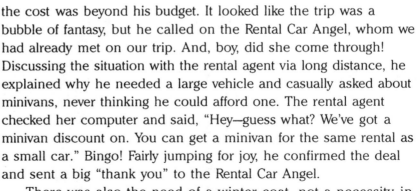

the cost was beyond his budget. It looked like the trip was a bubble of fantasy, but he called on the Rental Car Angel, whom we had already met on our trip. And, boy, did she come through! Discussing the situation with the rental agent via long distance, he explained why he needed a large vehicle and casually asked about minivans, never thinking he could afford one. The rental agent checked her computer and said, "Hey—guess what? We've got a minivan discount on. You can get a minivan for the same rental as a small car." Bingo! Fairly jumping for joy, he confirmed the deal and sent a big "thank you" to the Rental Car Angel.

There was also the need of a winter coat, not a necessity in Arizona. For years he had contented himself with hand-me-downs bought in thrift shops because his mother's health care was expensive and there was little to spare for luxuries. But he wanted to look nice for her, as well as get a little something special for himself. He went shopping for a leather jacket, not really expecting to find anything he could afford. Trying on one model, he was captivated by it; as in "Goldilocks," it was "just right." The price was $300. As he was lovingly stroking the soft fabric, the salesman came over and said, "This coat is going on sale next week at 40 percent off. If you want it, I can hold it for you until then." Is there an angel that looks after our apparel needs? There must have been one hanging around that shop on that day looking for a needy customer. When he returned the next week to pick up his purchase, that angel apparently followed him home, because on the way he bought a newspaper, that contained a coupon for 20 percent off any item in that store. Racing back to the store, he went up to the clerk and showed her the coupon and the unopened package. "Can I return this jacket and then buy it again with this coupon?" he asked hopefully. Barely glancing up, she said, "I don't see why not." In the end, the $300 jacket was his for just over $100! Now that's an angel we could all love.

Next was the question of lodgings. He wanted to have accommodations that would allow his mother to graciously receive her friends as guests, since she had limited mobility and couldn't go visiting. Consequently, he made reservations at a first-class motel in Westchester, which would be a central location, and he specified a room with two double beds and a walk-in shower to accommodate his mother's special needs. Everything was confirmed, and he sent the payment in advance.

As the costs of the trip mounted, he realized he would not have much spending money for himself, but he didn't care, as long as his mother had what she needed and enjoyed the trip with no hassles. However, sometimes angels invite themselves to the party without being asked, and out of the blue, he got a birthday check—in November, though his birthday is in July—from an old aunt who mixes up the birthdays of her various nephews. The last piece was in place, and off they flew in their first-class seats to New York.

Still, it was a long flight, with a tiresome overlay and plane change in Houston, and late evening before they arrived at LaGuardia in New York. By the time they arrived in Westchester, it was after midnight. Both were looking forward to an immediate trip to bed. But it was not to be so.

When he checked in to verify that the room had two double beds and a walk-in shower, he was told that the only available room had one king-size bed and a tub. Tired, anxious about his mother's fatigue, and furious that his reservation, made a month ago, hadn't been honored, he began yelling at the clerk, a plump black woman.

"My mother's a stroke victim. She needs a walk-in shower. I made this reservation a month ago! We'll never use a Holiday Inn again," he fumed.

"Slow, down, honey," the clerk said in calm tones. "Don't get your bones in an uproar. We'll work this out. Just get your mama inside and your luggage up to the room and then come back down."

Mollified by her placid attitude, he did as told, getting his mother as comfortable as possible under the circumstances. Then he went back to the registration desk, where, somewhat calmed down, he apologized for his outburst and explained the situation fully.

"You got all the care of your mama?" asked Clara, the clerk.

"Yes," he replied, "ever since she had the first stroke in 1986."

"Funny," mused Clara. "My mama had a stroke in 1986, too, and I'm the only one she's got to take care of her. We must be about the same age."

They compared birthdays and discovered they were the same age within a few weeks. Then they discussed the trials of being the sole caretaker for an invalid mother. Without preamble, she said, "Just you run downstairs and have a look at the suites and let me know what you think."

He did as instructed and found a luxurious two-bedroom suite, with two double beds in one room and a sofa bed in the sitting room. There was a walk-in shower and a tub in the large bathroom. He sighed, wondering how much extra such a suite would cost.

Back at the desk, he said, "One of those suites would be perfect—but," he hesitated forlornly, "I doubt we could afford it. How much extra would it be than for the room I originally booked?"

"Never you mind about that. Just move your stuff down there and get your mama settled in so she can get some rest. We'll talk about the extra money later."

Surprised but grateful for this late-night reprieve, he thanked Clara and said he'd straighten out the bill with her when they checked out, to which she agreed.

For eight days, they had a wonderful time, and everything went just as planned. Her friends came to visit, and he slept on the sofa bed in the sitting room to give her the privacy of the bedroom. It could not have been a more ideal situation.

Throughout the vacation, he hadn't seen Clara at the desk again and assumed she was on a different schedule. They planned an early morning departure, and on the afternoon before the day they were to leave, he went to the reception desk to check out in advance and pay the extra cost for the suite, hoping it wouldn't take every dollar in his small reserve.

"We're leaving very early tomorrow morning," he told the clerk. "So I'd like to check out now and pay the bill."

She asked his name and then pushed some keys on the computer, surveyed the screen, and said, "I'm showing you paid the whole week in advance, and since there aren't any mini-bar charges, you don't owe anything extra. Have a nice trip home," she chirped as she picked up a ringing phone.

He realized that the computer's records had not been changed to show that they had occupied the expensive suite. Had Clara forgotten or was it a gift—perhaps from an angel?

When the receptionist hung up the phone, he said, "I'd like to say good-bye to Clara. Will she be on duty tonight?"

"No. Clara doesn't work nights, not since her mother had a stroke a few years back. She's part-time now—noon to five."

If Clara didn't work nights, who had he talked to? Who was responsible for putting them in the suite and not changing the computer registration records? If not Clara, then who?

Was Clara an angel? My friend thinks she was, and I agree, for we'd already met the Motel Angel at a crucial point on a trip we took together.

We arrived past midnight at a motel in Nashville, where we had planned to spend the night. After a long, tedious drive through hard rain on roads under heavy construction, we were told that everything was full, due to a country music concert that weekend. "Not a room in town," said the desk clerk.

Tired, anxious, and dismayed, we collapsed in the lobby chairs, not knowing where to turn next. Then the desk phone rang. After talking a few minutes, the clerk turned to us and said, "That was a cancellation." She handed us the keys to a room. Ten minutes later, we were snugged in and ready to relax and restore our energies for the next day's driving.

As we poured a glass of wine to celebrate our "good luck," we both spontaneously raised our glasses and said, "To the Motel Angel." We gave thanks and felt blessed.

Angels Help People Find the Way

"Angels and angelic spirits serve us in many other ways during our life before death. When we need more strength or courage or clearer direction than we feel we have within ourselves, our appeals for help . . . bring angelic assistance if those appeals are genuine and if we are willing to accept help. . . . Most frequently, the support or guidance comes through spiritual depths that lie beneath our consciousness: when we become aware of them the strength or direction seems to have come from within—from some previously unknown resource."

—Robert H. Kirven, *Angels in Action*

Angels on the Road

In June 1997, I departed New York City to take up a secondary residence in rural east Texas, where, free of the distractions of the Big Apple, I could concentrate on my writing. My friend from Arizona, whose story is told above, graciously agreed to fly out from Tucson and be my driver; to make such a trek alone was beyond my capacities.

We loaded a rental truck with some of my belongings and set off. When planning the trip, I had asked AAA to give us a route that was both fast, using the interstate highway system, and scenic, with sections on little-used back roads. Since I chose a diagonal route (based on the geometrical tenet that the shortest distance between two points is a straight line), we were routed through Pennsylvania, West Virginia, Kentucky, and Tennessee.

Once we cleared the New York City traffic and exited the New Jersey Turnpike, we began to relax. My friend really enjoys driving, and I enjoy watching the scenery. Often we drove along in a companionable silence, talking when his attention to the road could permit conversation.

Somewhere along the way—I can't remember exactly when and where—the subject of angels came up. I began talking about them and about some of my experiences. He was a bit skeptical, but interested. He's had positive experiences with some metaphysical methods he had learned, and we had compared notes on our different results with these techniques, but angels were a new idea for him.

Almost as a game to amuse us, every time we passed a church along the many lonely back roads we traveled—and there seemed to be one every few miles—I'd say, "Here's another angel coming along for the ride with us," or I'd call out toward the church, "Is there an angel who wants to come along with us?" And then I'd announce that we had taken on another angel passenger.

The little country churches we passed had curious denominational names I'd never heard of such as Church of the Holy Light, and Church of Eternal Peace. One was even called Church of the Heavenly Angels. As I kept inviting angels to come with us, he began taking part in what he considered a game, partly to humor me, partly to make the long hours on the road less boring.

Then, odd things began to happen. It appeared that we had made a wrong turn and were lost, on a long, unmarked dirt road. Being a city person, this rural desolation made him nervous and tense. He wanted to ask someone for directions, but we traveled for more than an hour without passing another vehicle or any service place or country store. We saw nothing but churches along the side of the road.

"Don't worry," I reassured him (for I was the navigator and responsible for reading the route maps correctly). "I'm sure we're on the right road. And, anyway, our angels know how to get where we're going." This remark did nothing to allay his fears that we were hopelessly lost and hours out of the way.

As we continued on the road, never meeting another vehicle, for another hour, his anxiety became palpable. He was convinced we should retrace our route to get back to the highway where we had made the turnoff to this "scenic route," about which he was complaining bitterly.

Trying to calm his worries, for it was nearly sunset and darkness was looming ahead, I spotted up ahead a church with a tall spire. It was a small community church, but there weren't any houses in sight.

"Look," I said, "we'll ask an angel to hop aboard when we pass that church." He looked at me as though I had lost my marbles. As we passed the little white-painted building, standing stalwart and alone on the road, I made a beckoning gesture, waving out the window, saying, "Hi, there. We need an angel to show us how to get to the highway."

Despite my angel talk, he was in "worst-case scenario" mood, certain we were lost and would end up having to spend a night in the truck in the middle of nowhere. We were debating the wisdom of turning back and, restudying the map, I saw a little road that I'd not noticed before and realized we indeed might have made a wrong turn.

As this unwelcome, unpleasant thought entered my head, just beyond the church we came upon a welcome sight: two

Listening to Angels

"When we listen, we hear our angel voices in the shadows and the light places of peace and darkness within us. . . . The voices of our angels bear witness to the triumphs of Spirit."

—Karen Goldman, *Angel Voices*

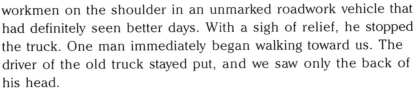

workmen on the shoulder in an unmarked roadwork vehicle that had definitely seen better days. With a sigh of relief, he stopped the truck. One man immediately began walking toward us. The driver of the old truck stayed put, and we saw only the back of his head.

Rolling down the window on my side, I greeted the man, asking if he was familiar with the area.

Laughingly, he replied, in a backcountry accent I'd never heard, "Ma'm, I'se *born* hereabouts. Not a square foot I don't know. Where you headin'?"

Showing him my map, I pointed to our destination. With his callused thumb, he traced a line on the map different from that marked by AAA.

"Yer goin' okay. Jus' take this here turn 'bout a mile down this road, then take a left for another three miles, and you'll hit the falls road."

With a chuckle he continued, "Yer cain't go wrong. Yer'll hear them falls long ere you git to the turn, make some noise they do!"

He laughed again, his blue eyes twinkling in his ruddy face, "Foller yer ears, and ye cain't miss them falls."

As I thanked him profusely, my friend—now in a state of relief and good humor—started the motor. As we began to move, I stuck my head out the window to wave a thankful goodbye, but saw nothing behind us but the long, empty dirt road and the tiny church in the distance. Where had they gone? The rearview mirror showed no image of anything, no men, no work vehicle. Did the angel I so playfully summoned from the little church really hop in with us and transform itself into a guide?

Following the directions we had been given, we indeed heard the roaring of the falls before we reached the turn. The sound of rushing water crashing down over cliffs of slate drowned out our conversation. For years I had wanted to visit the famous Falling Water house built by Frank Lloyd Wright, but I hadn't realized that there were massive waterfalls beyond the landmark structure, now a museum.

As we approached the turn, guided by the sound of the falls, my excitement mounted. At last I was going to actually *see* the famous structure about which I had only read and seen in photographs. As I chattered away about its history, we turned onto the main road and then soon came to the entrance driveway. Pulling in, we saw the way blocked by a chain. A small "Closed" sign dangled from it.

"Oh, no!" I cried. "I'll *never* have a chance to see it again." I was close to tears. Not knowing how to comfort me, my friend put the gear in reverse, preparing to back out. Just then, a man, apparently a gardener, in dirt-grimed blue overalls, appeared near the chain.

"Yer's wantin' to see the house?" he called out in the same accent used by the road workers.

"Oh, yes!" I said. "We're so sorry it's closed."

"Never yer mind, missy," he said, unhooking the chain. "Jus' yer drive right in thisa way."

Amazingly, we were given a private tour. As we thanked our guide before leaving and he rehooked the chain behind us, my friend muttered something under his breath.

"What?" I said.

"Angels."

One less skeptic in the world, I thought, and privately thanked our angelic companions for the wonderful private tour that to have missed would have broken my heart.

After that, every time we passed a church anywhere, in a city, a town, or on a country road, I invited angels to join us, and apparently they did, for we experienced numerous situations in which help just dropped out of the sky, so to speak. There were too many of them to relate here, so I will tell only one more.

When we arrived at our Texas destination, my friend turned in the rental truck in exchange for a rental car, staying with me at the house for a week to help me settle in, do shopping, and so on. I hadn't realized he had not taken out the extra insurance on the rented car until the day we came out of a restaurant and he yelped, "The car's been keyed." It was a phrase I'd never heard. Some local yokel had deliberately taken a key and made a deep scratch in the car's shiny surface.

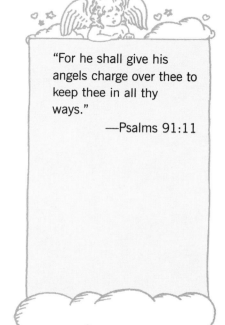

"For he shall give his angels charge over thee to keep thee in all thy ways."

—Psalms 91:11

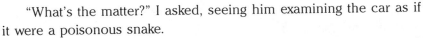

"What's the matter?" I asked, seeing him examining the car as if it were a poisonous snake.

"They'll charge me a mint for the damage," he cried angrily. I could see he was about to explode. "Don't worry," I said soothingly. "We'll just ask the Rental Car Angel to go along when you return the car."

Before he left to drive to the Houston airport for his flight back to Tucson, he said, "Could you send along an angel to get me upgraded into first class? I hate flying coach."

Why not? By this time, I was as prolific at creating names for angels as the old Hebrew patriarchs had been.

You won't be surprised at this point to learn that he called from Tucson to exclaim, "The angels work!" And then he told me what had happened when he turned in the keys: The receiving agent, bored and sleepy, didn't even bother to look at the car! Greatly relieved, he proceeded to his gate and waited for the flight to be called. Then, he heard a message over the public address system, asking him to check with the boarding gate agent. Doing so, he was told that his first-class upgrade had been approved! As you saw in the preceding tale, the Angel of the First Class Upgrade had evidently stuck close to him. And now he's a great believer in the angels. (He claims I have a personal hot line to them! But I make no such assertion. It's just a matter of getting—and staying—in touch.)

Close to the Edge

I'll close this chapter with a story by LouAnn Thomas of Plymouth, Indiana, that was published in the September/October 1999 issue of *Angels on Earth*.

In March last year, after weeks of excited preparation, my family finally arrived in Panama. My brother, Mike Hiser, an Army officer, was stationed there with his wife and young son, and we'd often dreamed of visiting them. Coordinating our adventure took work, including getting passports and visas for six of us—not to mention the packing! But handling details was an everyday task for me. As a supervisor for a national telecommunications company, I utilized a network of connections to keep things running smoothly for our customers.

Now I was on vacation. Jim and I had taken our three boys out of school, and our oldest son's girlfriend had joined us for this special trip. The isthmus of Panama connects North and South America, spanning from Costa Rica to Colombia. Seeing the famous canal was fun, of course, but we got as much enjoyment out of the lush tropical countryside and endless views of the water, the Pacific on one side and the Caribbean on the other. So different from the still wintry, landlocked home we'd left in Indiana!

One day Mike, Cindy and their son, Robbie, showed us around Old Panama City. The weather was sunny, so we packed a picnic and headed out to Colon, about two hours away on the northeastern side of the canal. Our destination was Fort San Lorenzo, 400-year-old ruins on a rocky site above the mouth of the Chagres River. Christopher Columbus landed there in 1503. With turrets and a history of pirates in search of gold, the place sounded irresistible, especially to the boys.

After an hour or so we crossed a picturesque bridge over Gatun Lake, and saw San Lorenzo standing prominently ahead. The area seemed desolate. "We're the only ones here," I said, vainly searching for other signs of life. It was too remote for me. I wanted to take a quick look and leave.

But the minute we parked the van, everyone set out in search of adventure. I strolled around the fort with my brother, snapping pictures. Finally, I saw a few other people. Mike and I found a ramplike incline leading to the top of the fort, and we slowly climbed up the crumbling structure. Cannon emplacements rusted along the walls. The sea crashed at the foot of the cliff below. Inside lay an open courtyard, strewn with fallen rocks. I shivered in the wind, and Mike put his arm around my shoulder.

Huge clouds gathered ominously in the sky. Staring upward at the shifting formations, Mikes said, "It looks like God is watching us." I looped my arm through his, trusting his words. Then my brother said he was hungry, so we began to round the kids up. I couldn't see Jason, Robbie, or my husband. I started getting worried. This was a big place; it could be dangerous.

Finally, I heard a welcome shout: "Mom!" It was Jason with Robbie at his side. They scurried up the incline, and I hugged them tight. "A quick picture," I said, "and then let's have that picnic."

Cindy and the boys posed together, flashing big smiles. I crouched slightly, ready to position the camera, wanting a perfect shot with that endless blue sea behind them. Glancing around, I decided to take a step backward to get a better view. I lifted my foot.

"Look out!" Jason yelled. "You're close to the edge!"

I lowered my foot, expecting to stand on the rim on the wall. But there was no rim. There was nothing to stand on!

I'm falling. I knew exactly what was happening. **In a second, I'll land on the ground.** But I was drifting, ever so slowly it seemed, like a leaf from an autumn tree. Then I heard a woman's voice, quiet and gentle. "You're going to fall much farther," she said. "Don't look down."

The voice soothed me. "Let your legs take the impact," she instructed. Relaxing, I closed my eyes, stretched my feet forward and extended my legs. The ground came up to meet me, and I felt as if my body exploded—quietly, though, like a drop of water on glass. There was no impact; no pain.

I opened my eyes, and I was lying twisted on the ground in the courtyard, my face in the dirt. Sean was at my side. Then I saw my husband, and my other two boys.

"Mike has his cell phone," Cindy said. "He'll get help." She hurried away to find him.

Soon there was a flurry of activity. Marines hovered around me. "We were training in the area," one said. "We got your brother's call." "I'm a medic," said another. He inserted an IV. Another medic told me I had multiple fractures. "Lie as still as you can," he said. That was easy. My elbow hurt, but otherwise I felt fine. Someone said I'd fallen 30 feet, but it didn't worry me. I was calm. Jim sat on the ground, holding my hand. Mike was beside me too. If I'd been told the woman who'd calmed me during my fall was somewhere close, I would have believed it. I heard her soothing voice all the while. "God is taking care of you," she said.

More people filled the courtyard: men from the film crew I'd spotted on the hillside, Air Force medics and an Army doctor from nearby Fort Sherman. The doctor told the medics I'd need pressure pants—huge plastic things pumped full of air to protect my legs. "They're sending a Blackhawk helicopter," a Marine said, holding a walkie-talkie to his ear. But a few minutes later he frowned and mumbled to a soldier, "She's not military. No helicopter," Everyone became quiet. The soldier whispered, but I caught his words. "Then she's done for," he said.

I still felt calm. **God's taking care of me**, I reminded myself. In a moment the walkie-talkie beeped, and the Marine put it to his ear. He smiled, and held up 10 fingers. The Blackhawk would arrive in 10 minutes. Jim squeezed my hand.

I was eased into the pressure pants, and put on a stretcher. Four Marines carried me slowly out of the fort, and into an open field. Soon the ground shook, and a roaring dragonfly of an aircraft landed nearby. I was carried over to it, and Jim climbed in with me as my stretcher was strapped into the helicopter.

An ambulance was waiting in Panama City when we landed, and the military police escorted us to the hospital. After taking the boys home, Cindy and Mike came to be with Jim and me.

Both of my legs had been shattered in the fall, and I'd also broken an arm, hip, and foot. I remained in the Panama hospital until I was stabilized for surgery. Sean had

Softly and gently, dearly
ransomed soul
In my most loving arms I
now enfold thee,
And, o'er the penal waters,
as they roll,
I poise thee, and I lower
thee, and hold thee.
And carefully I dip thee in
the lake,
And then, without a sob or
a resistance,
Dost through the flood thy
rapid passage take,
Sinking deep, deeper, into
the dim distance.
Angels, to whom the
willing task is given
Shall tend, and nurse, and
lull thee, as thou liest;
And Masses on the earth,
and prayers in heaven,
Shall aid thee at the
throne of the Most
Highest.
Farewell, but not for ever!
brother dear,
Be brave and patient on
thy bed of sorrow,
Swiftly shall pass thy night
of trial here,
And I will come and wake
thee on the morrow.
—Dom Wilmart, *Auteurs
spirituels et textes dévots*
(a book of ancient prayers
to the angel guardians)

to fly back to the States for college, but it was spring break for the other boys. Three weeks later we were home. I checked into a trauma center in the Indianapolis Methodist Hospital, and prepared for more surgery. Since the accident I've had 20 operations.

With regular physical therapy I'm walking again, and I've gone back to work full-time. I take pride in my job, but I'm even more aware that I can't do it alone. A support network has to be in place. It's true in life as well. "God is taking care of you," I was told at San Lorenzo. And he was, through one angel's comforting voice, and all the others he'd put in place to help me.

LouAnn's brother must have been right when he said, "It looks like God is watching us."

Angel Organizations

The AngelWatch Foundation, Inc.
P.O. Box 1397
Mountainside, NJ 07092
Publishes *AngelWatch*, a bimonthly maga-
zine about angels. Subscriptions are $16
yearly in the United States and $20 in
Canada. For information, send a SASE.

Angel Collectors Club of America
16342 West 54th Avenue
Golden, CO 80403
This large club is for collectors of angel para-
phernalia. It has local chapters, round-
robins, a biannual convention, a newsletter,
and a roster. Annual dues are $12.

Angels of the World
2232 McKinley Avenue
St. Albans, WV 25177
AWI is a general interest club for those interested in angels and related matters. It has
round-robins, a bi-yearly convention, and a
club newsletter. Write for information.

Be an Angel Day
Angelic Alliance
P.O. Box 95
Upperco, MD 21155
This organization sponsors the annual Be an
Angel Day. Write or call Jane Howard at
410-833-6912.

Opus Sanctorum Angelorum (Work of the
Holy Angels)
Marian Center
134 Golden Gate Avenue
San Francisco, CA 94102
This is a worldwide Catholic organization
devoted to explaining angels and encour-
aging devotion to them.

Tapestry
P.O. Box 3032
Waquoit, MA 02536
Tapestry sponsors an annual conference
on angels. For information, write to
K. Martin-Kuri.

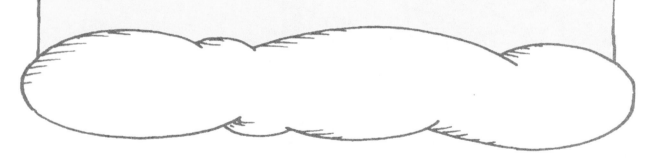

How to Recognize Angelic Presences

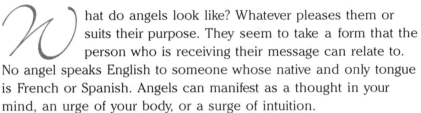

Angelic Presences

"One night as [June] lay in bed, she says, 'I felt a motion above my head, a slight moving of the air. I immediately knew it was the wings of an angel. I didn't see anything. There were no lights, no great drama. But I was so aware of a presence. I realized this is going on all the time; I just haven't known it. God's protective care surrounds me.' We yearn to know that the God who made us also holds our small lives in his hands. There is one sentence, writer Reynolds Price once wrote, that all humankind craves to hear: 'The Maker of all things knows and wants me.'"

—Timothy Jones, *Celebration of Angels*

What do angels look like? Whatever pleases them or suits their purpose. They seem to take a form that the person who is receiving their message can relate to. No angel speaks English to someone whose native and only tongue is French or Spanish. Angels can manifest as a thought in your mind, an urge of your body, or a surge of intuition.

This variability of angelic presences may account for the ease with which skeptics dismiss angel "sightings" or other evidences of these messengers, as if consistency of form were an appropriate characteristic for a divine messenger! We tend to see our angels as we have had them represented to us through our culture, which is actually as much a form of language as the tongue we speak. And just as languages are modified by dialect, so do angels fit their appearances to the circumstances involved.

The Christian West associates angels with white-robed, winged, humanlike figures. However, this popular conception of the angel is rarely what we actually perceive. Often, angels come in human or animal form, or they operate through the agency of a real human.

Angels are less often seen than they are *felt*—as presences, as thoughts, as ideas, as guidance. Often when I am searching for a reference, a book I wasn't looking for will catch my eye, and when I pick it up, it will fall open to precisely the information I need. Many writers have commented on this phenomenon, which the English writer Aldous Huxley called the Library Angel.

There are many ways you can tell if an angel is around. Sometimes there are sweet smells like flowers, or there can be a slight breeze. I have a hanging Tiffany glass lamp that sometimes sways gently back and forth when all the windows are closed and the air is entirely still. It's a signal that an angel is visiting me. Bodily sensations can also be caused by angels—in the form of heightened senses or in an altered state of consciousness that is conducive to the receiving of messages.

Some people hear sounds—bells, chimes, or trumpets. Some speculate that the sound of trumpets is actually the angels crashing through the sound barrier as they break into our dimension by lowering their vibrations.

Light is another angelic form of announcement. The word *angelos* in the original Greek means "messenger," and in this respect, the work of angels may be related to that of Mercury, or Hermes, one of whose daughters is called angel by Pindar. A daughter of Zeus, Iris—who, as the goddess of the rainbow, represents the magical bow of colored light we see in the sky—is described as an angel by the writer Hesiod. These terms suggest that an angel is a special carrier of messages from the gods, as was the case of the angel Gabriel announcing to the Virgin Mary that she was to become impregnated by the Holy Spirit. In paintings, angels with such messages often ride a beam of light.

The feeling of being suffused with love is another example of how one can feel or sense the presence of an angel, as was the case when I was visited by the pink glow and afterward felt that I was loved. Many others have reported this experience. It can be accompanied by some sort of phenomenon, such as the pink light I experienced, or it can just well up inside one on an ordinary day in one's usual routine of life. It's as if ordinary time suddenly stops and we are transported—even if only for a moment or two—into the sense that things are not as they seem, that someone or something is close by, looking after us and *caring what happens to us*. The chances of most of us having a dramatic angelic experience or vivid visionary tour of heaven's realms is relatively slim, but the *sensing* of angelic presence is available to all who are willing to pay attention. The mere fact that angels are all around attests to a myriad of unseen activities beyond our usual conscious awareness.

Ordinarily, we slip accidentally into such experiences, and they are fleeting and ephemeral. But they can be found regularly if only we become silent and wait for them to appear before our inner eye. These hints of another reality—these momentary liftings of the veil between the worlds—come to us when we are aware and *listening* for their soft tread in our inner landscape.

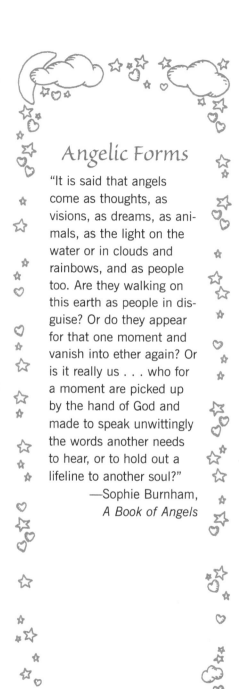

Angelic Forms

"It is said that angels come as thoughts, as visions, as dreams, as animals, as the light on the water or in clouds and rainbows, and as people too. Are they walking on this earth as people in disguise? Or do they appear for that one moment and vanish into ether again? Or is it really us . . . who for a moment are picked up by the hand of God and made to speak unwittingly the words another needs to hear, or to hold out a lifeline to another soul?"

—Sophie Burnham,
A Book of Angels

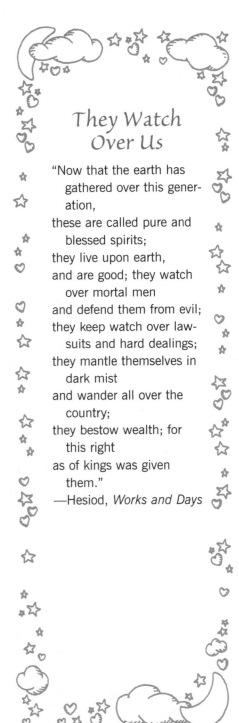

Silence

Contact with the angels occurs in the quiet stillness, when mind and heart are at rest. This point of silence is comparable to "the still point at the center of the turning wheel." This still center is the gateway between the striving ego and the angelic realm seeking our attention. To find our center, we must become quiet and still. Only then can we thread our way through the usual untidy jumble of our colliding thoughts to that place within where the spirit dwells.

Silence is the road to the center of the self. It is in our silences that we experience unity and recognize ourselves as being part of the All. This is the essence of sensing the nearness of angels. Almost everyone has had the experience at some time, perhaps while sitting by a lake in silence and solitude, gazing at a sleeping child, or caught alone and awestruck by a magnificent sunset on a country road. These are mystical moments that connect us to the larger totality of which we are an integral part. We are transfixed and transformed for the moment. It's difficult to describe the feeling, and we have no adequate words for that sense of having stepped outside our normal boundaries into something grand and inspiring. It always happens in silence.

Often, just slowing down a bit—letting ourselves be a witness to our own multilayered lives—is an illuminating experience. As we progress through our silence to the still point within, we peel away the layers of miscellaneous thought that have impeded our contact with the angelic world that lies beneath our every thought and action. Through the practice of silence we open ourselves to direct experience of the Most High.

Silence is not merely the absence of sound. It is a restful space that we inhabit when we are feeling our most free and uninhibited. Like pointers on a spiritual roadmap, silence leads to the next step we are required to take for our continued growth and development. Silence is a great spiritual master who guides us and illuminates our way when it is dark. In the silence of the inner self, we reach *gnosis*, or truth, and in so doing, we find our angels there, guiding and gracing us, delivering the messages we need to hear.

The angels want to help us, and they want us to be able to recognize their presence in our lives. But often their "still, small voices" cannot be heard through the jumble of sound and miscellaneous thought with which we entertain and occupy ourselves.

Why is silence so hard to bear? Do we fear that in silence we will hear what we do not want to hear? Are we afraid of discovering that life can be lived at different levels?

In order to experience the presence of angels, you must *dare to turn off the sound.* In order to come to your spiritual center, you have to stake out a territory of silence, wage a war of personal independence over the tyranny of noise pollution. To experience the angels is to be silent, at least for some of the time. Try turning off all the electronic sound conveyors and listening instead to the simpler sounds around you. You might hear a baby bird peeping, a child babbling, a cat's footfall, rain dripping, your own breathing—or perhaps the flutter of an angel's wings, or an angel singing.

As you allow yourself to become aware of the mystical power of *silence*, of the natural silences that fall in the interstices of the flow of sound, you open your senses to the perception of the presence of angels, for they are always there, just waiting to be recognized and given your attention.

The angels are everywhere around us, but it is our responsibility to make ourselves open to their presence by eliminating the excess noise we permit and even encourage in our lives.

Demanding silence for one's self in this society requires a major leap of faith. Not only must we overcome obstacles merely to obtain some silence in our busy lives, but we must also jealously guard that silence against noisy invaders, including the ones inside who may try to sabotage our efforts to be silent. Given silence unexpectedly—whether a few moments or a few hours—most of us apprehensively reach out for the nearest sound with which to distract ourselves. Realize that silence is not the enemy. It is the great mother lode of the angelic realm.

Fortunately, you do not have to retire to a monastery or become a hermit to experience the contemplative silence that is at the heart of experiencing the angelic world. You can achieve your

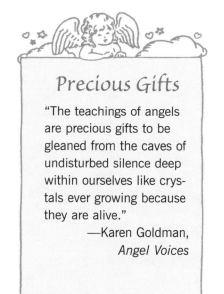

Precious Gifts

"The teachings of angels are precious gifts to be gleaned from the caves of undisturbed silence deep within ourselves like crystals ever growing because they are alive."
—Karen Goldman,
Angel Voices

own silence, contact your still center, and recognize the presence of angels by practicing silence on a daily basis.

Solitude

If silence is golden, solitude is a precious jewel. The historian Edward Gibbon called solitude "the school of genius," and Karen Goldman, in *Angel Voices*, echoes the sentiment: "Our angel voices come from a place where we do not think, from a quietness inside us and all around us, from a pristine place . . . perfect within us."

Solitude, that necessary adjunct to recognizing the angelic presences that surround us at all times, is, in our socially driven society, as difficult to attain as is silence. If we fear silence, we see solitude as the ultimate negative state. Instead of being recognized as a treasure-house of sublime gifts, all too often, being alone is viewed as a noxious condition to be remedied at once. And if we cannot fill the empty spaces with living people, the flickering color images on the TV set or the chattering of the endless supply of radio talk shows will do as well.

Yet, like silence, solitude is "the necessary thing." Without it we are consumed in the backwash of others' lives. Lacking solitude, we are lonely despite the presence of others . . . lonely because we are not in touch with our deepest selves. When we fill up our hours, days, years, whole lives with the constant presence of others, we forfeit the opportunity to know ourselves. Neglecting or abandoning this innermost self reaps a bitter harvest. We feel we don't know who we truly are, and indeed we do not, having never bothered to go within where the true self dwells, the self that is open to recognizing the angel within who only awaits awakening to give us a glimpse of our personal paradise. The angels do not conceal themselves from us; we hide from them by refusing the gifts of solitude.

Somehow we feel that the solitary individual is to be pitied as inferior, deficient in some way—unable or unwilling to make "significant" relationships with others. Yet, the world's most creative artists

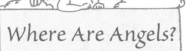

Where Are Angels?

"Angels are found hovering in the pauses and spaces between our imaginings; between our feelings and thoughts and perceptions; whenever we forget ourselves for a moment and do not hold on too tightly to our pain. The angels need room to enter in and, likewise, to come out."
—Karen Goldman,
Angel Voices

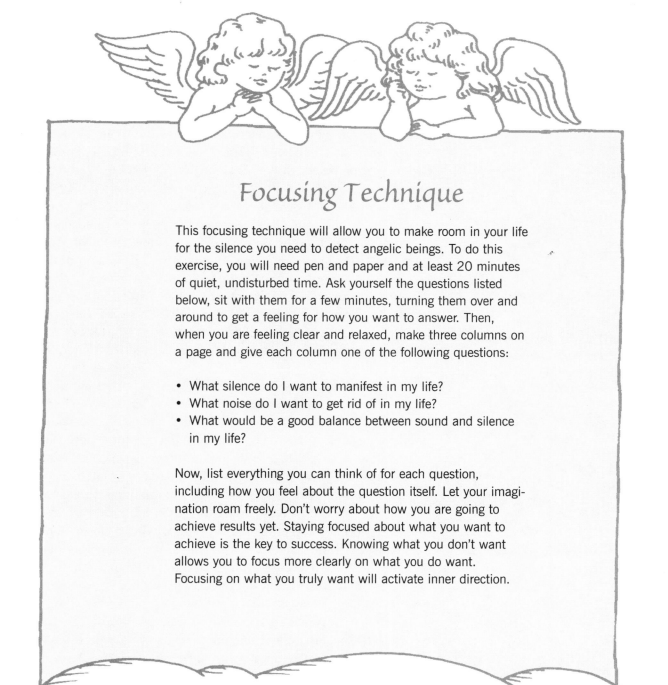

Focusing Technique

This focusing technique will allow you to make room in your life for the silence you need to detect angelic beings. To do this exercise, you will need pen and paper and at least 20 minutes of quiet, undisturbed time. Ask yourself the questions listed below, sit with them for a few minutes, turning them over and around to get a feeling for how you want to answer. Then, when you are feeling clear and relaxed, make three columns on a page and give each column one of the following questions:

- What silence do I want to manifest in my life?
- What noise do I want to get rid of in my life?
- What would be a good balance between sound and silence in my life?

Now, list everything you can think of for each question, including how you feel about the question itself. Let your imagination roam freely. Don't worry about how you are going to achieve results yet. Staying focused about what you want to achieve is the key to success. Knowing what you don't want allows you to focus more clearly on what you do want. Focusing on what you truly want will activate inner direction.

and writers have by and large preferred solitude to company. And the great visionaries whose encounters with angels have come down to us through various sources such as the Bible, the Koran, and other mystical religious writings like those of St. Catherine, have had their experiences of angels alone. The prophets of old retired to mountain caves for days of solitary meditation before their visions occurred. It would seem that solitude is indeed "the necessary thing" if one wants to experience the presence of angels.

Abraham Maslow, the psychologist who identified *peak experiences*, those moments of feeling total unity—a recognition of the Self in the All—said that the ability to have peak experiences is dependent upon being free of other people, "which in turn means that we become much more . . . our authentic selves, our real identity." Maslow's approach differs considerably from those who propose that the entire meaning of life is derived from interpersonal relationships.

Complete happiness, that oceanic feeling of perfect harmony between the inner and outer worlds is at best an infrequent experience, but the most profound psychological and spiritual experiences invariably take place internally, witnessed only by the "indwelling self." Rarely, and then only distantly, are these experiences related to interaction with other human beings. Human adaptation to the world is largely a product of the imagination and the development of an inner world in which to shield the self from the vagaries of the outer world. Without this inner world, without a strong and well-built structure within, the outer world seems threatening and dangerous. The ability to remove one's self, to be "totally immersed, fascinated, and absorbed in the present, in the here and now, enables us to interact with those angelic presences from whom we receive much guidance and protection. When we are in this state, we invite the angels in, and they in turn answer questions emanating from our depths, questions that we may not have known needed to be asked.

It seems that the human psyche is so constructed that the discovery or creation of unity in the internal world produces a sense of wholeness or unity in the outer world; it's like a mirror reflection. This is what is meant by the New Age saying, "You create

The Power of Silence

"Daily silence experienced in humility and fervour as an indispensable exercise in spiritual nourishment gradually creates within us a permanent state of silence. The soul discovers in such a silence unsuspected possibilities. It realizes that life can be lived at different levels."
—Pierre Lacout, *God Is Silence*

your own reality." Outer happenings and inner experience interact with one another. Mind and matter are not only inseparable; they affect one another. Thus, when the inner plane is in harmony with itself, the outer world seems to follow suit, almost magically.

We do not know for certain *how* and *why* this works, but the evidence suggests that communion with the inner self aligns us with the cosmos, with the right and natural order of all things. One might say that we are deliberately getting in tune with the harmonic chords of the universe. And when we are in tune, we produce effects.

Angels in Dreams

Angels can also appear in dreams. Though I have dreamed of angels frequently, one dream stands out from all the others. I call it Dream of the Angelo. To explain the fascinating interweaving of the dream process, I should also note that when I lived in Italy I was close to a man named Raphaelle (a form of the name Raphael), who was a Caprese. It happens that the people who live on the island of Capri are genetically closer to their forebears than are others in Italy, and one finds there faces that are startlingly similar to the faces seen in the art of the Renaissance. For example, I took a photograph of a Caprese child who looked as though he had just stepped from a painting by one of the great Italian masters. My friend Raphaelle had such a fifteenth-century face and could have posed for a portrait by his famous namesake.

Dream of the Angelo:

I am asleep in my own bed when I am awakened abruptly by a loud knocking at the door to my apartment, which alarms me, as it is the middle of the night. I call out, "Who's there?" and am answered by a rough, gangster-type voice that says, "Angelo!" in a preemptory manner, commanding and demanding. As I know no one named Angelo, and as the voice was threatening—I thought of the "mob"—I don't answer. The knocking grows louder and more insistent, as if to say, "Open up or else."

The Sanctuary Within

For many people, solitude is a difficult commodity to come by; there are constant demands on one's time and physical presence. While you are working your way through to finding more solitude in your life, you can find a place of solitude within. Once you have done this and it has become real for you, a sense of calm and ease will suffuse you. Think of this as your inner sanctuary, a place where you can recharge your batteries and make contact with your deep inner self. Creating a place of inner solitude is not difficult. Here's how it is done:

To create your own private sanctuary, find a time when you can be alone and undisturbed for a half-hour. Spend a few minutes breathing slowly and rhythmically and allowing your body to relax completely.

Now, create in your mind a picture of a lovely place. It might be a secluded spot in a woods or a cove on a beach. It can be outdoors or indoors. Letting yourself feel relaxed and free, think in a leisurely way about what a sanctuary would mean to you. As this picture emerges (you don't actually have to *see* it, you only have to *know* it), let yourself be absorbed into its quiet, beauty, silence, and sense of comforting solitude.

When you have an image in your mind or a feeling about what your sanctuary is like, continue to fill in all the details. Imagine what a "room of your own" would be and feel like. What would you put there? A comfortable chair? A bowl of fresh flowers? Pictures on the wall? Make this picture as complete as you possibly can, with colors, smells, and textures. Walk about the environment you are creating and claim it for your own personal place of inner solitude.

When you feel that you have taken complete possession of your special place, perform a symbolic gesture—such as writing your name or placing a favorite object there—that will enable you to return to you sanctuary at will. The purpose is to make it easy for you to recall this experience. Then, breathe slowly and quietly for a few minutes before returning yourself to normal waking consciousness.

You have now created a place of inner solitude. It is yours to command. You can return anytime you want, whenever you choose or need a space to practice being alone and quiet.

I call out, "What do you want?" and the answer is unintelligible, like rapidly spoken dialect, which bears little resemblance to the language from which it derives. (The Italian island of Capri, where I lived for a year, has such a dialect, and even those who speak Italian fluently cannot understand these variations.)

I do not answer the door, and the man finally goes away. The dream progresses to evening. I am giving a party. My friend Raphaelle suddenly appears on the little balcony outside my living room window, sitting cross-legged like an elf. He is handsome and smiling as I remember him. As I go to the window to welcome him and invite him inside, I wonder how he got up the three flights to my balcony. Inside, he guides me through the throng of partygoers and out into the hall, where he says he has something to tell me. We sit on the steps above my landing, and he relates a fascinating story to me about my ancestry, disclosing the history of four generations, about whom in real life I know virtually nothing. He says that each generation has written a book about itself. This history was, however, incomplete because I was not included. I was, he said, "a missing character."

The stories he told me about four generations of my family were absolutely fascinating, and I longed to read these books. I asked about the book of my own generation, and he replied, "It is already written. It only needs for you to make it complete."

Sitting with him in the dimly lit hall with the noise of the party in the background was cozy and comforting, and I was mesmerized by the family story he related. I thought about writing such a book. But the books—all of them—were already written. I wondered how I fit in. How could I get myself into the books so that they could be complete? I didn't know the answer, and he didn't tell it to me.

He said he had to leave, and I was sad to see him go. I woke feeling that he had actually been there, and it took several minutes for me to realize it had been a dream. Though I could not remember what was in the books, I woke with the same thought I had had in the dream: that I would dearly love to write such a book as he had described to me.

My interpretation of this dream is that Angelo, unable to gain entry through the front door, a symbol for the conscious mind, had transformed himself into a figure with which I was familiar and could therefore accept. Raphael is, of course, the name of one of the powerful archangels, and Angelo had scared me with his power. The message was clear: I do have ancestors, and though they are unknown to me, I am not unknown to them. The angel has come to tell me that "I" am missing—that is, that I have a book to write that will put me in the family archives. For a long time, I had wanted to research both the maternal and paternal sides of my family and to write an autobiographical book about my search for my roots. The angel's message was not only that the time to write the book had come but that *the book is already written*, as indeed all books are already written in the divine mind. One has only to set one's fingers to the keyboard or take pen to paper and allow the doors of the great cosmic repository to open and present their treasures.

Recognizing the Presence of an Angel

Be on the alert. If you feel the presence of an angel, become still and wait for a message. As you become more and more aware of their presence, you will draw them closer and experience them more often. Many of them are coming closer to the human realm in this period of the birth of a new age. They are coming to serve as a bridge between our many individual souls and the ultimate cosmic consciousness that is ready to manifest in all who are ready to receive its energy and message of love and peace to all everywhere. Listen with your ears, eyes, mind, emotions, body, and—above all—your heart.

If you travel without an inner stillness, you are at risk of being cut off from the wisdom of angel guidance. But once you allow yourself to claim your right to be silent, to enjoy solitude, you will be able to sense the presence of the angels and hear them singing.

Working with Breath

Angels, we are told, are pure spirit, and we can enhance our connection to that world simply by using breath techniques (*breath* is synonymous with *spirit*). God "blew upon the waters and the world was created." By becoming aware of our breathing, we become aware of our spiritual nature, for breath is life. Thus, we can use our life breath, as a yogi does, to elevate our consciousness to the realm where the angels dwell.

Breath is the gateway to the sacred angelic dimension. It is something we take for granted, for we could hardly function if we had to consciously remember to breathe. Most of us are unaware of our breathing until it becomes impaired, by a cold or by shortness of breath. When we become aware of our breathing, we connect to the link we have with our spiritual selves. Awareness and control of breath allows us to consciously open ourselves to our innate sacred realm.

Most Eastern philosophies teach that we live in a sea of vital energy and that we absorb and activate this with our breath. The Hindu yogi tradition calls this energy prana. Oriental mind-body balancing techniques such as acupuncture and shiatzu refer to this vital force as Qi (chi). The Hawaiian Huna tradition calls it mana (mana loa in its highest form). In the Hawaiian language, the word *mana-o* means "to think."

Working with breath is a form of spiritual practice. Controlled breathing permits us to extract new energy from the air. Our physical bodies can store this energy in the same way food is stored as fat. When this subtle energy is in short supply, you feel down, listless, and tired, and you can become ill. When it is in abundant supply, you feel "up," energized, optimistic, and full of energy. Though the energy is subtle, it is very real.

You can prove this to yourself by paying attention to the ion content of the air you breathe. Air is charged with positive and negative ions, and a surplus of the former results in an oppressively heavy atmosphere, like that before a thunderstorm. Positive ions sap our energy. Think of how you feel when a storm is brewing and the sky lowers darkly. Negative ions release uplifting energy into the air. When the storm breaks and the rain comes pelting down, the

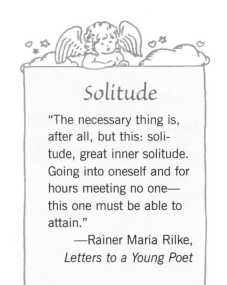

Solitude

"The necessary thing is, after all, but this: solitude, great inner solitude. Going into oneself and for hours meeting no one— this one must be able to attain."

—Rainer Maria Rilke, *Letters to a Young Poet*

air is clear and refreshed. Your spirits lift, and your mood brightens. You feel energized and ready to go. Proper deep breathing has the effect of saturating your system with negative ions, contributing to the release of tension and to mental calmness, the state in which angels visit you.

This energy is subtle, but it is real. Yogis claim that it not only gives vitality to the body but that it also nourishes the spiritual self. A high content of prana in the system causes the unfolding of natural abilities—mental, physical, emotional, and spiritual. Prana is there whether or not we are aware of it. But when we make a deliberate effort to increase it, blocked channels of information open up. The breath is a powerful tool for bringing forth the sacred dimension in ourselves. Conscious breathing develops a communications link between body and mind, between conscious and unconscious, between spirit and angels.

Relaxation

Another important clue to being able to recognize angelic presences is the ability to *relax*. When we are in a state of tension, which is the habitual condition of most of us, we wouldn't be able to recognize an angel if it poked us in the eye with a beam of heavenly light.

Most of us are just too busy to leave uncluttered time and space open for an angel to enter into. We lead lives dominated by such hectic schedules that relaxation seems to evade us most of the time. Why? The answer is not completely clear, but clues can be found in our outlook on life. When we look upon life as an adversary or threat, we are in a perpetual state of "fight-or-flight." Instead of releasing the tension when danger is past, we store it; this retention results in a dangerous buildup that can bring on stress-related disease such as high blood pressure, ulcers, and the like. It seems almost superfluous to add that in such a state, the gentle presence of an angel will go unnoticed.

In the late 1960s, Harvard cardiologist Herbert Benson was involved in some physiologic tests on meditators. He discovered that relaxation methods, of which there are many, caused both

Rhythmic Breathing

Rhythmic breathing is simple, but if practiced daily, it will release inner power to you. A simple basic exercise, it is a way to harmonize body, mind, and spirit. This breathing technique can be used anytime, and you can do it almost anywhere, whether sitting quietly at home, in your car, or on a train.

Relax and close your eyes. Observe your breath pattern, but do not make any attempt to alter it. Merely pay attention to the breath going in and coming out. Now, begin to breathe slowly and deeply. Breathe in through the nostrils and out through the mouth. As you breathe in, feel the coolness of fresh air coming in. Then, feel the warmth of used air leaving your body. Imagine yourself being cleansed and energized by each breath.

Next, listen to any sounds you make while breathing. Do not judge; just listen. Also notice whether you breathe in shallow or deep breaths and where the air goes, into the diaphragm or into the belly. Does your chest rise and fall or does your abdomen rise and fall?

As you inhale each breath, be aware of the flow of air coming into and leaving your body. Follow the inhalation/exhalation cycle and see whether you can find the point at which they intersect. Actually, breath is one continuous movement, but we tend to separate the in-breath from the out-breath when we think about breathing. Continue doing this for several minutes. The object is to become aware of your own breath, to monitor its natural cycle of movement, and nothing more. Imagine it filling up all the cells of your body like you would fill a balloon by blowing air into it. Let the sense of being filled with prana spread throughout your body. Do not force or strain.

Guidelines for Attracting Angels

Make room in your life for silence every day.

Create a space in your life for the practice of solitude.

Practice focused breathing daily.

Practice relaxation meditations regularly in a calm, comfortable surrounding, away from distractions.

psychological and *physiological* changes that served to counterbalance the body's response to "fight-or-flight." He called this the "relaxation response." Not a technique but a coordinated series of internal changes occurring when the mind and body become calm and tranquil, the relaxation response can be achieved by numerous means, including deep breathing, muscle relaxation, meditation, visualization, and prayer. The simplest of these is called "focused meditation." Benson's tests showed that persons who simply sat quietly with their minds focused on a single word, idea, or thought could markedly change their physiology, decreasing metabolism, slowing heart and respiratory rates, and exhibiting brain waves comparable to the dream state. We already have shown that the dream state is a prime source of angelic communications, as are the altered states of consciousness we tend to call a "brown study," or reverie.

Physical relaxation can be an important adjunct to a spiritual practice. Using a relaxation technique regularly will make you more aware of the soft tread of an angel's feet or the beat of angelic wings.

Breathing Relaxation

This is a simple technique that takes only a little time. Sit or lie down in a safe and comfortable spot where there are no distractions. Loosen any tight clothing; unbutton or untie anything that is restrictive on your body. Begin to breathe *consciously*, following your breath in and out of your lungs. Breathe in through the nostrils and out through the mouth. Pay full attention to your breath, in and out, in and out. Listen to the sound and feel the rhythmic pulsing of it. Continue this until you begin to feel calm and relaxed, a state usually signaled by the breath becoming slow and even.

You can deepen your relaxation using breath by imagining that you are breathing in prana, or the vital force of life, and exhaling all tension and negative feeling or experience. One way to do this is to choose one color for the prana and another color for the negative energy and then to see a stream of the positive color coming into your body as you inhale and a stream of the negative color flowing out of you as you exhale. White and black are easy; white is the pure energy of light, and black represents any dark thoughts. But feel free to use the colors that represent to you the positive and the negative energy. Don't worry if distracting thoughts arise. Let them float away (you can tell them you will attend to their needs later) like soap bubbles in the air and return your attention to your breathing.

CHAPTER SEVENTEEN

Communicating
with Angels

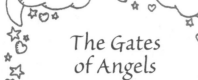

The Gates of Angels

"There are two gates to the realm of angels. Through one we can move toward them; through the other they can come to us. At night before sleeping we can look back over the day, recalling events, seeking to find the wisdom behind them. Our gratitude for what comes to meet us strengthens the connection with our angel and makes it easier for him to help. Prayer before sleeping prepares our souls for the inspirations we can receive during sleep. The other gate opens in the morning upon waking . . . we become conscious of the 'plan for the day,' of the gifts from the spirit waiting for us. . . . Merely being aware of their existence opens the soul to their influence."

—James H. Hindes, *Angel and Mortals*

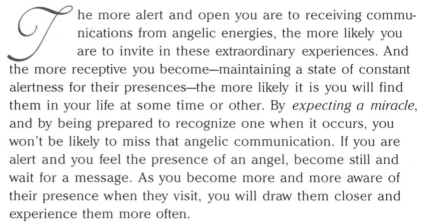

The more alert and open you are to receiving communications from angelic energies, the more likely you are to invite in these extraordinary experiences. And the more receptive you become—maintaining a state of constant alertness for their presences—the more likely it is you will find them in your life at some time or other. By *expecting a miracle*, and by being prepared to recognize one when it occurs, you won't be likely to miss that angelic communication. If you are alert and you feel the presence of an angel, become still and wait for a message. As you become more and more aware of their presence when they visit, you will draw them closer and experience them more often.

Many of them are coming closer to the human realm in this birth of a new age. They are coming to serve as a bridge between ourselves and the ultimate cosmic consciousness that is ready to manifest in all who are ready to receive its energy and message of love and peace. Listen with your ears, eyes, mind, emotions, body, and—above all—heart.

Angels are everywhere. You might not see them, but you can always sense them. And when you begin to have contact with them, such experiences are likely to occur frequently. There are many ways to contact angels. But the three methods most effective and easily used are *invoking*, *dreaming*, and *writing*.

Invoking the Angels

To call forth an angel or a spirit, practice this invocation. First, enter your sacred space and sit in silence and stillness. Center yourself. Then ask the spirits to come forth. As you say the words, imagine that you see a beautiful white angel with its wings spread protectively.

Angels have long been associated with the four corners, or the four directions, or the four elements. As you speak the invocations, stand facing the direction indicated.

Spirits of Fire (West)

I call upon the Angels of Fire to bring love, protection, and safety. May the warmth of the lifegiving fire come into my being and guide me. May the strength of the sun come to me and illuminate me on my way.

Spirits of Earth (North)

I call upon the Angels of Earth to bring love, protection, and safety. May the regenerative and restorative power of the earth ground me and guide my way. May the renewing power of the moon come to me and light my path.

Spirits of Air (East)

I call upon the Angels of Air to bring love, protection, and safety. May the gentle winds of heaven blow always and imbue me with their airborne energies. May the communication power of Mercury come to me and guide my way.

Spirits of Water (South)

I call upon the Angels of Water to bring love, protection, and safety. May the waters of heaven cleanse and purify me. May the flowing and regenerative powers of water come to me and guide my way.

Before your perform any invocation, decide what spot or area is the center, or heart, of the situation or matter. If the home is the center, choose the area of the home that seems appropriate. For some, the family room is the heart-center of the house, for others, the kitchen, and so on. Once you have located the center—even if it is not a material space but an inner condition, such as your desire for a happy marriage, or a child, or a new job, sit in perfect silence and stillness for a few minutes, visualizing an angel coming forth at your request. Imagine this angel beaming a beautiful bright white light at you from its head. Ask for the blessing or help you desire. Afterwards, thank the angel for coming.

Angels for Specific Needs

To invoke an angel for a specific purpose, concentrate your thoughts on that purpose and perform appropriate rituals. For example, if you want to call forth an angel for your home, especially if you have just moved into a new place, first do a thorough cleaning of the premises. *Always* get rid of what you don't need, don't use, or don't like. Angels are repelled by unnecessary clutter; it inhibits their freedom of movement and entry. And, quite naturally, they appreciate being invited into a clean environment, just as any guest would.

Children have a special affinity for angels. If you have them, you might want to invoke an angel for each of their bedrooms.

Writing to Angels

Letter Writing

Another way to contact angels is through letter writing. Writing to the angels is a wonderful way to align with their energies and connect with them, and writing them will allow you to gain clarity on your personal issues. When you write to the angels, you establish a mind-heart link between them and you.

Angels of Fire would bring more active love energy, protect outdoor adventures, and make safe courses of action. Angels of Earth would bring more stable love energy, protect the home and family, and make safe the hearth, childbirth, or feminine concerns. Angels of Air would bring more variable love energy, protect intellectual pursuits, and make safe enterprises having to do with air, such as flying. Angels of Water would bring more spiritual love, protect creative pursuits, and make safe anything having to do with water, such as boating or taking a cruise.

You can write to your personal angel, or you can write to all the different kinds of angels mentioned in Chapter 11. Also, you can write to angels on behalf of other people or about other people. For example, if you are uncertain about how someone feels about you, you can write and ask that person's angel for clarification. Or if a person is ill, you can write and ask his or her angel for healing.

Angel letters are no different than letters you write to friends. Just begin with the salutation "Dear Angel of . . . " It's always a good idea to do a breathing relaxation exercise to center yourself before writing to an angel. It's best to write in silence and solitude, though I've written letters to angels on airplanes and in hospital waiting rooms filled with people. Angels aren't bothered by exterior noise so much, but they don't like mind-noise interfering with the communication. So, try to keep your celestial hot line free of static.

When writing, don't be intimidated by the blank sheet of paper. Just let the words flow from your heart. Don't worry about grammar, spelling, punctuation, or writing style, your angel is your spiritual guide, not your English teacher. Date your letter, give thanks in advance for the answer, and sign it. You won't need a stamp!

Then make your own angel postbox. It can be any kind of a receptacle, even a shoe box covered in pretty paper. Or, you can put the letter under your pillow or in a place where you keep special mementos. Once you have "mailed" your angel letter, put it out of your mind. Don't hang about worrying when you'll get an answer. It will come at the appropriate time and in the appropriate manner.

Journal Writing

Angel journals provide another way to contact angels. In fact, keeping a journal about your angels is a spiritual practice. Such a journal can tell you where you have been, and show you where you are going. It can serve as a channel into your higher self.

At times when life seems like a lonely trek through an unknown and unpopulated wilderness, an angel journal can offer wonderful companionship. It is truly a friend. Often people say to me, when they learn that I write books, "You should write about *me*. My life would make a great book." And it is true. Everyone's life would make a great book, and everyone should write the book of his or her life to honor our uniqueness.

Such writing puts you in touch with your celestial helpers because it clears out the "forebrain chatter"—that never-ending inner dialogue we have with ourselves, mostly criticizing our faults—that interferes with clear reception from your angels. Talk to your angels as you would talk to a trusted confidante whose advice you trust.

Think of your angel journal as "The Book of My Life" and consider it a friend who will always be there to heal, uplift, and celebrate with you. Going back to pages you have written in the past can be an illuminating experience. You may wonder if the person who wrote those lines a few weeks ago was really you.

Special Angelic Colors

Angels have special colors. You can either wear the appropriate color when writing or use paper in the color of the angel to whom you are writing.

Rose, soft green—
   guardian angels of
   the home
Deep sapphire blue—
   healing angels
Sky blue—Angels of
   maternity and birth
White—Ceremonial angels;
   music angels
Apple green—
   Nature angels
Yellow—Angels of art
   and beauty

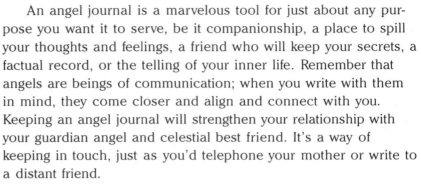

An angel journal is a marvelous tool for just about any purpose you want it to serve, be it companionship, a place to spill your thoughts and feelings, a friend who will keep your secrets, a factual record, or the telling of your inner life. Remember that angels are beings of communication; when you write with them in mind, they come closer and align and connect with you. Keeping an angel journal will strengthen your relationship with your guardian angel and celestial best friend. It's a way of keeping in touch, just as you'd telephone your mother or write to a distant friend.

Your angel journal will allow you to communicate with the many layers of yourself, to experiment with forms of expression, and to mirror your many facets. A superb exploratory vehicle, writing about your life's experiences, both inward and outward, can bring fascinating insights and be full of delightful surprises, as well as connect you with your celestial partner, who is interested in all the facets of your life, both light and dark.

To begin an angel journal, you don't need much, just a pen and some paper, a private space if it is available, perhaps a lighted candle or some incense. But these enhancements aren't necessary. I know people who can write in the middle of a traffic jam. One man carries his notebook in his glove compartment just for that purpose. He says writing about angels while those about him are "losing it" keeps him calm and collected. Others comfortably write while commuting on a train or bus.

The charm of angel writing is that it is entirely private. You can think of this activity as a way of manifesting into concrete reality all the thought forms and feelings that float around inside you. No matter where you are in your life—at the beginning, in the middle, or near the end—I would encourage you to begin an angel journal, lest you miss them unawares!

Whatever you are doing now, wherever you are in your life, you are on a spiritual quest. You may call it something else—a search for meaning, finding yourself, or getting in touch with what you really want to do in life. Labels are unimportant. The spiritual quest *is* life, and life is a spiritual quest. It is the center, the still point at the hub of the turning wheel of fortune, out of which all else comes, and the angels are our companions and helpers on this quest.

Remember that there is a special angel for every day of the week. Sunday is Michael, Monday is Gabriel, Tuesday is Samael, Wednesday is Raphael, Thursday is Sachiel, Friday is Anael, and Saturday is Cassiel. You can address your letters or communications to these angels on their own days. There is also a special angel for every hour of each day of the week! That's too many angels to list here, but you don't have to address them by name; they'll know. You can send a celestial e-mail to the angel of 2:00 P.M. on Friday if, say, you have a presentation to make at that time, or a medical procedure scheduled.

The real core of our spirit is tucked away in the corners of everyday life. We can sense an angel presence when we are diapering the baby, washing the car, taking a shower, vacuuming the rug, building a shelf, raking the lawn, or shopping for groceries. Angels accompany us when we stand in line at the bank, make a travel reservation, eat at a restaurant, or spend the day lounging around at home. Although angels do appear in extraordinary circumstances (the ones we most often hear about), the comingling of the inner, private self with the details of life's commonplaces is the means by which we most often meet angels. It is in this living of our everyday lives that we find the spirit, the real soul food that nourishes us.

Our angel journal, and the keeping of it as a record, is a transformational process not unlike what artists undergo as they work on the material that forms their artwork while simultaneously working on the needs of their souls. By following our soul-directedness—what I call the "internal imperative"—we keep on the course that will fulfill who we truly are, without the societal and personal-traumatic overlays that have obscured the gold of our authentic selves.

Many people are plagued with self-consciousness when confronted with a blank page. They feel shy, as if meeting a powerful stranger for the first time. Worries about "how to do it" rise up and keep the mind from transmitting to the hand what needs to be written. But it need not be so. A journal is a private place and should be guarded from intrusion. We only need start the flow, and

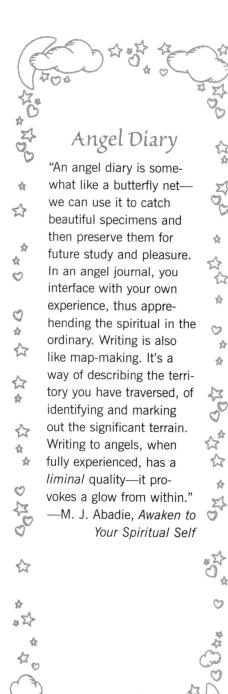

Angel Diary

"An angel diary is somewhat like a butterfly net— we can use it to catch beautiful specimens and then preserve them for future study and pleasure. In an angel journal, you interface with your own experience, thus apprehending the spiritual in the ordinary. Writing is also like map-making. It's a way of describing the territory you have traversed, of identifying and marking out the significant terrain. Writing to angels, when fully experienced, has a *liminal* quality—it provokes a glow from within."
—M. J. Abadie, *Awaken to Your Spiritual Self*

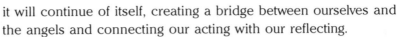

Angel Gold

"I often imagine what it must have been like for Howard Carter when after years of searching and digging in the inhospitable desert, he peered from amidst the outside rubble into the gold-filled tomb of Tutankhamen and stood stunned and speechless at the wondrous sight of wall-to-wall gold and bejeweled riches beyond comparison. Metaphorically speaking, this is the experience waiting for you as you proceed with what I call "soul excavation" and begin to unearth your own inner treasures. After much hard work and patient digging you will find *gold*, not the common gold of the marketplace, not even the polished gold of great treasure, but the gold of the soul."

—M. J. Abadie, *Awaken to Your Spiritual Self*

it will continue of itself, creating a bridge between ourselves and the angels and connecting our acting with our reflecting.

The nineteenth-century American writer Willa Cather spoke of "the furniture of the mind." She said, "Miracles seem to rest . . . upon our perceptions being made finer so that for a moment our eyes can see and our ears can hear that which is about us always." In other words, we can furnish our minds with our conscious observations of what is about and inside us.

A renaissance of personal writing is going on all around; people are writing their histories, probing their parents and grandparents for personal recollections. And autobiography, which was once considered naive in academic writing courses, is again popular. Many of today's angel books are filled with the recollections of those who have had angel encounters, but have heretofore kept quiet about them. Ordinary people living ordinary lives are "coming out of the closet" about angels and how they interact with our lives. Moreover, they are *writing* about these experiences.

Writing is a sorting process. It is also a great teacher. A dialogue with an angel is never dull or uninteresting. Once you get to know your angel, your deeper levels will become activated. And you will have the ultimate reward of actually experiencing your own life firsthand, not just living vicariously through TV and newspaper accounts of others people's stories about meeting and conversing with angels!

Please lay aside your fears that somehow you won't get it right. There's no right or wrong. You can have terrible handwriting or be a master at calligraphy. You can be a high school dropout or possess a doctorate in literature. And if you lack writing skills, what better way to improve them? Write. That's all. And don't worry about the details. Just put them down as you see fit. You can also draw angels as you picture them, or as you have seen them, and paste in cutouts of angel pictures if that pleases you. If you like structure, be neat and orderly. If you don't, scribble any old way, so long as you can read it.

When thoughts and feelings arise from the inner self, do not ignore them or push them away; record them either mentally or physically so that they do not vanish in the well of forgetfulness.

The Monitoring Technique

As we go about our daily lives, we usually are in a blur of automatic, preprogrammed thoughts and activities. Our mental processes most of the time are like a slightly out of focus photograph. We ordinarily only go into sharp focus in times of crisis. As a result, we are often bored and "not there." So much of our everyday life is such a blur of routine that we miss what our angels are trying to tell us. To combat this tendency, I have developed and teach a technique I call monitoring, which is a way of consciously focusing on the day's input, either as it is happening or during brief periods of reflection.

If the idea of learning to monitor your thoughts and feelings at first seems daunting, do not let that prevent you from attempting it. Like learning to ride a bicycle, it at first will seem clumsy and impossible, and then, suddenly—bingo!—you will be off and away with ease.

Begin by consciously storing in memory your thoughts, feelings, and reactions with regard to the events of the day. If you have trouble remembering them, train yourself to take brief notes during the day, either during or after their occurrence. Note the particulars of the situation, along with your reactions. A few words will do; you will develop a kind of shorthand in time. The purpose is to jog your memory later and enable you to recall the entire event, complete with "feeling tone."

Angel Writing Helps with Weight Loss

A friend had ballooned up to nearly 300 pounds following her divorce and the death of her mother. She worked in the fashion industry as a makeup artist and was constantly depressed looking at all the thin, beautiful models. I told her about keeping an angel journal, and she started writing about her stress instead of eating to suppress it. Within a year and a half, she had dropped from a size 24 to a size 10, with practically no conscious effort. She found she just wasn't hungry. So if you have a weight problem, call on the Weight Loss Angel!

During the day, whenever you have a spot of unoccupied time—waiting for a bus, sitting on a train, standing in line—review what you have noted to fix it firmly for later evaluation.

At the end of the day, set aside a few minutes of time to examine the entire day's input for clues to messages from angels. Record your thoughts and feelings along with any physical or environmental circumstances.

In time, you will perceive patterns of meaning. Your life is not an accidental or random event; it has meaning and purpose. Keeping an angel journal will help you to discover this.

If you are new to journal keeping, you may need some time to acclimate yourself to writing about your angelic experiences on a regular basis. One friend makes it a habit to write down a self-created angel prayer every day. Here is a sample prayer:

"Dear Angel—Be with me today and keep me safe. Let me be aware of your presence around me."

Use any form of journal you please. I find a bound notebook is best, as I tend to lose separate pieces of paper. A simple spiral notebook is inexpensive, or you may prefer a cloth-bound book.

Rereading what you have written either the next day or even a year later can be an illuminating experience. For one thing, you won't forget any of your angel messages and experiences! Enjoy your angel journal; think of it as a dear friend with whom you spend intimate time.

Write when and for as long and as much as it suits you each time. If you are a person who responds well to a scheduled activity, by all means put it in your schedule. If not—and I think this preferable—let your writing be spontaneous. Whatever works for you at the time is best.

In addition to keeping your journal on a regular basis, you can benefit by writing out your feelings about any particular experience, angelic or otherwise. James W. Pennebaker, Ph.D., a professor in the Department of Psychology at Southern Methodist University, developed an effective technique in which you spend 20 minutes writing nonstop and without concern about spelling or grammar. If you do this, emotions will likely pour forth, even tears—but these are tears of release. This is an excellent method to gain insight into the meaning of your life.

Your angel journal can also be a way to help you lessen stress and handle anxiety or depression. Making a commitment to writing on a regular basis is the key to success.

Tips for Angel Journal Writing

Here are some helpful angel writing tips:

- Decide whether to write by hand or keyboard.
- If by hand, select loose-leaf paper or a bound book.
- Choose a book that opens flat.
- Decide whether to use lined or unlined paper.
- The writing implement you use should be one that is permanent and does not smear. You may want to keep a special pen or pencil just for this purpose.
- If using a keyboard, you can use paper that is three-hole punched and keep your pages in a ring binder. Or, you can create a file folder or a computer file.
- Browse in a stationery store for an assortment of pens, markers, and colored pencils, and use them for a variety of moods and experiences. One client writes all her dreams in purple.

Exercises for Angel Journal Writing

Here are some angel writing exercises:

- Practice "flow writing." To do this, simply write anything that comes to mind for 15 minutes.
- Write an outline of the major turning points of your life for later elaboration.
- Ask yourself where you are *now* and write about it.
- Write a short essay about your angel journal.
- Create a piece of angel artwork for your journal.
- Imagine yourself meeting an angel and draw the scene.
- Write about how you felt about the angel.

Angelic Communication

"The very presence of an angel is a communication. Even when an angel crosses our path in silence, God has said to us, 'I am here. I am present in your life.'"

—Tobias Palmer, *An Angel in My House*

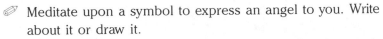

- Meditate upon a symbol to express an angel to you. Write about it or draw it.
- Find some pictures or symbols of angels and make a collage of them.
- Write a description of your recorder self.
- Write a description of your actor self.
- Write a dialogue between them.
- Write a letter to your angel about your journal.
- Write a letter to your guardian angel and invite him or her to be a participant in your writing.
- Write a letter to someone else's angel.

An angel journal can in itself be a spiritual practice, or it can be an adjunct to whatever else you practice. In it you keep a *private* record of your spiritual growth. Keeping an angel journal will help you to understand your individual pilgrimage on this earth. You will be having the adventure of your life, that is, the discovery of your authentic self. Journal writing is a rewarding and important facet of your overall spiritual development.

When Should You Write in Your Angel Journal?

There is no "right" time or "right" length of time. Follow your own rhythm; let the angel "speak" to you when it wants your attention. I do recommend writing frequently, daily if possible. The quiet period just before bedtime works well because pre-sleep writing can influence your dreams. And just after waking also is excellent. I like to use this time to fit together the experiences of the previous day and the night's dreams.

Are There Ideal Conditions for Writing in Your Angel Book?

Conditions will vary for each person depending on his or her personal situation of space and privacy. Ideally, you should have a quiet, private spot you use regularly, perhaps your study, bedroom, or the kitchen table. Using the same place enables your angel to more easily sense that you are in your writing spot and ready to make contact.

How Much Should You Write in Your Angel Book?

This is a question that can only be answered by you. My only advice is that you write what you want for as long as you want. If you feel you have nothing to say to your angel, don't write at all. You may write copiously or sparsely, and do either or both at different times in your life. There's no minimum and no maximum. Sometimes I jot down a few words; at other times, I write several pages. For those accustomed to taking notes, jotting a few lines in their own brand of shorthand suffices to jog their memories when they want to reread. For others, there is an outpouring of immense detail.

Make a Covenant with Your Angel Journal

Think for a few minutes about your purpose in keeping a journal and whether you are willing to make a commitment to writing regularly. Then put your thoughts onto paper. Study what you have written and see whether you are satisfied with your purpose; if you are not, make changes. Your statement of purpose might go something like this:

I'm keeping my angel journal for the purpose of getting in touch with the angels who guard and guide me, with the aim of generating more consciousness.

My goal is to become more aware of messages from my angels and to act on this information for my spiritual growth and development.

I believe that keeping a journal will aid this process by providing me with a framework in which I can record and reflect upon my experiences and wherein I can chart my progress.

When you are satisfied with your written statement of purpose, write out a contract. It might go something like this:

[Statement of purpose.]
Therefore, I make a covenant with myself to pursue this effort on a regular basis.
I promise to write in this journal _____.

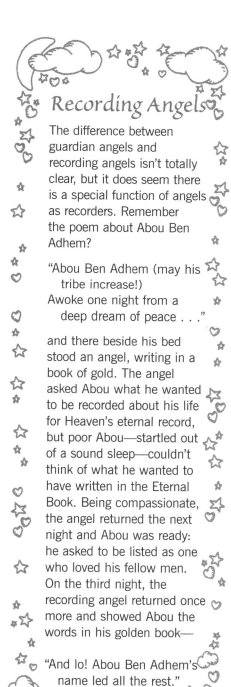

Recording Angels

The difference between guardian angels and recording angels isn't totally clear, but it does seem there is a special function of angels as recorders. Remember the poem about Abou Ben Adhem?

"Abou Ben Adhem (may his tribe increase!)
Awoke one night from a deep dream of peace . . ."

and there beside his bed stood an angel, writing in a book of gold. The angel asked Abou what he wanted to be recorded about his life for Heaven's eternal record, but poor Abou—startled out of a sound sleep—couldn't think of what he wanted to have written in the Eternal Book. Being compassionate, the angel returned the next night and Abou was ready: he asked to be listed as one who loved his fellow men. On the third night, the recording angel returned once more and showed Abou the words in his golden book—

"And lo! Abou Ben Adhem's name led all the rest."

Here, you will fill in the blanks. You might say "every day" or "when I feel the need" or whatever else suits you.

Remember, you are making this agreement with yourself, and it is up to you to abide by the terms. Trust your angel to keep up its half of the bargain.

Let your angel journal be a gift to yourself. You might think of it as a spiritual practice or as a way of learning the skill of communicating with angels. Rereading what you have written is a pleasant way to bring back memories of your angelic experiences.

Think of your angel as a friend and companion, one to whom you can turn whenever you need a boost or someone to talk to. Enjoy him or her as you would enjoy spending time with any dear friend who is *genuinely interested* in you, your problems, your daily life, your successes, your setbacks, your dreams, your goals.

Consider the time you spend with your angel as time spent with your Higher Self, or the Source, or God, whichever term fits your personal belief system.

Consciousness

There is a well-known mythological symbol of two birds sitting in a tree—one is eating; the other is watching the one who eats. The symbol represents the two sides of ourselves: the *doer* and the *observer*. These might also be thought of as the *actor* and the *recorder*. The actor represents your outward existence, your struggles and achievements, your movements toward others, your *participation*.

The recorder represents your inward life, your thoughts, feelings, attitudes, beliefs, hopes, and dreams. This self reflects on what the actor is doing; it contemplates.

Together, the actor and the recorder create *consciousness*. Just as thought without action is invalid, action without thought is mere movement. Both are necessary to create a being conscious of itself and its actions. Do you remember your first conscious moment? There is a time when we first open our eyes to the world around us and see ourselves as both participating in it and separate from it. Child specialists debate just when this happens in terms of age, but I see it as a continuous process attendant upon the spiral ascent. At each further turn of the spiral, we gain more consciousness. We become more conscious of our own consciousness. And we do this through the interaction of our actor and our recorder.

Consciousness is our most precious possession. Without it, we are mere robots, only going through the motions of life, not really *living.* In the ability to think, reflect, and wonder, we possess treasures greater than found in all the tombs of Egypt, or the immense riches of the Orient, or the vast diamond mines of South Africa. Without consciousness, we do not know who we are and cannot find out. This greatest of gifts should be guarded carefully and used wisely. The human mind can observe itself thinking—subject and object simultaneously. We can "see" ourselves doing what we do. Consciousness is the inner companion who never goes away. It is even attested that some surgical patients emerge from under anesthesia with memories of what happened in the operating room. The reason for this is simple: Consciousness is *always there*, at some level.

We confuse the terms *conscience* and *consciousness.* Conscience guides us in matters moral and ethical, but without being conscious of exactly what our actions mean, we cannot judge them. This is where consciousness comes in. Consciousness is our ability to *be aware.* When we become conscious of some behavior or thought pattern, we are in a position to change it for the better.

The purpose of angelic communications to the pilgrim on a spiritual journey is a consciousness-raising mission. As we progress along the way, consciousness emerges into the light of spirituality, and we become aware not only of our true selves but also that others possess true selves, and we want to know those selves, not the false ones we are most often presented with. The emerging of consciousness is like the peeling away of the layers of an onion.

It takes consciousness of "all the distinctly different components of the self" to make us aware of the whisperings of angel guidance. So often our angel guidance is drowned out by the noise—both external and internal—with which we surround ourselves. Consciousness thrives in the silence of reflection.

Consciousness

"We learn to live consciously through becoming aware of inner and outer events *as they are happening.* Building a conscious self means becoming increasingly aware of inner events, bodily events and interpersonal events. A conscious self is able to experience in full awareness all the distinctly different components of the self, including feelings, needs, drives, and values. A conscious self lives consciously."
—Gershen Kaufman and Lev Raphael, *The Dynamics of Power*

The angel message may reach us merely as a vague sensation, either mental or emotional. It can be a tension or a sense that something is about to happen. Consciousness may register as no more than an ephemeral state of being, like the feeling that one has forgotten something important but cannot for the life of one remember what it is. Ideas communicated to us by our angels may come to us as feelings, or we may find ourselves undergoing a change in values as the result of a crisis.

When we listen and pay attention to "the still small voice," we find angel guidance is available. The directions we need most often come from within, yet they can be mirrored by what is happening without. The question is, How can we sort through our multiplicity of feelings, sensations, intuitions, thoughts, and reactions to get to the spiritual core of the matter?

Angels Who Visit in Dreams

The great Swiss psychologist Carl Jung called dreams "the royal road to the unconscious." They are also the gateway to the subtle realms where spirits abide. Sometimes they are like long letters we write to ourselves. A friend of mine says an unremembered dream is "an unopened letter from God."

Dreams speak their own language, and angels who visit in dreams come through that portal to bring their messages, which we often need to interpret. The reason the dream state is so propitious for contacting angels is that it is approximates the way angels function—fluidly, openly, timelessly. When we go to sleep, we let go of the tightly organized, highly regimented linear left-brain thinking that usually dominates our waking hours. While asleep, we have no schedule; we float freely in a magical substance in which swim creatures of the deep and that creates visions of incredible creativity. Dreams are angels' territory.

When one goes on a journey into unfamiliar territory, it is best to have a knowledgeable guide who knows the terrain, speaks the language, and is familiar with the customs. Classical Greek Hermes, the "guide of souls," also called *angelo*, is emblematic of such guides. The classical scholar Karl Kerényi speaks of the "activity of Hermes" as referring to "alternatives of life, to the dissolution of fatal opposites, to clandestine violations of boundaries and laws"—in other words, the overturning of the rational mind-dictated world and the discovery of the magical powers of the inner world.

A guide is actually a symbol for our own deepest wisdom, which resides in the self and connects us to the celestial energies, to nonhuman life, to nonorganic life, to the cosmos itself.

During my life, I have encountered many angels who came as guides. You too will have more than one angel during your lifetime, but you can call upon these cosmic tour guides at any time you feel you need guidance.

An angel may appear as an archetype—an old man or a wise woman, a human figure you may or may not recognize, an animal that talks or communicates telepathically, a spiritual entity such as an "intelligence" from another dimension, or even a rock or body of water. These symbols are likely to shift and change over time and with the subject for which you are asking guidance.

For example, asking for guidance with healing may produce a figure consonant with your idea of a healer. Accept what comes, for it arises from your deepest core, where your sacred self dwells.

By making the effort to meet and talk with your angel, you will be setting a precedent for getting help on a regular, sometimes unasked-for basis. Your angel can warn you of problems in advance, it can provide you with penetrating insight, and it can reveal subtle nuances of meaning that are imbedded in your everyday experience.

For example, about 15 years ago, I encountered a group of nine men in an exceptionally vivid dream.

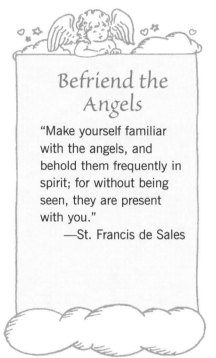

Befriend the Angels

"Make yourself familiar with the angels, and behold them frequently in spirit; for without being seen, they are present with you."
—St. Francis de Sales

The Dream of Green Fire

I am in a large house in a wooded area with a young woman friend. Outside, there is a blizzard. I hear my name called. I cannot imagine who would be calling my name late at night with a storm raging, but I know I must go and find out whether someone in trouble needs my help.

Bundling up, I forge out into the snow, in the direction of the voice calling my name. Going through dense woods, I come upon a clearing, surrounded by a ring of green fire. Inside the ring of green fire there is no storm; all is quiet, placid, peaceful, and warm. Nine men robed and hooded like monks, in long woolen olive-brown gowns, tied at the waist with knotted golden ropes, sit in a circle inside the ring of green fire. In the center of the circle there is a small bonfire that glows with the same emerald green light as the fire ring.

By gesture, they invite me to enter the circle. From the maelstrom of the raging storm, I step into this center of absolute calm, safety, and warmth. A great sense of peace descends over me, as if I have at long last come home. Beneath their hoods I can see their faces; all are very old, wrinkled, and wizened, and have deep, dark eyes like pools of unfathomable wisdom. I feel a sense of protection coming from them.

One rises and steps toward me, and I see that he has my cat, Fuzz, cradled in his arms. I realize that the voice I heard calling my name was that of my precious Fuzz, who was lost in the terrible storm and needed rescuing. He is handed to me ceremoniously, like a gift on an important occasion. I can tell he is perfectly all right and has suffered no injuries from the traumatic experience of being lost in the cold and snow. Taking him from the monk's wrinkled old hands, I feel a sense of complete and utter peace and safety.

When I awoke from the dream, I pondered the symbolism, and the answer came immediately: Fuzz was my heart. They had told me that my *heart*—most fearfully broken more than once, in essence lost in the dark cold—had been rescued and kept safe. In the dream it was returned to me intact and healed.

The nine men appeared to me several different times over the next several years, always accompanied by ice and snow, to which they were immune and within which they created a warm center. Though they appeared to be human, I knew they were from the angel world.

In another dream, they gave me a large book made of parchment sheaves, ancient and yellowed but not fragile, the pages covered with a mysterious writing that I could not decipher but that I understood to be important esoteric knowledge. I realized that the nine men were celestial sages from the world of no time. I came to call them the Council of Nine. Later, I was inspired to write a poem, "The Return," about the experience of this wondrous group.

When I read Betty Eadie's *Embraced by the Light*, I was astonished to find that one chapter was entitled "The Council of Men." In her vision, she met 12 men, seated around a kidney-shaped table, who radiated "absolute love" to her. She also learned from this council of men many fascinating things about herself and her life. In addition, she describes three men who meet her at the beginning of her near-death experience. The numbers 12, 9, and 3 are all related, each being divisible by the core number *3*. The number *3* represents the trinity, or the triangle, of mind-body-spirit and the threefold nature of divinity, of great symbolic importance and spiritual significance. The number *9* represents completion, humanitarianism, and universal compassion. The number *12*, which is the number of the signs of the zodiac, reduces back to *3* using the numerological formula 12 = 1 + 2 = 3.

We are all capable of experiencing contact with our own deeper dimensions symbolically. It is through the use of symbols that we can connect with what cannot be seen, heard, touched, tasted, or smelled. Whatever symbolic form your angelic guides take will depend on which forms you are most open to and able to respond. In my case, these often have to do with art and books.

The Dream of the Great Library

I am visiting the house of a man who goes by the nickname Winnie (which may be a pun on the word win*). He tells me that if I will forgo getting my Ph.D., he will teach me everything contained in the books in his library. He shows me a magnificent collection of ancient texts on papyrus, handwritten tomes from*

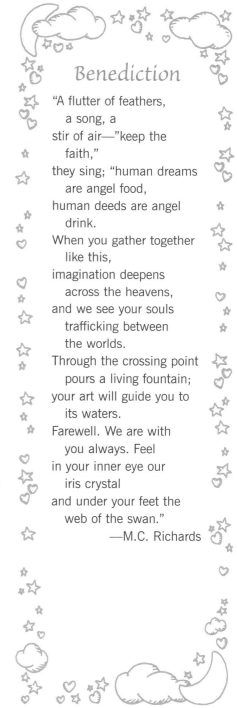

Benediction

"A flutter of feathers,
  a song, a
stir of air—"keep the
  faith,"
they sing; "human dreams
  are angel food,
human deeds are angel
  drink.
When you gather together
  like this,
imagination deepens
  across the heavens,
and we see your souls
  trafficking between
  the worlds.
Through the crossing point
  pours a living fountain;
your art will guide you to
  its waters.
Farewell. We are with
  you always. Feel
in your inner eye our
  iris crystal
and under your feet the
  web of the swan."
            —M.C. Richards

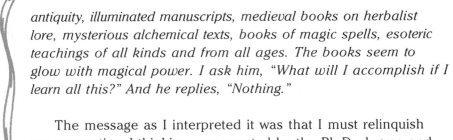

antiquity, illuminated manuscripts, medieval books on herbalist lore, mysterious alchemical texts, books of magic spells, esoteric teachings of all kinds and from all ages. The books seem to glow with magical power. I ask him, "What will I accomplish if I learn all this?" And he replies, "Nothing."

The message as I interpreted it was that I must relinquish my conventional thinking, represented by the Ph.D. degree and our society's obsessional fixation on credentialing as the only path to a successful life, and replace it with the powerful ancient tradition, which is far superior to dry, academic "book learning" that places all value on the rational-linear mode of thought and what can be proven in a laboratory. However, learning the ancient wisdom will not "accomplish" anything in the usual sense of our limited thinking about what accomplishment means. That is not the purpose of esoteric knowledge. Though it can be used on the mundane plane, that is, to enrich one's self in a material way, its true purpose is for the development of the spiritual life.

The teachings we receive from our angels may not be remembered after the particular altered state of consciousness in which we experience them is gone, but they nevertheless make an impact, as do unremembered dreams.

There was a lot you learned at school that you "forgot"—who can recall their high-school algebra or Latin? But somehow those subjects sunk in as part of an overall pattern of learning to think.

Some fortunate people are able to regularly receive angel communications while in an altered or dream state, and they can remember everything and record it. Viola Petitt Neal, who wrote *Through the Curtain*, reports how she attended "night classes," which she dictated to Ms. Shafica Karagulla while in the altered state. In this book, the authors speak of a Council of Seven (the number of archangels, which combines *3* with *4*, the number of the four directions, each of which is represented by a different angel; the number *7* is often diagrammatically represented as a triangle enclosed within a square, symbolizing the trinity and the four directions).

Other Altered State Experiences

It's even possible for one person to receive guidance from another person's angel. I had such an experience when I first began to practice astrology professionally. My friend, Josephine Corado, a blind psychic, had invited me to spend the weekend at her home on Long Island and had arranged for me to read the charts of several of her clients. I arrived on a Friday afternoon carrying some astrology books. At that time, I was accustomed to spending three or four hours of preparation time on each chart, and although I had prepared most of the charts I was to read over the weekend, one remained undone.

That evening as we sat chatting in Jo's living room—she in the recliner and me on the couch—she suddenly burst out laughing.

"What's so funny?" I asked in puzzlement.

"Akenaton," she replied. "He's standing right in front of you."

I knew Akenaton was what she called her angel, but there was nothing in front of me but the coffee table.

"Where?" I asked, looking around.

"Right *there*," she pointed a finger to the spot where my tummy was.

"What does he want with me?" I asked perplexedly.

"I haven't the faintest idea," was her unhelpful reply.

Shortly after this conversation, she announced that she was going to bed early because she didn't feel well. I reminded her that I had a chart to prepare the next morning before my first reading at noon, and she promised to get me up by 9:00 A.M. It was about 10:00 P.M when she retired, and as I'm a late-night person, I was at loose ends to occupy myself. Since Jo was blind, there were no books and no TV. I wasn't in the mood to study astrology, the only books I had. I lay on the couch to meditate.

As I lay there, wide awake but very relaxed, a curious thing happened. My entire body began to vibrate as if someone had plugged me into an electric socket. It was very intense, though not actually uncomfortable. The source of the sensation seemed to be the center of my forehead (where the "third eye" is located). I didn't understand at all what was happening to me, but as I was in

"Coming to God"

"The true mystic is not merely involved in esoteric thoughts or beautiful images of God in heaven. He is totally absorbed in a life movement, a journey in which his essential self—his real self—comes into life with and in God. This 'coming to God,' as it has been called, is the journey."
—Marsha Sinetar,
*Ordinary People
as Monks and Mystics*

An Angel in the Corner

"When my daughter was three or four years old, she and I used to go to the Theosophical bookstore in Seattle. She would always run to one corner of the store. There were not any children's books or toys in this corner, or anything else that would have particularly held her interest. But she would nonetheless run and stay there while I browsed through the rest of the shop. I happened to mention this to an elderly Theosophical author I knew who also frequented the bookstore. She looked surprised and said, 'Oh, my dear, don't you know? There's an angel in that corner!'"

—Denise Linn,
Sacred Space

what I knew to be a spiritually saturated atmosphere, I made no effort to get up. The room was not dark; there was a streetlight just outside the uncurtained window. I looked about myself, but I saw nothing out of the ordinary.

The sensation finally stopped—*three hours later*. As unexpectedly and inexplicably as it had started, it stopped, like the switching off of a light. Whatever circuit I had been connected to went dead. I felt none the worse for the experience, and I got up and went to bed. In the morning as promised, Jo woke me and I sat at her dining-room table to prepare the chart. I worked away, consulting my books only occasionally, and when I had finished, I asked Jo, who had a talking watch, for the time. "It's nine forty-five," she told me.

I knew this could not be right, for I had finished three hours' worth of work, and I had not started until a bit after 9:00 A.M. "That's impossible," I said. "Could you check your watch again?" She came over to me and held out her wrist. I heard a little mechanical voice say, "Nine forty-six." How could that be? I wondered. I had not felt any sense of time speeded up, had worked at my usual slow and thorough pace, or so I thought, and yet I was done. To make sure, I called the time service. Then I remembered the previous evening's strange experience and Jo's having told me her angel was standing in front of me. Could there be a connection?

In the weeks that followed, it became evident to me that I had a far greater understanding and knowledge of astrology than I had before I went to Long Island that weekend. At a conference at which I was a lecturer a thoroughly seasoned astrologer who had been practicing for 20 years came up to me and said that I was the "best technical astrologer" she knew. Amazed, I understood that I had received a powerful teaching that night, like an intravenous injection straight into the brain. Since then, my readings have risen to a level of comprehension that still amazes me, for I know that I didn't earn the knowledge I have, that it was a gift from an angel. Is there an Angel of Astrology?

Angelic guides are a very personal, sometimes profound, experience. There is no way any of us can pass on information about them except by relating our own experiences.

One such experience occurred on a bleak, snowy February evening, the last night I spent in my house in Woodstock, New York.

I was leaving Woodstock very reluctantly to return to New York City. Overcome with sadness, for the house had provided me with rich spiritual experiences, I was packed and ready to go when my friend who was driving me back to the city called to say he would be a couple of hours late. There was nothing to do in the empty house, so I lay down on the bed to meditate and pass the time. I slipped into a mild trance state.

I saw bright light, like that of the full moon, and I roused to go and look at the moon shining on the new snow, a scene I love. But when I got up, I discovered the moon wasn't full, or even visible in the cloudy sky. The room was in darkness. Puzzled, I lay down again. Then, I felt a presence touching me gently. It told me I was going to receive a healing treatment. For more than an hour, I felt a gentle pulsing going through my body; I felt connected to parts of myself that had long been outside of my awareness. My legs, which had been damaged by childhood polio, felt alive for the first time I could remember. I felt myself open like a flower under the beneficence of this healing vibration. It was a parting gift from the angel of my beloved house.

This story is an example of the deeply mysterious region of the invisible world, which includes angels of all sorts. I have been asked, "What is the difference between an angel and a guide?" and, quite honestly, I do not know. There may not be a difference. Angels and guides may be different forms of the same basic energy. Since all of life is energy, and since energy has the ability to take any form, there is no certain way of knowing. When we venture into the invisible world, we encounter mystery, for there exist no neat categories that serve to divide our rational world into recognizable events and objects. In the invisible world, all is shifting and changing, like a dream.

When you open yourself up to Hermes's world, do not be surprised at what may happen. I myself have had many fantastic and surprising adventures in this most wonderful and mysterious realm of the invisible world.

Angelic Forces

It is not necessary to perceive an actual angelic *figure*—though this seems to be the most usual form in which angels appear to us. One can simply *sense or feel* the presence of an angelic energy.

Qualities of Angels

Angels of different qualities have revealed themselves to me. For example, during one period when I was studying the tarot, I received information and guidance through specific sounds. I identified three different energies, one of which was a thin, high-pitched tone, barely audible but piercing nonetheless. The second was lower, but still in the high range, and seemed to cover a slightly wider band of the sound spectrum. The third sound was much lower, almost a bass, and broader. Each of these sounds conveyed a different type of information.

For example, when I heard the highest note, I knew it was time to sit quietly and meditate, that a "message" was coming in through this vibration. These sounds occurred at all times of the day and night, in my home as well as other places. They seemed to follow me around. So be aware that you can receive guidance from angels in many guises.

Here is a method for making contact with an angel guide. You can do this anytime you feel the need. One angel guide may stay with you for a long or a short time. You may meet different angels at different periods of your life. There is no right or wrong way to contact an angel, although some do appear spontaneously without your asking.

Meeting Your Angel

In the following meditation, you are going to meet someone whom you can trust and rely on. To prepare yourself, do the following:

1. Articulate a question you wish to ask your angel. Formulate the question clearly and succinctly. Vague questions beget vague answers. Be specific.
2. Do not ask a question requiring a yes or no answer. The purpose is to make contact with your angel.
3. Stick to your present situation; avoid generalities.
4. Do not ask a question requiring a prediction. This is usually interpreted as lack of faith. Asking for guidance is

always good. State the subject about which you wish to receive angelic guidance.

5. Be willing to trust your angel and to take whatever form appears to you. If you draw a blank, try again later when you are more relaxed.

6. When your angel appears, pay attention to how he or she looks. Ask your angel for a name or a symbol by which you can recognize him or her in the future.

After you have prepared yourself for your encounter with your guide, find the time to be alone and undisturbed for half an hour. Using any of the breathing and/or relaxation methods already given, relax completely and let go of the day's tensions and cares.

Mentally take yourself to a place somewhere in nature—a forest, the seaside, a flower-filled meadow, a lakeshore, a cove, a wood—whatever appeals to you. See in front of you, in this pleasant place, a veiled object, full of mystery. A puff of wind may come along and blow away the covering, and your angel will be revealed to you. Take whatever image comes and begin to engage in a dialogue with it. Ask your question and wait for an answer. If one doesn't come at once, be patient. The answer may come in words, through intuition, or telepathically, as an image, even as a snatch of song or an instruction to read a book or magazine article.

The specifics are not as important as making the contact. Whatever springs into your mind is the right answer. Your angels are in touch with the deepest part of your being, which is connected to all reality everywhere at all times and places.

When you have met your angel, introduce yourself, and ask your question. Notice the details of the place so that you can return here whenever you like. Fix it in your memory. When you get the answer to your question, thank your angel and say you will look forward to future meetings.

If you do not get an answer, or if the answer doesn't seem to make sense, accept that also and try again later. Remember, you are learning a new skill.

Angelic Influence

"Angels cannot directly determine acts of the human will. The inviolability of its freedom exempts it from such determination either by angels or by men. But just as one human being can influence the will of another by efforts at persuasion, or by motivating it in one way or another through arousing emotions, so angels have even greater power to influence the will of individuals in these indirect ways."

—Mortimer J. Adler, *The Angels and Us*

Angels in Today's World

n 1943, Mortimer J. Adler, one of the leading philosophers of the time, was selected to edit the publication of *The Great Books of the Western World*, sponsored by the *Encyclopaedia Britannica*. The publication would enable readers to have access to the major books responsible for shaping our culture. Eventually, the series would become the basis for literally thousands of book discussion groups.

Adler was enthused about the project and he identified 102 "great ideas" about which he would then write essays, in order to make the books themselves more understandable to the general public. His advisory board approved all of his ideas but one—the subject of angels.

Senator William Benton, the publisher, was amazed that anyone would regard angels as a great idea with cultural value, as were Robert Hutchins, president of the University of Chicago, and other board members. Adler, however, stood his ground. Talk of angels, he said pointedly, ran through all of the great books that had been selected for inclusion in the series.

In the end, Adler had his way. His volume of essays, titled *The Syntopican*, had as its first article "Angels," and the text ran to 5,000 words!

Billy Graham, the well-known evangelist preacher and spiritual advisor to several U.S. presidents, decided in 1975 to preach a sermon about angels. Commencing to do some research, he discovered to his surprise that his own library contained little on the subject. Further investigation revealed that, during the preceding 75 years of the twentieth century, few books about angels had been published.

In an attempt to rectify this situation, Graham wrote and published *Angels, God's Secret Agents*, which almost immediately hit the best-seller lists and was reprinted several times. He brought out an expanded edition in 1986, and since that time there has been a literal explosion in interest about angels.

Angels, angels, everywhere—a recent check of Amazon.com, the on-line bookstore, produced dozens of titles of angel books, and an additional several *thousand* references to angels in various forms! Wherever you look, there are angels, including dozens of

Angel Jewelry Makers

Angel World, P.O. Box 210425, Columbia, SC 29210

Martha Powers's angel-inspired designs are executed in pewter, silver, and gold. Her story was told in *Touched By An Angel*. She conceived the idea of wearing a guardian angel pin on one's shoulder.

Hand and Hammer, Woodbridge, VA, (800)-SILVERY

H and H produces elaborate sterling silver angels cast by the lost-wax process, as ornaments or for wear as pins and pendants. Call for a catalog showing pictures of their designs.

Jeff Stewart Antiques, P.O. Box 105, Newton, SC 28658

Send $2 for a catalog of silver angel ornaments and jewelry, including old H and H designs.

James Avery Craftsman, P.O. Box 1367, Kerrville, TX 78029, (800) 283-1770

James Avery Craftsman makes silver and gold angel charms, earrings, bracelets, and rings. Angel items are available in retail stores or call for a catalog.

gift shops selling angel-related items all over the country. There are dozens of angel "things" in mail-order catalogs—everything from angel jewelry and figurines to angel hangings, angel-printed sheets and towels, angel-embossed treasure boxes, Teddy bears in angel garb, angel greeting cards for all occasions, and angel oracle cards (an angel tarot).

Today, angels are speaking to or visiting all those who can find the silence and proper frame of mind with which to perceive, see, or hear them. Additionally, the current preoccupation with angels has gone way beyond the traditional religious format.

Angels have invaded the entertainment industry in a big way. *Highway to Heaven* started the popular angel TV programs, which now include *Touched By An Angel* and several others. Angels are discussed quite openly in secular contexts as well as religious ones, and everyone today seems quite comfortable with the idea of angels.

There's even a Roman Catholic nun who owns a cable TV station called the Eternal Word Television Network. Its founder, Mother Mary Angelica, with absolutely no knowledge of how television worked, along with a coterie of other sisters, brought the network into being.

Millions of viewers watch EWTN, and visitors to the TV complex outside Birmingham, Alabama, are always impressed with what this nun—with God's help of course—has accomplished. There stands a nunnery, network facilities, a big satellite dish, a print shop, and a chapel, all in the center of the Bible Belt.

Mother Angelica's story is unique. She grew up Catholic. Her parents were divorced. And she herself endured a miserable marriage.

As a child she wasn't at all interested in becoming a nun. She found them dreary and sour-faced: "I was convinced they were the most unhappy people I'd ever seen," she says. But an amazing event changed all that.

At age 11, she was walking on a busy downtown street one evening, feeling sad and lonely. "I started to cross a busy street, then heard a woman's shrill scream behind me." Looking around to see if someone was in distress, she saw a car speeding toward

Angel Gift Resource

For a list of angel gift shops where you can buy everything from angel weather vanes to angel night-lights, see the book *Angelic Healing* by Eileen Elias Freeman.

Metaphysical Books about Angels

Living with Angels, Dorie D'Angelo, First Church of the Angels

Ask Your Angels, Alma Daniel, Timothy Wyllie, Andrew Ramer, Ballantine

The Angel Book and *Angel Voices*, Karen Goldman, Simon and Schuster

The Kingdom of the Gods and the Brotherhood of Angels and Men, Geoffrey Hodson, Quest Books (classic theosophical work)

Commune with the Angels, Jane M. Howard, A.R.E. (personal statement of her experiences with angels)

Working with Angels, Robert Leichtman and Carl Japikse, Enthea Press

To Hear the Angels Sing: An Odyssey of Co-Creation with the Devic Kingdom, Dorothy Maclean, Lindisfarne Press (Findhorn founder discusses her experiences with angels)

The Kingdom of the Shining Ones, Natives of Eternity, and *Rediscovering the Angels*, Flower Newhouse, The Christward Ministry (three volumes by the well-known mystic)

Angels and Mortals: Their Co-Creative Power, Maria Parisen, ed., Quest Books (a compilation of excerpts and articles from many sources)

The Ministry of Angels, Here and Beyond, Joy Snell, Citadel Press (Subtitled *A Personal Account of What Lies Beyond*)

Creating with the Angels, Messengers of Light, and *Guardians of Hope*, Terry Lynn Taylor, H.J. Kramer (three volumes)

her. Its headlights blinded her, and she had no time to reach the safety island in the middle of the broad street. Rita, as she was then named, simply closed her eyes and waited to die as the car inevitably hit her small body.

She felt two strong hands grasp her and lift her high into the air. A moment passed, and she opened her eyes to find herself standing on the sidewalk on the other side of the street! Witnesses to the event thought they saw the child hit, her body hurled into the air by the force of the impact, her crumpled little body lying on the pavement. They expected to find a corpse, not a healthy, if terrified, little girl on the far sidewalk. Onlookers were totally mystified by her uninjured condition.

Another witness, a bus driver who had the vantage point of a high seat, reported in astonishment that he had seen Rita either jump or be catapulted high enough to clear both the safety island and the speeding automobile. Others were shaking their heads in puzzlement.

After that incident, little Rita gained confidence in the angels and came to feel protected and cared for by them. After her divorce, she entered the Poor Clares convent, later founding Our Lady of the Angels Monastery, to honor her angel friends, where she now lives and directs her TV network. She appears twice weekly on her own show, Mother Angelica Live, on which she takes phone calls from across the country to minister and give counseling "to those who, perhaps, can't reach out any other way."

"Angels as people" are cropping up everywhere these days. The December 1999 issue of *Good Housekeeping* had a feature, "Profiles: The Angels Next Door," about regular humans who are considered "angels" because of the good works they perform. One, a doctor, only charges her patients $9 an hour. When the interviewer asked her daughter what she thought of a mother who worked so hard for so little money, the girl replied, "I think it's so cool. My friend said you only hear about people like her in the movies. So it's really great that there's somebody out there who actually does it!"

Along with TV programs about angels, Hollywood has gotten into the angel act with such films as *Angel on My Shoulder, The*

General and Reference Books about Angels

The Angels and Us, Mortimer Adler, Collier Books (a philosophical enquiry in a popular style)

Angels and Men, Ladislaus Boros, Seabury (introduction to angels)

A Book of Angels, Sophie Burnham, Ballantine (the book that started the flood of angel books)

The Angel Book, Ann Cameron (a general resource on the subject)

In Search of Angels, David Connolly, Putnam (general introduction)

A Dictionary of Angels, Gustav Davidson, Free Press (an indispensable resource book; has a bibliography that comprises dozens of pages)

Angels: The Role of Celestial Guardians and Beings of Light, Paola Giovetti, Samuel Weiser (a translation of an Italian work that mixes metaphysical, Catholic, and artistic elements, with plates)

The Blessed Angels, Manly P. Hall, Philosophical Research Society (a short monograph on the subject, with illustrations)

The Many Faces Of Angels, Harvey Humann, De Vorss Publications (general book that includes the Bible, Edgar Cayce, William Blake, and so on)

Angels: Ministers of Grace, Geddes MacGregor, Paragon (serious treatment from many perspectives, with bibliography and indices)

Do You Have a Guardian Angel? John Ronner, Mamre Press (chatty style)

Know Your Angels, John Ronner, Mamre Press (highly informative volume; offers interesting facts and lore about angels in history, art, literature, religion, and so on)

Bishop's Wife, *The Milagro Beanfield War*, and, that old favorite, *It's a Wonderful Life*, starring the angel Clarence. German film-maker Wim Wenders has created a movie featuring angels called *Wings of Desire*, which demonstrates what a wonderful medium film is for depicting angels.

And books about angels also continue to proliferate. Author Joan Wester Anderson has collected dozens of angel stories from ordinary people and published them in her books, as have William and Marilynn Carlson Webber, authors of *A Rustle of Angels*, a book resulting from an article about Marilynn that was picked up by the Associated Press.

Sophie Burnham, author of *A Book of Angels*—the book that jump-started the whole angel explosion—received thousands of letters from ordinary people all over the country in response to her book. People everywhere, in all walks of life, felt they had been touched by angels, and they were eager for their stories to be told. As a result, Burnham published a second book, *Angel Letters*, which contains many of these first-person accounts.

Novelists have not ignored angels either. Andrew Greeley wrote *Angel Fire,* which was mass-marketed and found in paperback racks in supermarkets and convenience stores. This popular book, all about guardian angels, is written in a form that is easy to read.

Children's books about angels also abound. For a partial list of popular titles, see Eileen Elias Freeman's *Angelic Healing*, or check Amazon.com on-line. One children's book, *The Tiny Angel*, comes with an angel necklace!

Music, too, has been a popular venue for angels. Angels seem to be using this medium to make their presence felt in contemporary culture. Beginning with the 1950s, angels are frequently components of lyrics in songs like "Earth Angel," "Angel Eyes, "Johnny Angel," "I'm Living Right Next Door to an Angel," "Where Angels Fear to Tread," and, the hit song, "You Are My Special Angel."

Not only music, but *people* are getting angel happy. There are cities, charitable activities, aviator groups (e.g., the famous U.S. Navy flying acrobats, "The Blue Angels,"), and even sports teams named after angels. In New York City, young people have organized themselves into voluntary street and subway patrols, calling themselves

Religious Groups

Philangeli (Friends of the Angels)

1115 East Euclid Street
Arlington Heights, IL 60004
Catholic prayer organization

Opus Sanctorum Angelorum

Marian Center, 134 Golden Gate Avenue
San Francisco, CA 94102
Catholic prayer organization

First Church of the Angels

P.O. Box 4713
Carmel, CA 93921
New church that focuses on angels and
healing

Questhaven

P.O. Box 20560
Escondido, CA 92029
Sponsors religious retreats and workshops
emphasizing angels; Rev. Flower
Newhouse organization

Angel Walk

P.O. Box 1027
Riverton, WY 82501
Nondenominational, religious-metaphysical
center

"Guardian Angels" and wearing T-shirts with an emblem featuring an eye, wings, and a shield. Curtis Sliwa, the founder and director of this extraordinary volunteer group of protectors of ordinary citizens, says, "angel-like protection is offered to everyone, even those who don't want us looking out for them."

Then, there is the Angel Collectors Club of America, a national association of angel lovers. It has a newsletter and an annual convention. In Tucson, Arizona, a children's boutique named Angel Threads specializes in angel "stuff" for children. In Cleveland, Ohio, there is a day nursery called Angels in Heaven. And an angel collectible mail-order business operates out of Riverside, California.

In Toronto, six-time Canadian figure-skating champion Toller Cranston lives in a house filled with angel paintings, mobiles, and other celestial art because, he says, "they can leave gravity behind," something a champion figure skater does every time he or she competes!

Writers Alma Daniel, Timothy Wyllie, and Andrew Ramen, in their book *Ask Your Angels,* have this to say about their involvement with angels:

We noticed billboards sporting our celestial friends beaming down at us; lyrics, ads, TV, and jingles dropped references to our unseen companions with astonishing regularity. Cab drivers named Angelo turned up with delightful frequency and at invariably significant moments.

Wherever we went, we heard the same tales, from countless people. It isn't just happening to us—or to you. The angels are reaching out to everyone, in every way they can, and to a degree that they never have before.

Index

A

Abadie, M.J. (author), 5, 231, 232
  altered states and, 245–247
  angels and, *xiii–xvii*, 90–92,
    93–95, 188–190, 196–200
  dreams of, 215, 217–218,
    241–244
  poem by, 157
"Abou Ben Adhem," 237
Abraham
  Isaac and, 21–22, 83–84
  Sarah and, 16, 18, 36, 45
Adler, Mortimer J., 125, 131,
  249, 252
Ahura Mazda, 7, 8, 9, 53, 54
Air
  invoking spirit of, 227
  writing to angel of, 228
Akhenaton, 6–7, 9
Alexander of Hales, 42
Altered state experiences,
  244–247
Ambrose, Saint, 134
Anahel, 80
Anderson, Joan Wester, 19, 28,
  178, 258
Angel Collectors Club of
  America, 259–260
Angel Fire (Greeley), 258
Angelica, Fra, 148
Angelos, 5, 209
Angels, 125

books about, 158, 160, 176, 182,
  252, 255, 257, 258
creation of, 28, 41–42
definition of, 74, 189
descriptions of, 76–79
humanization of, 42–43, 98
in modern world, *xiv–xvi*, 178,
  180, 252–263
organizations about, 205
perceptions of, 90–99, 208–209,
  218–223
proving existence of, 166–176
as pure intellect, 43–46, 74
work of, 130–141
Angels, God's Secret Agents
  (Graham), 252
Angra Mainyu, 8, 53
Annunciation, 30–31, 85
Anquetil-Duperoon, Abraham
  Hyacinthe, 55
Anselm of Canterbury, 108
Anthroposophy, 73, 132
Aphrodite, 104
Apocrypha, *see under* Bible
Aquinas, Thomas, 47, 123, 124
  on angels as intellect, 43–46
  canonization of, 42
  saints and, 110
  sin and, 108
  writings of, 45, 166
Archai, 134
Archangels, 80, 82–83, 125,
  133–134

origins of, 82
  see also Gabriel; Michael;
    Raphael (archangel); Uriel
Aristotle, 46
Armaiti, 8
Art
  angels in, 72, 76–77, 79, 93,
    152–161
  angels of, 73
  music in, 148
Ascension of Isaiah, 34–35
Ashi, 8
Assyria, 4–5, 76–77
Astrology, 172
Atkov, Oleg, 185
Auden, W.H., 179
Augustine, Saint, 28, 29, 98, 122
  saints and, 110, 111
  sin and, 107
Azazel, 114

B

Beauty, angels of, 73
Beecher, Henry Ward, *xii*
Bendit, Laurence J., 167
Benson, Herbert, 220, 222
Benton, William, 252
Bernard of Clairveaux, Saint,
  134, 145
Besant, Annie, 73
Bible
  Apocrypha, 33–34, 86

We Have
EVERYTHING!

Everything® **After College Book**
$12.95, 1-55850-847-3

Everything® **American History Book**
$12.95, 1-58062-531-2

Everything® **Angels Book**
$12.95, 1-58062-398-0

Everything® **Anti-Aging Book**
$12.95, 1-58062-565-7

Everything® **Astrology Book**
$12.95, 1-58062-062-0

Everything® **Baby Names Book**
$12.95, 1-55850-655-1

Everything® **Baby Shower Book**
$12.95, 1-58062-305-0

Everything® **Baby's First Food Book**
$12.95, 1-58062-512-6

Everything® **Baby's First Year Book**
$12.95, 1-58062-581-9

Everything® **Barbeque Cookbook**
$12.95, 1-58062-316-6

Everything® **Bartender's Book**
$9.95, 1-55850-536-9

Everything® **Bedtime Story Book**
$12.95, 1-58062-147-3

Everything® **Bicycle Book**
$12.00, 1-55850-706-X

Everything® **Build Your Own Home Page**
$12.95, 1-58062-339-5

Everything® **Business Planning Book**
$12.95, 1-58062-491-X

Everything® **Casino Gambling Book**
$12.95, 1-55850-762-0

Everything® **Cat Book**
$12.95, 1-55850-710-8

Everything® **Chocolate Cookbook**
$12.95, 1-58062-405-7

Everything® **Christmas Book**
$15.00, 1-55850-697-7

Everything® **Civil War Book**
$12.95, 1-58062-366-2

Everything® **College Survival Book**
$12.95, 1-55850-720-5

Everything® **Computer Book**
$12.95, 1-58062-401-4

Everything® **Cookbook**
$14.95, 1-58062-400-6

Everything® **Cover Letter Book**
$12.95, 1-58062-312-3

Everything® **Crossword and Puzzle Book**
$12.95, 1-55850-764-7

Everything® **Dating Book**
$12.95, 1-58062-185-6

Everything® **Dessert Book**
$12.95, 1-55850-717-5

Everything® **Digital Photography Book**
$12.95, 1-58062-574-6

Everything® **Dog Book**
$12.95, 1-58062-144-9

Everything® **Dreams Book**
$12.95, 1-55850-806-6

Everything® **Etiquette Book**
$12.95, 1-55850-807-4

Everything® **Fairy Tales Book**
$12.95, 1-58062-546-0

Everything® **Family Tree Book**
$12.95, 1-55850-763-9

Everything® **Fly-Fishing Book**
$12.95, 1-58062-148-1

Everything® **Games Book**
$12.95, 1-55850-643-8

Everything® **Get-A-Job Book**
$12.95, 1-58062-223-2

Everything® **Get Published Book**
$12.95, 1-58062-315-8

Everything® **Get Ready for Baby Book**
$12.95, 1-55850-844-9

Everything® **Ghost Book**
$12.95, 1-58062-533-9

Everything® **Golf Book**
$12.95, 1-55850-814-7

Everything® **Grammar and Style Book**
$12.95, 1-58062-573-8

Everything® **Guide to Las Vegas**
$12.95, 1-58062-438-3

Everything® **Guide to New York City**
$12.95, 1-58062-314-X

Everything® **Guide to Walt Disney World®,
Universal Studios®, and
Greater Orlando, 2nd Edition**
$12.95, 1-58062-404-9

Everything® **Guide to Washington, D.C.**
$12.95, 1-58062-313-1

Everything® **Guitar Book**
$12.95, 1-58062-555-X

Everything® **Herbal Remedies Book**
$12.95, 1-58062-331-X

Everything® **Home-Based Business Book**
$12.95, 1-58062-364-6

Everything® **Homebuying Book**
$12.95, 1-58062-074-4

Everything® **Homeselling Book**
$12.95, 1-58062-304-2

**For more information, or to order, call 800-872-5627
or visit everything.com**
Adams Media Corporation, 57 Littlefield Street, Avon, MA 02322